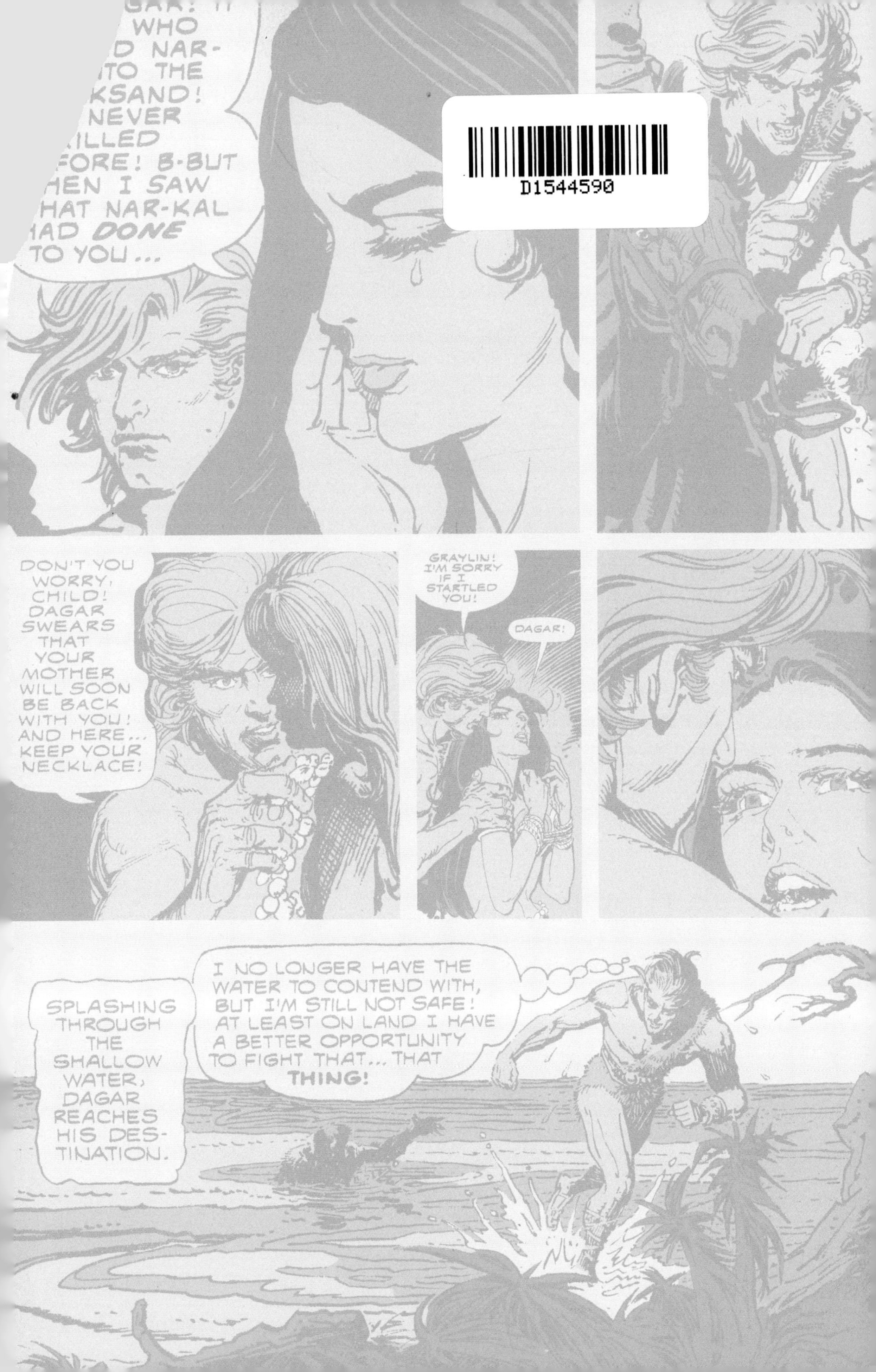
WHO
D NAR-
TO THE
KSAND!
NEVER
ILLED
FORE! B-BUT
HEN I SAW
HAT NAR-KAL
HAD DONE
TO YOU...
DON'T YOU WORRY, CHILD! DAGAR SWEARS THAT YOUR MOTHER WILL SOON BE BACK WITH YOU! AND HERE... KEEP YOUR NECKLACE!
GRAYLIN! I'M SORRY IF I STARTLED YOU!
DAGAR!
SPLASHING THROUGH THE SHALLOW WATER, DAGAR REACHES HIS DESTINATION.
I NO LONGER HAVE THE WATER TO CONTEND WITH, BUT I'M STILL NOT SAFE! AT LEAST ON LAND I HAVE A BETTER OPPORTUNITY TO FIGHT THAT... THAT THING!

DAGAR

THE INVINCIBLE™

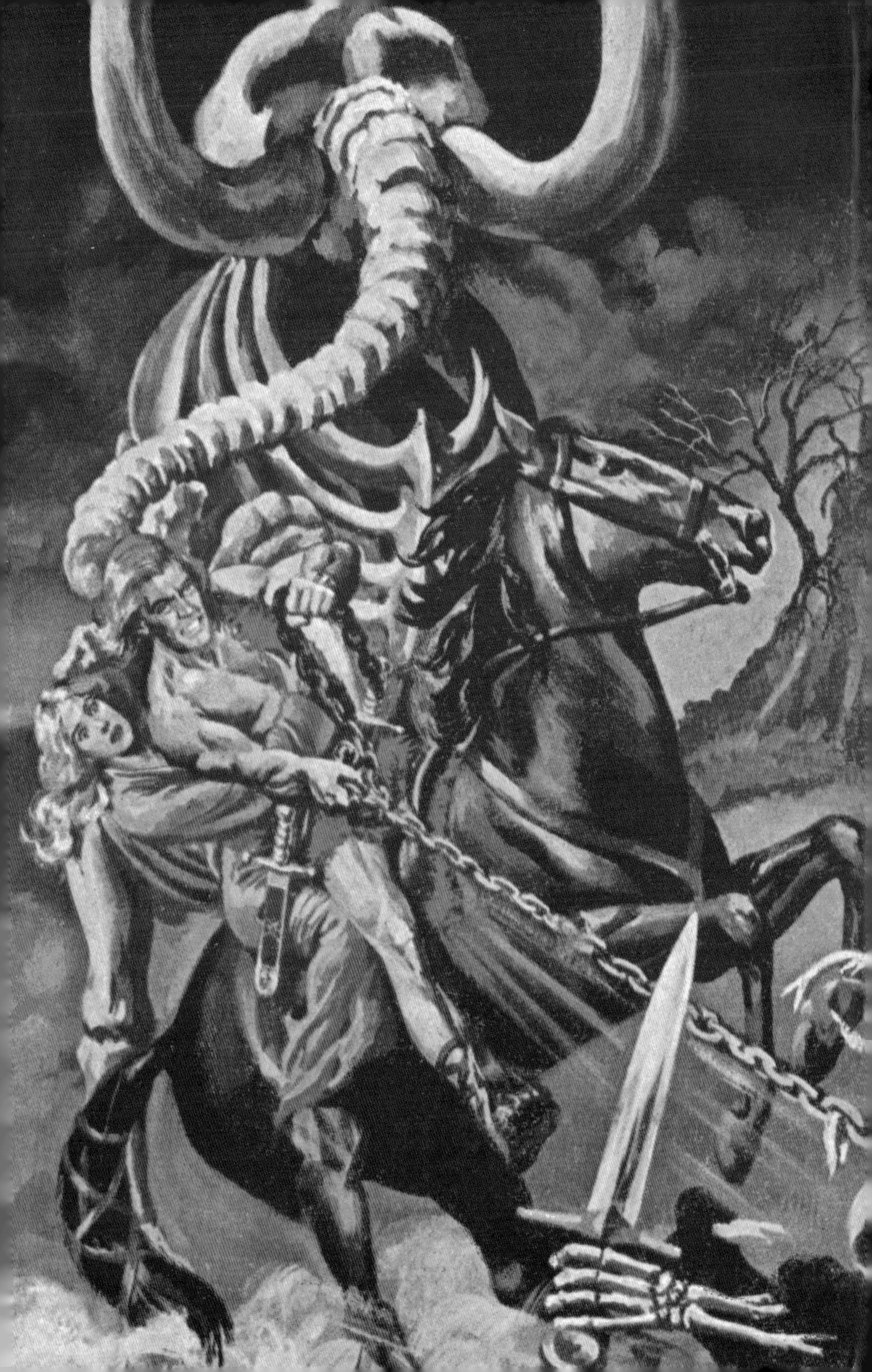

DAGAR
THE INVINCIBLE™

DARK HORSE ARCHIVES | VOLUME ONE

Written by
DONALD F. GLUT

Art by
JESSE SANTOS

Introduction by Donald F. Glut

Dark Horse Books®

Publisher
MIKE RICHARDSON

Collection Editor
JEMIAH JEFFERSON

Collection Designer
KAT LARSON

Published by
Dark Horse Books
A division of Dark Horse Comics, Inc.
10956 SE Main Street
Milwaukie, OR 97222

DarkHorse.com

To find a comics shop in your area, call the Comic Shop Locator Service: (888) 266-4226

First edition: November 2011
ISBN 978-1-59582-818-7

10 9 8 7 6 5 4 3 2 1

This volume collects *Tales of Sword and Sorcery: Dagar the Invincible* #1–9, originally
published in 1972, 1973, and 1974 by Gold Key Comics.

Printed at 1010 Printing International, Ltd., Guangdong Province, China

MIKE RICHARDSON president and publisher NEIL HANKERSON executive vice
president TOM WEDDLE chief financial officer RANDY STRADLEY vice president of
publishing MICHAEL MARTENS vice president of book trade sales ANITA NELSON
vice president of business affairs MICHA HERSHMAN vice president of marketing
DAVID SCROGGY vice president of product development DALE LAFOUNTAIN vice
president of information technology DARLENE VOGEL senior director of print, design,
and production KEN LIZZI general counsel DAVEY ESTRADA editorial director SCOTT
ALLIE senior managing editor CHRIS WARNER senior books editor DIANA SCHUTZ
executive editor CARY GRAZZINI director of print and development LIA RIBACCHI art
director CARA NIECE director of scheduling

TABLE OF CONTENTS

INTRODUCTION

By Donald F. Glut

The origin of Gold Key Comics' *Dagar the Invincible*—not the *fictional* origin of the hero of that name, but the *real* origin—is long and rather convoluted, spanning three publishers and more than a half-dozen character names.

The "sword-and-sorcery" genre, long familiar to readers of prose pulp fiction, became a popular comic-book trend in the early 1970s, largely thanks to the success of Marvel Comics' *Conan the Barbarian*. When *Conan* debuted, my career as a comics scriptwriter was just beginning, all of my published work seeing print in magazines like Warren Publishing Company's *Creepy*, *Eerie*, and *Vampirella*.

Although I was not much of a sword-and-sorcery fan, I decided to give the genre a try. In spring 1971, I wrote another spec script for Warren, not intended to become a series, entitled "Castle of the Skull" and featuring a sword-toting barbarian character I named Shaark. The Warren magazines published the occasional sword-and-sorcery tale, and I already had an in at the company, so submitting "Castle of the Skull" seemed reasonable. Without explanation, Warren editor J. R. Cochran rejected it.

Having the attitude of never letting anything with potential die, I next tried Skywald, Warren's main competitor in the field of black-and-white illustrated horror. Again the script came back, but not as an outright rejection. An accompanying note explained that "Castle of the Skull" was acceptable, but Skywald had a huge backlog of scripts. The note further suggested that I resubmit the story later.

In the meantime I'd begun selling comic-book scripts and text pieces to the West Coast branch of Gold Key Comics, initially working under editor Chase Craig, but soon directly for associate editor Del Connell. Most of my comics work consisted of horror, science-fiction, and fantasy scripts, most of them ten pages in length, for Gold Key's new *Mystery Comics Digest*. Among my earliest submissions to this title was "Lizard Sword," another presumably one-shot sword-and-sorcery tale with another barbarian character, this one named Daggar. Neither Chase nor Del seemed to be familiar with the genre; intrigued by something new, they bought the story. They liked the story but not its title, which I changed to "Wizard of the Crimson Castle."

I went ahead and scripted a second story starring Daggar, "Demon of the Temple." Neither Chase nor Del, however, was keen on a follow-up story using the same character, opining that most likely no reader would see both stories. Finally, though, I managed to convince Chase and Del that it didn't matter if a reader read just one of the stories or both. There was no real plot continuity linking them, so there would be no need for flashback or footnotes (which neither editor liked using); and, since the hero needed a name, there would be no harm in using the same name twice.

"Wizard of the Crimson Castle" was mailed to the editors' new "discovery," San Jose, California—based Jesse Santos. In 1967 Jesse had been elected vice president of the Society of Philippine Illustrators and Cartoonists and three years later joined the Society of Western Artists. He worked in virtually all media, and seven of the comic books he drew while in the Philippines had been made into movies. Jesse's rugged style was atypical of the usual Gold Key stories and perfectly suited to sword and sorcery. Being also a portrait artist, Jesse could convey a wide range of emotions through his characters' expressions. Often he emoted and posed in front of a mirror, doing double duty as both model and artist.

As Jesse Santos was busy drawing "Wizard of the Crimson Castle" for *Mystery Comics Digest*, Chase and Del began to view that story, plus its sequel, "Demon of the Temple," in more expansive terms.

Taking the two stories together, the editors began to consider the possibilities of doing an actual sword-and-sorcery *series* featuring Daggar as a continuing hero in his own book. Told to forge ahead and write a presentation, I came up with an origin for Daggar (one coincidentally similar to that concocted by my director friend John Milius for his later motion picture *Conan the Barbarian*) and a break down of the character. If approved, he would soon be appearing in his first twenty-five-page story. The West Coast editors submitted the concept to their counterparts in New York, who, shortly afterwards, green-lighted the project.

Seeing a grander picture, I remembered "Castle of the Skull." Changing that story's protagonist from the original Shaark to the new Daggar, giving him more characterization while toning down the violence and sex that would never have met Gold Key's more rigid standards, I revamped and expanded the story for Daggar's premiere issue. That first issue was to include two complete stories—the origin tale and also "Castle of the Skull." Del, never knowing that "Castle of the Skull" had its own pre–Gold Key history, bought it. His *only* objections were the title of the book and the name of its lead character.

For reasons never explained to me, Del did not like naming a book after its lead character. He seemed to prefer titles that began with the words "Tales of . . ." and wanted to name the Daggar book *Tales of Sword and Sorcery*. Furthermore, Del felt that the name *Daggar* sounded too much like "dagger." Actually, that *was* my intent, as symbolically shown on the third page of the hero's origin story, whereupon he kills a saber-toothed cat with a dagger rather than a sword.

Del suggested we rechristen the character *Dragar*, until I pointed out him that it could potentially lead to jokes about our hero wearing women's clothes. Then he came up with *Zagar*, even drawing a rough mockup of the first issue's cover and a hastily executed logo with that name—until I informed him

that Skywald was currently publishing a comic book about a Tarzan clone named Zangar. Finally we settled on *Dagar* (which I for a while still pronounced like "dagger" until forced to acquiesce to the longer "dag-are" pronunciation that became the norm). It wasn't until the third issue of the book saw print that someone informed me that *Dagar* had already been used for a 1940s desert sheik from Fox Publications.

I continued to push the title *Dagar the Invincible*, which I felt had strength, while Del still wanted *Tales of Sword and Sorcery*. The two first-issue scripts—"The Sword of Dagar" and "Castle of the Skull"—were sent off to Jesse Santos for drawing and Bill Spicer for lettering. When the printed books finally arrived at the office, they boasted the compromised title *Tales of Sword and Sorcery: Dagar the Invincible*. To my delight the *Tales* portion of the title was small, with the *Dagar* part much larger and bolder. (To this day I don't recall encountering anyone who has referred to the book as *Tales of Sword and Sorcery*.)

Nomenclatural issues aside, problems with the character were hardly over. By coincidence the first sword-and-sorcery story I'd sold to Gold Key—"Wizard of the Crimson Castle," now under the more encompassing title *Tales of Sword and Sorcery,* a recurring feature in *Mystery Comics Digest*—was scheduled to appear on the newsstands in *Mystery Comics Digest #7*, just one month before the first issue of *Dagar*. Del Connell believed that having Dagar appear in a short story in the digest book while almost simultaneously starring in his own title somehow diminished the character's prestige; thus, he changed the name of the digest-tale swordsman to Duroc.

Jesse Santos, meanwhile, was assigned to create Dagar's look based on my basic description, making his physical features different from those of Duroc. In short order the artist submitted to Del a detailed drawing of his interpretation of Dagar. Except for a long cape, which arguably made the character appear a bit *too* civilized and even noble, the drawing was a perfect rendition. Jesse was ready to start drawing Dagar's first issue.

There were other matters to consider. Both "Wizard of the Crimson Castle" and "Castle of the Skull" had quite similar surprise endings; both were illustrated in the same style; both featured characters who, despite their different names, were much alike in both appearance and behavior, even in the weapons they wielded. In essence, though the editors may not have realized it, Gold Key now had *two* sword-and-sorcery heroes! And there was yet another paid-for Duroc story waiting to see print in *Mystery Comics Digest*.

Again seeing things a bit differently than Del, I began to envision two separate sword-and-sorcery series, one featuring Dagar and the other Duroc. To accomplish this dream I needed to make sure that these characters remained significantly different. Dagar had already been established as having blond hair, while Duroc's was brown. A year later Duroc, in "The Evil of Xorkon," *Mystery Comics Digest* #14 (October 1973), not only had longer hair than Dagar's, but was also sporting facial hair.

More than just making cosmetic changes, I wanted to separate Dagar and Duroc in terms of their personalities. Most sword-and-sorcery heroes, like Conan, tended to be barbarians. To be different I wanted to establish Dagar as having belonged to a *civilized* community; consequently he was *not* a barbarian. Duroc, on the other hand, *was* a barbarian, no question about that. Moreover, Dagar was a more serious-minded, often brooding, mercenary who fought only (usually, anyway) for payment, while Duroc might leap into battle simply for the thrill of it. I thought of Dagar as more of a Kirk Douglas/Spartacus type (decades later, Jesse admitted to me that Dagar's features were based on Douglas's) and saw Duroc in the Errol Flynn/Robin Hood mold.

Controversy over Duroc's name was by no means over. Following his cameo in "Death between Floors," published in the fourth issue of *The Occult Files of Doctor Spektor* concurrently with his second *Mystery Comics Digest* appearance, the East Coast Gold Key editors finally noticed that the character's name rhymed (and might be confused) with that of the lead character of their *Turok, Son of Stone* comic-book title. And two additional Duroc scripts had not yet been published. The first of these stories would soon be transformed into a Dagar story, "The Golden Curse"; the second, scheduled for *Mystery Comics Digest* #15, had already been penciled by Jesse and was awaiting lettering by Bill Spicer, when Del Connell was instructed by the New York editors to change the Turok-sounding name. Del promptly came up with, in my opinion, the stronger Durak. This time, the name finally stuck.

"The Golden Curse" was Durak's last solo adventure. But the character would continue his adventures, eventually crossing over into Dr. Spektor's modern-day story line, and in the third issue of the reprint book *Dr. Spektor Presents Spine-Tingling Tales*, two of the barbarian's original stories from *Mystery Comics Digest*—with his name spelled Durak—would be seen again.

As neither Jesse Santos nor I were yet getting name credit for these stories, I constantly sought new ways of sneaking my name into places so, if ever called upon to explain that I'd written these stories, I could offer up some proof. As established in the first issue's opening story, "The Sword of Dagar," our hero hailed from the nation of Tulgonia. If Del Connell or Chase Craig ever noticed what the first four letters of that word spelled when reversed, they kept that knowledge to themselves. Also, upon release of the first *Dagar* comic book, various friends accused me of basing the spelling of the hero's name on my own, the *D* and *G* beginning each syllable of his name being my initials. Although their suspicions made perfect sense, and I was surprised that I hadn't thought of this myself, in this case any resemblance between Dagar's name and my own was entirely—or at least consciously—coincidental.

Del Connell, suggesting that Dagar's horse have a name, came up with the exotic-sounding *Kasa*. Del's suggestion was a wise one, because, in my mind, it reinforced the idea of Dagar being civilized and not a barbarian.

The second story, "Castle of the Skull," introduced both the villain Scorpio (astrology was quite big at the time) and the subordinate villain Ostellon. As would later be revealed (although at the time I wrote this story I had no idea what awaited in the future story), Ostellon, "master of living bones," would one day

cross paths, although in different time periods, with both Dr. Spektor and the caveman hero of *Tragg and the Sky Gods*, another series I created and wrote for Gold Key, establishing continuity between these characters and Dagar.

At first Del did not completely approve of my introducing in that initial book a villain—Scorpio—who didn't get his moral comeuppance by story's end and, assuming that very few, if any, people would read two consecutive issues, whose presence would spread over at least several issues. I assured Del that, despite Scorpio's pervading menace in subsequent issues, each story involving the villain would be complete in and of itself and could be read, understood, and enjoyed as a standalone piece. Del allowed Scorpio to continue, providing Dagar defeated him by the end of the fourth issue. I assured my editor that Dagar would honor his demand.

"The Beast Within," appearing in *Dagar the Invincible* #2 (1972), was a more-or-less standard werewolf tale in a sword-and-sorcery setting. Its plot introduced the lobrostone, a mineral with transformation-suppressing powers. The concept would later spill over to Dr. Spektor's continuity.

The script I turned in for the third issue of *Dagar the Invincible* was titled "City of the Vampires," which Del, probably thinking it too bland, changed to "Wrath of the Vampires." I wanted to do a vampire story for the series but, taking into account the ancient time period in which Dagar's stories were set, I didn't want the vampires he encountered to be in the black-cloaked Dracula mode. Therefore I presented the vampires as a race unto themselves, a concept that has, in more recent years, become quite fashionable in literature, comic books, and movies. It was Jesse's idea, however—not mine—to depict only the female vampires as human beings with fangs. The really weird alien look he gave to the male vampires came as a complete surprise to me.

In "Vengeance—Sweet Vengeance" (Del's title; I no longer recall what I'd named this story, although it most likely included Scorpio's name), published in *Dagar the Invincible* #4 (July 1973), I kept my promise to Del, with Dagar, upon defeating his archfoe and avenging the slaughter of his people, free to find new adventures.

"Another World . . . Another Time," in *Dagar the Invincible* #5 (October 1973), was my chance to combine the sword-and-sorcery comic-book genre with one of my favorites, the dinosaur and/or caveman story. The story that I originally wrote and sold to Del, however, was not exactly the one that saw print. As scripted, the tale was a straightforward crossover between heroes Dagar and Tragg, the latter a prehistoric character who had not yet been awarded his own book. Until then, in fact, Tragg had only appeared in a couple of *Mystery Comics Digest* short stories, one of them under the Tales of Sword and Sorcery heading.

After approving and paying for the script, Del Connell began to have second thoughts about the inclusion of Tragg in the story. A caveman whose Cro-Magnon appearance was the product of genetic tinkering by a race of alien invaders, Tragg did, like Durak when drawn by Jesse, look suspiciously like Dagar. Del surprised me, after Jesse's penciled and inked pages arrived at Gold Key, by showing me how he had changed Tragg to a more primitive Neanderthal-type caveman that he named Jarn. Of course I was not happy with what Del had done to my story, especially without telling me beforehand. Again not letting an idea go to waste when Tragg finally acquired his own comic book, I brought back Jarn, identifying him as Tragg's nongenetically altered brother. Nonetheless, despite Tragg's departure from the Dagar story as a major character, I managed to get Jesse to sneak him into that tale in a small, one-panel cameo appearance (you have to look closely to find him).

As already stated, author and artist credits were not yet being given at Gold Key. Consequently I named many of the characters in my Dagar and other Gold Key stories after relatives and friends. Two Dagar stories—for reasons both practical and economical—appeared in the sixth issue (January 1974). The first story, "Treasure of Nai-Po-Gah," allowed me to slip a friend's name into the very title, as the name of the "forbidden city" was, spelled in reverse, that of my longtime Chicago friend Richard Hagopian. Also, the story introduced the character of Graylin, for a while at least Dagar's companion. Graylin, like Nai-Po-Gah, was another attempt to sneak in a personal reference, named this time after my then-girlfriend Linda Gray.

"Demon of the Temple" was a retooling of what was originally intended as the third Durak tale. The apish horned monster of the story was inspired by the "sacred Orangupoid" ape monster I'd remembered Buster Crabbe fighting in an episode of the first *Flash Gordon* movie serial.

"Two Swords against Zora-Zal," in *Dagar the Invincible* #7 (April 1974), finally brought Dagar together with that other hero with whom his history was so intertwined, Durak the barbarian. "The Red Ruby of Garloth" ends the issue, introducing Graylin's more dynamic fighting outfit, which she would wear for the rest of her Gold Key appearances.

Shaark . . . Daggar . . . Duroc . . . Durak . . . Dragar . . . Zagar . . . a lot of names that all come back to the same sword-toting guy, Dagar. I am happy that Dark Horse has brought him back in his original adventures and made them available again both to old and new readers. And remember to come back; more of his exploits will be re-presented in volume 2!

—**Don Glut**
May 2011

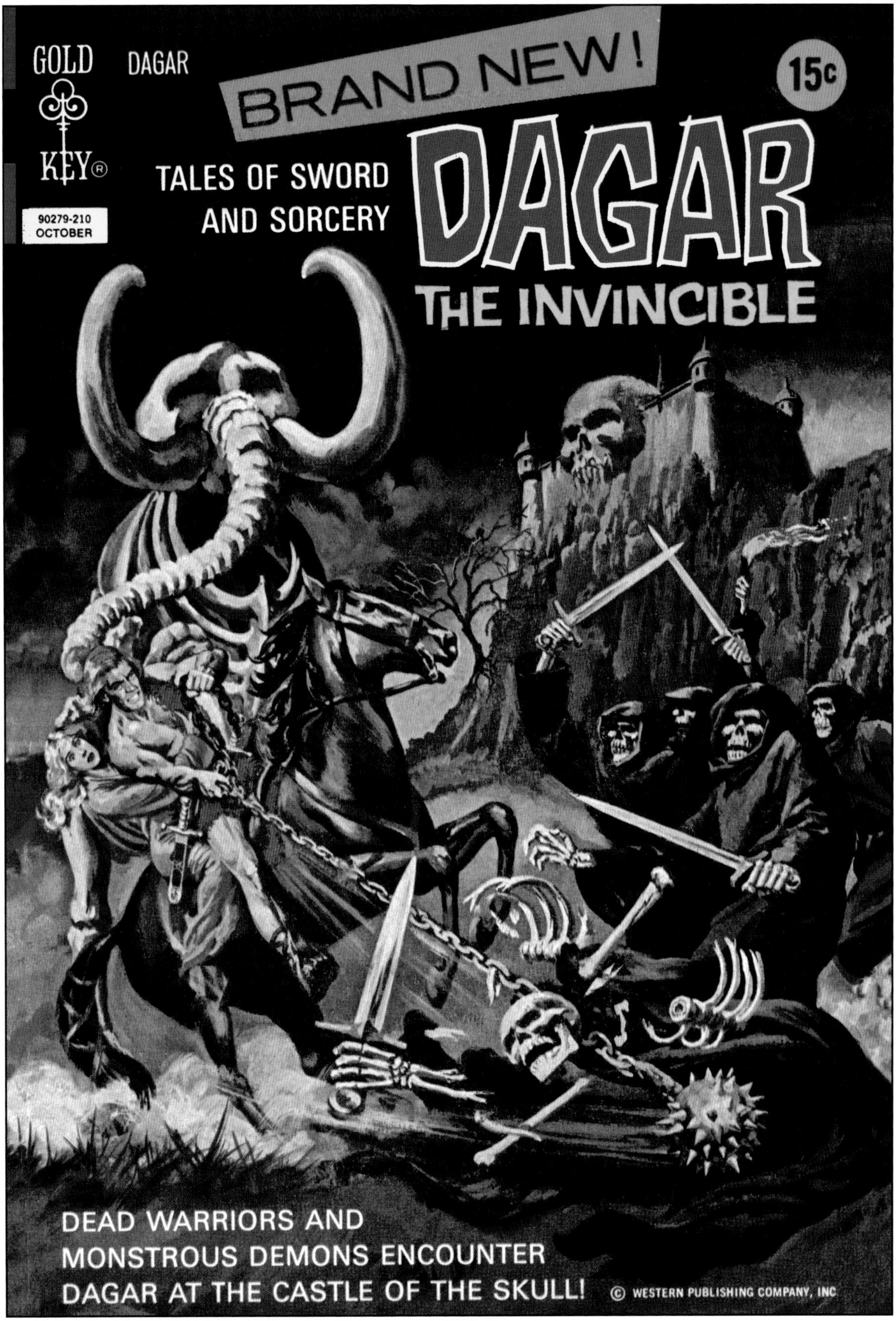
GOLD KEY®
DAGAR
90279-210
OCTOBER
BRAND NEW!
15c
TALES OF SWORD
AND SORCERY
DAGAR
THE INVINCIBLE
DEAD WARRIORS AND
MONSTROUS DEMONS ENCOUNTER
DAGAR AT THE CASTLE OF THE SKULL!
© WESTERN PUBLISHING COMPANY, INC.

Dagar character sketch by Jesse Santos.

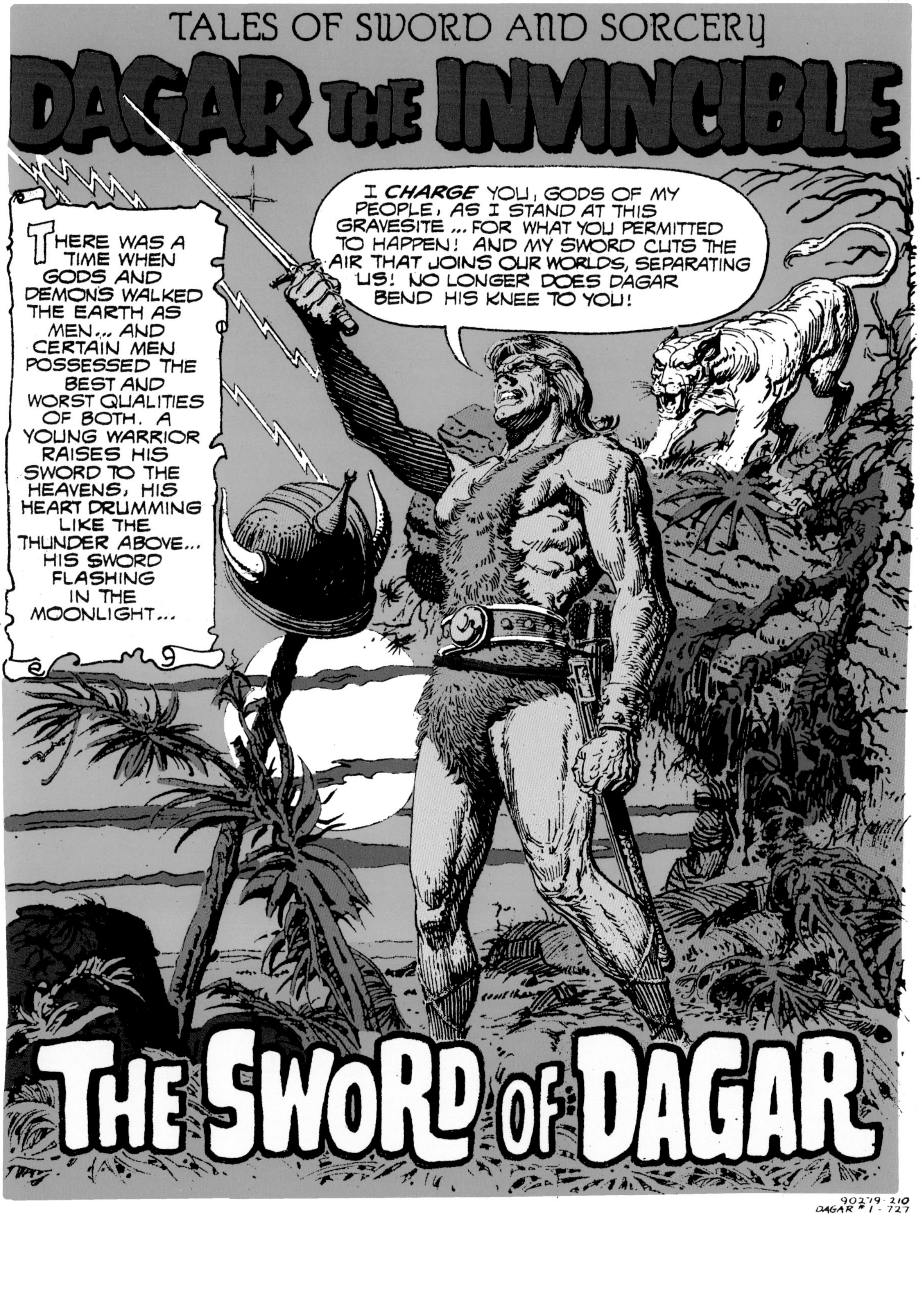
TALES OF SWORD AND SORCERY
DAGAR THE INVINCIBLE
THERE WAS A TIME WHEN GODS AND DEMONS WALKED THE EARTH AS MEN... AND CERTAIN MEN POSSESSED THE BEST AND WORST QUALITIES OF BOTH. A YOUNG WARRIOR RAISES HIS SWORD TO THE HEAVENS, HIS HEART DRUMMING LIKE THE THUNDER ABOVE... HIS SWORD FLASHING IN THE MOONLIGHT...
I CHARGE YOU, GODS OF MY PEOPLE, AS I STAND AT THIS GRAVESITE ... FOR WHAT YOU PERMITTED TO HAPPEN! AND MY SWORD CUTS THE AIR THAT JOINS OUR WORLDS, SEPARATING US! NO LONGER DOES DAGAR BEND HIS KNEE TO YOU!
THE SWORD OF DAGAR

90279-210
DAGAR #1-727

AS IF IN ANSWER TO THE BRAZEN WARRIOR, A STREAK OF FIRE SPLITS THE SKY...

THE GODS DO NOT LIKE BEING DEFIED! BUT WHY SHOULD I FEAR THEIR WRATH!

EVEN THROUGH EXPLOSIVE THUNDER, DAGAR'S KEEN SENSES ALERT HIM TO IMPENDING DANGER...

SOMETHING BEHIND ME!

A SABRE-TOOTH TIGER PEERS AT DAGAR. THEN, LIT BY A BLINDING BOLT OF LIGHTNING...

ROMMROOMMMM!!!

SABRE-TOOTH!

THE YOUTHFUL WARRIOR PREPARES FOR THE ATTACK... BUT THE SABRE-TOOTH IS TOO SWIFT!

UGHHH! M-MY SWORD!

GRRRRRRR...

THE GODS HAVE ABANDONED ME! BUT I'LL NOT NEED THEIR AID... IF I CAN REACH MY DAGGER!

...HIS **OWN FANG!**

Thughhh!

I HAVE IT! NOW, FANGED ONE, TRY YOUR BEST TO VANQUISH ME! FOR NOW DAGAR HAS...

THE HEART OF THE WARRIOR RACES AS THE FELINE MONSTER WRITHES... THEN FALLS ASIDE. THE CONFLICT IS OVER.

BUT WHO IS THIS MAN CALLED *DAGAR*... THIS SUPERB WARRIOR WHO HAS RENOUNCED THE COUNTLESS GODS OF HIS HERITAGE... AND STANDS ALONE BESIDE A WATER-DRENCHED GRAVE?

THE EARTH WAS A REALM OF UNSURPASSED BEAUTY... AND *TERROR*... IN THE TWILIGHT YEARS BETWEEN THE END OF THE STONE AGE AND THE BEGINNINGS OF BABYLON. THE WORLD WAS NOT GOVERNED BY SCIENCE... BUT *MAGIC*... EVEN AS CERTAIN *HIGHLY ADVANCED* PEOPLES ERECTED GREAT CITIES...

SOME OF THE PREHISTORIC CREATURES OF THE STONE AGE HAD NOT YET DIED OUT. THEY BATTLED MAN...AND EACH OTHER AGAINST EXTINCTION...

BUT THE RULERS OF THIS PLANET CONTROLLED IT WITH THE POWERS OF GOODNESS AND EVIL...MOSTLY *EVIL*.

CERTAIN CIVILIZATIONS DID *NOT* REQUIRE THE POWERS OF SORCERY TO LIVE HAPPILY. *TULGONIA* WAS A PEACEFUL NATION... SMALL, HARDLY MORE THAN A CITY... BUT A NATION NONETHELESS...

IT WAS IN TULGONIA THAT A YOUNG ORPHAN GAZED AT A METAL BATTLE HELMET AND FELT A THRILL OF ADVENTURE...

YOU WERE ONCE OUR *GREATEST WARRIOR*, GRANDFATHER, AND WORE THIS HELMET!

AYE, DAGAR! EVERYONE FEARED AND RESPECTED *ANDO* IN THOSE DAYS!

SOMEDAY *I* WILL BE A WARRIOR LIKE YOU AND... *BY THE GODS!* LOOK WHAT'S *APPROACHING!*

LIKE A GHASTLY SWARM OF STARVED LOCUSTS, THE INVADERS STRUCK — SAVAGELY WIELDING BLADES THAT SPARED NO ONE ...

HAH! THESE TULGONIANS ARE A PUNY LOT! SEE HOW THEY FALL TO OUR SWORDS!

AAAIIIIIIEEEEEEE!!!

COME WITH ME! ANDO IS NO LONGER CAPABLE OF BATTLE! AND YOU HAVE NO EXPERIENCE!

NO! PLEASE! I MUST GO BACK!

IT SEEMS THE ENEMY'S DEMONS ARE MORE POWERFUL THAN OUR GODS!

OUR PEOPLE! ALL OF THEM ... BEING SLAUGHTERED LIKE SHEEP!

DAGAR AND ANDO GAPED — WITH FEELINGS OF NAUSEA AND INCOMPARABLE HATRED — AS THE LAST OF THEIR COUNTRYMEN FELL BEFORE THE INVADERS.

SCORPIO WAS RIGHT WHEN HE COMMANDED THAT WE WIPE OUT THIS SMALL NATION! IT WAS A BLIGHT ON HIS DOMAIN ... AND IS RICH IN SPOILS!

AYE! HE'LL BE PLEASED!

AS THE STRANGE ARMY RODE OFF, DAGAR REALIZED THAT TULGONIA NO LONGER EXISTED...

DID YOU HEAR HIM, GRANDFATHER? SOME FIEND NAMED *SCORPIO* ORDERED OUR PEOPLE DESTROYED!

I...HEARD, DAGAR!

I NEVER KNEW MY PARENTS, FOR THEY WERE KILLED DURING THE GREAT WARS! AND NOW— EVERYONE I'VE EVER KNOWN, *ALL MY PEOPLE*, LIE *DEAD* AT MY FEET!

YOU! WHY DIDN'T YOU LET ME FIGHT? I MAY BE YOUNG, BUT I'D HAVE GLADLY DIED ALONGSIDE MY PEOPLE!

NO, DAGAR! YOU *MUST NOT* DIE!

YOU MUST *LIVE,* DAGAR! FOR WHEN *I* DIE, YOU WILL BE ALL THAT IS LEFT OF OUR PEOPLE! YOU WILL *BE* OUR NATION...AND OUR NATION MUST HAVE *VENGEANCE* UPON THOSE *FOUL MASS MURDERERS!*

I WAS ONCE THE MIGHTIEST OF WARRIORS...BEFORE THE GRAYNESS OF *TIME* ENTERED MY BODY! BUT I STILL KNOW HOW TO TRAIN ONE TO FIGHT AS NO OTHER! I WILL TEACH YOU MY FORMER SKILLS, DAGAR...AND YOU SHALL BE... *INVINCIBLE!*

THUS, DAGAR BEGAN HIS LONG PERIOD OF TRAINING... UNDER THE CONSTANT SUPERVISION OF THE ONCE MIGHTY ANDO...

DRIVEN BY AN ALMOST INSANE DESIRE FOR REVENGE, THE YOUNG MAN DROVE HIMSELF ALMOST BEYOND ENDURANCE ...DEVELOPING HIS ABILITIES TO PERFECTION...

AND AS THE YEARS TOOK EFFECT, DAGAR BECAME AN UNEQUALED MASTER OF THE SWORD...

THEN CAME THE INEVITABLE DAY THAT DAGAR DREADED...

I AM TOO OLD, DAGAR! THE GODS HAVE KEPT ME ALIVE THIS LONG...TO MAKE *YOU* INTO THE GREATEST OF WARRIORS...

YOU HAVE LEARNED WELL... FIND THE DESTROYERS OF OUR PEOPLE... *VANQUISH THEM!* UNNNNHHHH...

GRANDFATHER!

DAGAR MADE A SOLEMN VOW...

YOU HAVE GONE TO THE SPIRITS, BUT *I EXIST! I AM* THE NATION OF TULGONIA! I WILL BECOME A MERCENARY WARRIOR, FIGHTING ONLY FOR PAY...FOR I BEAR *NO* LOVE FOR MANKIND!

AFTER BURYING HIS MENTOR, THE YOUNG WARRIOR GRASPED HIS WEAPON...

BY MY *SWORD* AND THIS *GRAVE*, I SWEAR NOT TO REST UNTIL I'VE FOUND THE MURDERERS OF MY PEOPLE AND THEIR MONSTROUS MASTER!

NOW THERE IS NOTHING LEFT BEHIND BUT GRIM MEMORIES... AND A *REASON* TO EXIST...

FASTER, KASA... AWAY FROM HERE!

DAGAR RIDES OFF ON THE LONG-FADED TRAIL MADE BY HIS ENEMIES...AS BUT ONE CLUE BURNS WITHIN HIS MIND...

I MUST FIND...AND *KILL*...THOSE WHO WEAR THE SIGN OF THE *SCORPION!*

LATER, EAST OF TULGONIA...

I'VE COME FOR ANCIENT FORAK! THIS TIME HE *WILL* BE RETURNED TO OSTELLON!

I'VE STOPPED VILLAINS BEFORE, I'LL—

WHA—?! YOU DIDN'T EVEN JERK AS MY BLADE STRUCK!

HAH! HAH! HAH! BY NOW YOU SHOULD KNOW BETTER, WITLESS FOOL!

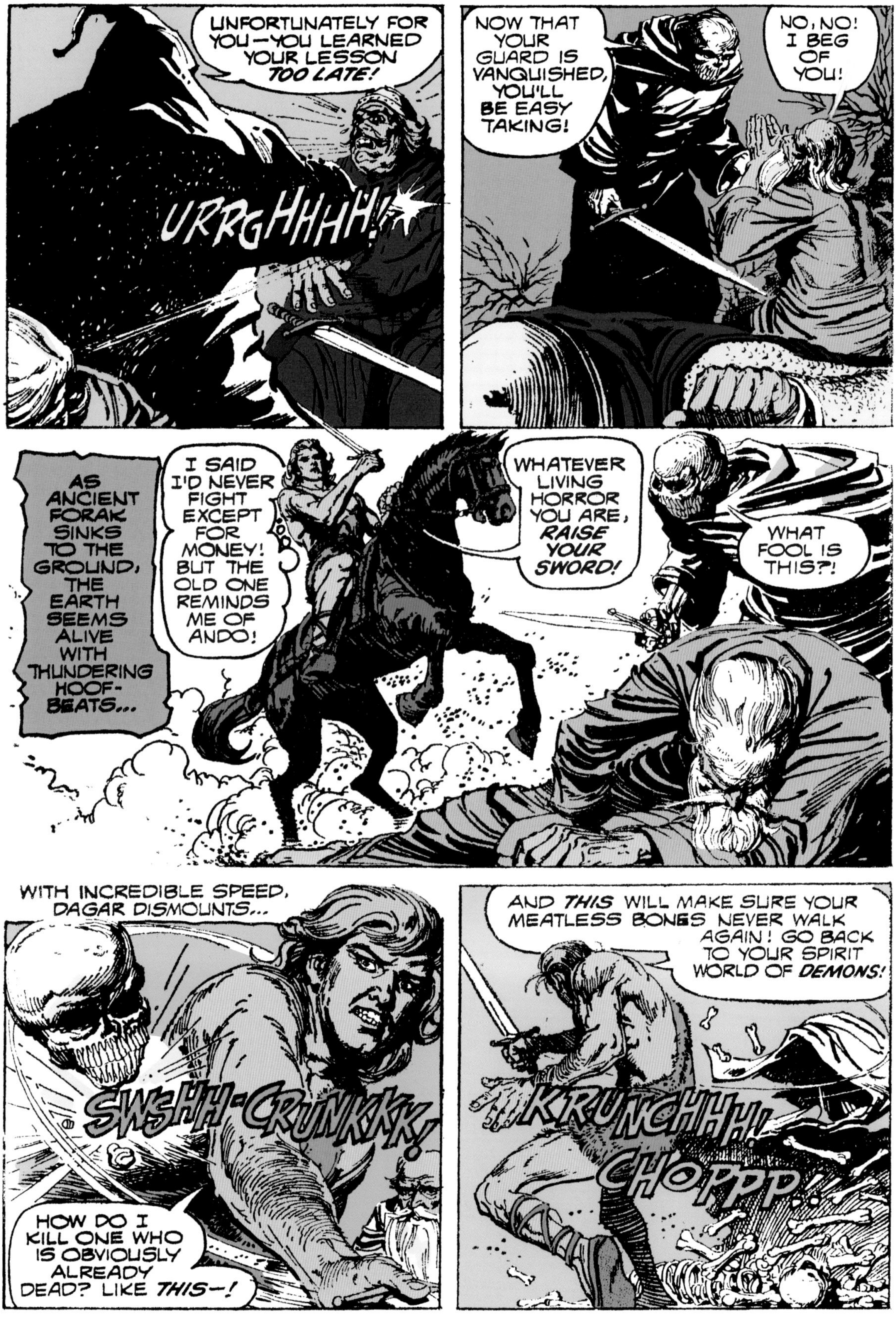
UNFORTUNATELY FOR YOU—YOU LEARNED YOUR LESSON TOO LATE!
URRGHHHH!
NOW THAT YOUR GUARD IS VANQUISHED, YOU'LL BE EASY TAKING!
NO, NO! I BEG OF YOU!
AS ANCIENT FORAK SINKS TO THE GROUND, THE EARTH SEEMS ALIVE WITH THUNDERING HOOF-BEATS...
I SAID I'D NEVER FIGHT EXCEPT FOR MONEY! BUT THE OLD ONE REMINDS ME OF ANDO!
WHATEVER LIVING HORROR YOU ARE, RAISE YOUR SWORD!
WHAT FOOL IS THIS?!
WITH INCREDIBLE SPEED, DAGAR DISMOUNTS...
SWSHH-CRUNKKK!
HOW DO I KILL ONE WHO IS OBVIOUSLY ALREADY DEAD? LIKE THIS—!
AND THIS WILL MAKE SURE YOUR MEATLESS BONES NEVER WALK AGAIN! GO BACK TO YOUR SPIRIT WORLD OF DEMONS!
KRUNCHHH! CHOPPP...

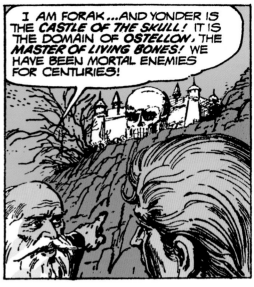

YOU'VE DONE IT, VALIANT ONE! DONE WHAT MY HIRELING FAILED TO DO!

DAGAR HAS LITTLE TIME, OLD ONE! TELL ME HOW A SKELETON LIVED...AND WHY HE WANTED YOU!

I AM FORAK...AND YONDER IS THE *CASTLE OF THE SKULL!* IT IS THE DOMAIN OF *OSTELLON,* THE *MASTER OF LIVING BONES!* WE HAVE BEEN MORTAL ENEMIES FOR CENTURIES!

FOR AGES, OSTELLON HAS WORKED HIS EVIL UPON THE LAND! THAT DREADED *SORCERER* HAS SUSTAINED MY LIFE, THOUGH I LONG FOR THE PEACE OF DEATH!

AND *WHY* HAS THIS OSTELLON KEPT YOU ALIVE FOR SO LONG?

BECAUSE HE HAS *WANTED* SOMETHING OF MINE...SOMETHING WHICH NOW, CURSE HIM, HE *HAS!* COME, I WILL SHOW YOU!

HIS CURIOSITY AROUSED, DAGAR FOLLOWS THE OLD MAN INTO A CAVE...

LOOK, DAGAR, INTO THE HOURGLASS BY WHICH I HAVE SOME CONTROL OVER VISIONS!

GAZE INTO THE GLASS AND SEE A TIME WHEN FORAK STILL HAD HIS MEAGER POWERS... AND WHEN OSTELLON FIRST FEASTED HIS EYES UPON *HER!*

BEHOLD ARRANNA, MY DAUGHTER...WHOSE BEAUTY ONE DAY ATTRACTED THE EVIL EYES OF *OSTELLON*...

WHO... WHO ARE YOU? WHAT DO YOU WANT?

I AM OSTELLON...AND YOU MUST BE MY BRIDE! I OFFER YOU *ETERNAL LIFE*... JUST AS I AM IMMORTAL!

N-NO! YOUR EYES... THEY SHOW ONLY *EVIL!* AND *DEATH!*

"ARRANNA ESCAPED THE SORCERER... AND I FLED WITH HER FROM THAT LAND..."

WE'LL GO WHERE OSTELLON CAN NEVER FIND US! HE CANNOT PURSUE US FOREVER!

"BUT ARRANNA'S BEAUTY HAD *BEWITCHING* POWER... AND OSTELLON WOULD INDEED SPEND ETERNITY PURSUING HER..."

I GIVE BOTH OF YOU A SHARE OF MY IMMORTALITY... SO THAT ARRANNA WILL ALWAYS BE MINE NO MATTER HOW LONG IT TAKES TO FIND HER... AND SO FORAK NEVER KNOWS THE PEACE OF *DEATH!*

"FOR AGES WE FLED AND HID FROM THE FIEND, EVENTUALLY FINDING THIS CAVE..."

WE WILL STAY HERE! AND I SHALL *PAY* SOME WARRIOR TO DEFEND US SHOULD OSTELLON FIND US!

BUT OSTELLON FOUND US AND SENT HIS SKELETONS TO ABDUCT ARRANNA! SHE IS NOW WITHIN THE *CASTLE OF THE SKULL!*

NEVER HAVE I SEEN SUCH A BEAUTIFUL WOMAN! I'LL *RESCUE* ARRANNA... AND MAKE HER MY *BRIDE!*

YOU SHALL HAVE MY DAUGHTER! BUT YOU'LL NEED *MORE* THAN YOUR SWORD TO BATTLE THE UNNATURAL HORRORS CREATED BY OSTELLON!

WHEN I FIRST DISCOVERED THIS CAVE, I FOUND *THIS!* THE LEGENDARY MACE AND CHAIN OF A WARRIOR GOD! IT MUST HAVE BEEN HERE FOR EONS!

THEY SAY THAT IN THE HANDS OF ONE NOBLE ENOUGH TO WIELD IT, ITS ENCHANTED POWER IS WITHOUT LIMIT! MY HIRED GUARD TRIED, BUT FAILED! I HAVE LITTLE MONEY, BUT...

SLOWLY AT FIRST, DAGAR'S STEEL-LIKE MUSCLES STRAIN TO LIFT THE INCREDIBLY HEAVY WEAPON...

YOU NEED PAY ME *NOTHING!* THIS TIME I FIGHT FOR A CAUSE! A *BEAUTIFUL* CAUSE!

THEN... THERE IS NO FURTHER NEED TO STRAIN...

THE *WEIGHT* IS GONE! THE WEAPON SEEMS *MADE* FOR MY HAND!

AND WITH THIS MAGIC WEAPON I'LL GO TO THE *CASTLE OF THE SKULL!* I'LL RETURN WITH ARRANNA.... OR NOT AT ALL! *THIS SWEARS DAGAR!*

PART TWO

CASTLE OF THE SKULL

IT IS STILL DAYLIGHT BUT THE DARK CLOUDS SWELL AND SPREAD AS IF TO SHIELD THE HEAVENS FROM THE MASSIVE SKULL. ONLY ONE WARRIOR DARES RIDE INTO THE GAZE OF THOSE HOLLOW EYES... *DAGAR* THE *INVINCIBLE!*

THE CASTLE OF THE SKULL! ACCORDING TO FORAK, EVEN THIS CASTLE WAS CONJURED UP BY OSTELLON, WHO MAKES IT APPEAR WHEREVER HE CHOOSES!

I SAID I'D NEVER FIGHT EXCEPT FOR PAYMENT! AND NOW I'M ABOUT TO CHALLENGE A POWERFUL SORCERER, AFTER BUT A GLIMPSE OF A YOUNG GIRL IN AN HOUR-GLASS!

COULD IT BE THAT FORAK WAS RIGHT ABOUT ARRANNA'S BEAUTY HAVING BEWITCHING POWERS? SOMEHOW JUST THE SIGHT OF HER MADE ME FEEL STRANGE!

EVEN AS DAGAR CONTEMPLATES HIS FEELINGS FOR THE GIRL, ARRANNA BROODS WITHIN A CHAMBER IN THE CASTLE OF THE SKULL...

WHAT IS THE MATTER, MY LOVELY ONE? YOU DO NOT LOOK HAPPY, EVEN THOUGH I OFFER TO SHARE MY THRONE WITH YOU... AND MAKE YOU OSTELLON'S QUEEN!

QUEEN?

I'M A *PRISONER* IN THIS GHASTLY PLACE!

PRECAUTIONS, MY DEAR! ONCE YOUR FATHER IS BROUGHT HERE, YOU WILL NOT DESIRE TO ESCAPE!

SOON ONE OF MY SKELETAL SLAVES WILL CAPTURE THE OLD TOAD! THEN IT WILL BE A DUNGEON FOR HIM, WHERE HE CAN *ENJOY* HIS ETERNAL LIFE!

THE GUARD MY FATHER HIRED WILL DESTROY YOUR SKELETONS! THEN HE'LL FREE ME FROM THIS JAIL!

BELIEVE THAT IF YOU LIKE, ARRANNA! BUT NO ONE *HUMAN* CAN SURVIVE THE HORRORS I CONTROL HERE!

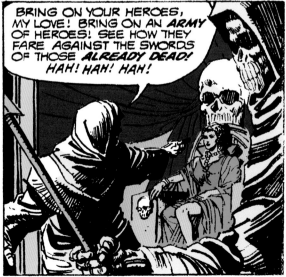

BRING ON YOUR HEROES, MY LOVE! BRING ON AN *ARMY* OF HEROES! SEE HOW THEY FARE AGAINST THE SWORDS OF THOSE *ALREADY DEAD!* HAH! HAH! HAH!

AT THAT MOMENT, OUTSIDE THE GRIM CASTLE...

I HOPE THIS MACE AND CHAIN IS AS ENCHANTED AS FORAK SAYS! ...HUH? WHY DO I HEAR A VOICE WHEN THERE IS NO VOICE? A VOICE IN MY *HEAD?!*

LET MY WORDS ENTER YOUR BRAIN, DAGAR! YOU HAVE THE MACE AND CHAIN OF THE WARRIOR GOD! NOW NOTHING CAN STOP YOU, SINCE YOUR CAUSE IS *JUST!*

"SUCCEED, AS I KNOW YOU CAN, DAGAR... SO THAT MY DAUGHTER WILL BE FREE OF OSTELLON'S CLUTCHES...AND I MIGHT KNOW *REST* FOR MY TIRED BODY!"

I HEAR YOU, OLD ONE!

MY HEART IS SAD FOR DAGAR! IF ONLY I COULD TELL HIM THE *MONSTROUS TRUTH!* BUT THEN HE WOULDN'T GO OFF TO VANQUISH OSTELLON!

THE YOUNG WARRIOR WILL LEARN THE TRUTH ONLY TOO SOON! WHEN THAT HAPPENS, I HOPE HIS HEART IS STRONG ENOUGH TO ENDURE IT! AND I'LL THANK THE GODS THAT I WILL NOT BE ALIVE TO FACE HIM!

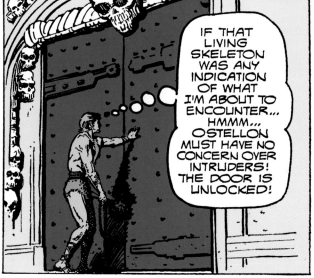

IF THAT LIVING SKELETON WAS ANY INDICATION OF WHAT I'M ABOUT TO ENCOUNTER... HMMM... OSTELLON MUST HAVE NO CONCERN OVER INTRUDERS! THE DOOR IS UNLOCKED!

DAGAR BUT TOUCHES THE DOOR...AND, AS IF POSSESSING LIFE OF ITS OWN, IT OPENS TO REVEAL ONLY *BLACKNESS*...

CCRREEEEHAAAKKKKKKK!!!

...*BLACKNESS*...AND FIVE GLOWING THINGS OF *WHITE*!

BY THE WARRIOR GODS!

SOMEONE SEEKS ENTRANCE TO THE CASTLE!

THEN LET US SHOW HIM THAT HE HAS FOUND ONLY... *DEATH!*

THERE ARE TOO MANY OF THEM TO FIGHT WITH MY SWORD! BUT I HAVE THE ADVANTAGE WITH THIS MAGIC WEAPON!

SWWW-KARUNKKK!!!

GO BACK! BACK TO THE UNHOLY GRAVES WHICH SPAWNED YOU! NO DEAD MEN WILL MAKE A CORPSE OF *DAGAR!*

BUT EVEN AS DAGAR REGAINS HIS BREATH, AN AWESOME WHITE FORM EMERGES FROM THE SHADOWS OUTSIDE THE CASTLE...

MUSTERING ALL HIS UNEQUALED STRENGTH, DAGAR PREPARES TO SWING THE WEAPON NO OTHER MORTAL HAS EVER WIELDED...

THE SKELETON OF A *MAMMOTH* CHARGING DOWN AT ME! IF I HADN'T RENOUNCED THE GODS OF MY PEOPLE, I'D PRAY TO THEM THAT THIS MACE BE AS POWERFUL AS FORAK PROMISED!

...AND RELEASES THE *FULL FORCE* OF THE *MACE* ONCE USED BY A *GOD!*

SWSHHH--CRKK--RMBL!

THAT'S IT, DAGAR! AS LONG AS YOU HAVE THE POWER OF THAT MACE AND CHAIN, YOU ARE LIKE A GOD! YOU ARE TRULY... *INVINCIBLE!*

"NOW GO...*GO!* EVEN OSTELLON IS NOT PREPARED FOR A WEAPON FORGED IN THE LAND OF GODS!"

WITH NO LIGHT SAVE THAT THROWN BY THE ENCHANTED MACE, THE MERCENARY SOLDIER BOLDLY PROWLS THROUGH THE BLACK CORRIDOR... SPURRED ONWARD ONLY BY THE COURAGE IN HIS BREAST AND THE STRANGE, SUDDEN LOVE FOR THE GIRL ARRANNA...

SO FAR THESE BONES HAVE NOT SPRUNG AGAINST ME! PERHAPS OSTELLON IS STILL UNAWARE OF MY PRESENCE IN THE CASTLE!

"KEEP GOING, DAGAR! THE MACE ITSELF WILL LOCATE THE ONLY OTHER GOOD HEART IN THE CASTLE! BY THE WEAPON'S VIBRATIONS YOU WILL FIND **ARRANNA!**"

FORAK IS RIGHT! THE MACE FILLS ME WITH WEIRD *SENSATIONS* THAT GET *STRONGER* THE FARTHER I GO IN THIS DIRECTION!

AND THEN...

HERE THE FEELING IS THE *STRONGEST!* THAT MEANS ARRANNA IS BEHIND THIS DOOR! NO WEAPON COULD CUT THROUGH THAT BARRIER! NO WEAPON...EXCEPT...

THIS *ENCHANTED* ONE!

CLANG-
GASHHHHH!

THEN DAGAR **SEES** HER... THE BEWITCHING BEAUTY WHOSE IMAGE IN THE HOURGLASS HAD CAPTURED HIS HEART...

WH-WHO ARE YOU? IF OSTELLON HAS SENT YOU...

I HAVE NOT COME FROM OSTELLON!

I'VE COME TO **SLAY** OSTELLON! LOOK AT ME, ARRANNA! AM I NOT MADE OF LIVING FLESH...AND NOT DRY BONES?

I DON'T KNOW! I AM SO CONFUSED! AND YET, YOU HOLD THE ENCHANTED MACE!

YES, I WAS GIVEN THE MACE AND CHAIN BY YOUR FATHER! HE IS STILL ALIVE! BUT NEITHER OF YOU ARE SAFE UNTIL THE EVIL OF OSTELLON IS BROUGHT TO AN END!

THAT IS WHY **DAGAR** IS HERE! THE IMAGE I SAW OF YOU IN FORAK'S HOURGLASS BEWITCHED ME! I MUST HAVE YOU FOR MY WIFE!

B-BUT... OH, NO...

NO! DAGAR, PLEASE DON'T FALL IN LOVE WITH ME! THERE IS SO MUCH YOU DON'T UNDERSTAND...THAT YOU ARE BLIND TO!

I NEED ONLY KNOW **ONE** THING!

AND THAT IS... I LOVE YOU!

BUT DAGAR! YOU *MUST* LISTEN TO ME!

THERE IS NO TIME TO LISTEN! ONLY TO ACT! I PROMISED TO FREE YOU AND FIND ETERNAL PEACE FOR YOUR FATHER! I MUST SLAY THE FIEND CALLED OSTELLON!

THERE IS THE SOUND OF RATTLING *BONES* AS...

OSTELLON! WITH HIS ARMY OF SKELETON MEN!

SO — SOMEONE HAS FINALLY SUCCEEDED IN BREAKING INTO MY STRONGHOLD!

NO MATTER! YOU WILL NEVER DEFEAT THE HUNDREDS OF WARRIORS SOON TO DESCEND UPON YOU! THEN *YOUR* BONES WILL JOIN THEIR RANKS!

FORAK SPEAKS TO ME AGAIN!

"DO NOT TRY TO FIGHT THEM INDIVIDUALLY! THE MACE CAN SERVE A BETTER PURPOSE! THINK, DAGAR, **THINK!**"

"...THINK!"

HAH! I SEE YOU BACK AWAY! PERHAPS EVEN WITH SUCH A WEAPON, YOUR COURAGE DOES NOT EQUAL YOUR STRENGTH!

BUT DAGAR IS HARDLY AFRAID... EXCEPT FOR THE GIRL'S SAFETY...

STAND BACK, ARRANNA! AND GET READY TO FLEE! THIS WILL ALL HAPPEN *FAST!*

NOW RUN, WOMAN! RUN TO THE FAR WALL! IN A MOMENT I'LL BE AT YOUR SIDE!

HIS WEAPON IS LIKE *NOTHING* I HAVE EVER SEEN! IT CUTS THROUGH STONE AS IF IT WERE BREAD!

RUMMMBLLLE!

Thkkk!

OOOOH...

RUMMMBLLLE!

ARRANNA!

DEATH FILLS THE CHAMBER... NOT THE DEATH OF BLEACHED SKELETONS... BUT THE DESCENDING DEATH OF TONS OF STONE...

THERE IS ONLY *ONE* CHANCE! IF I CAN *REVERSE* THE SPELL WHICH BROUGHT THIS CASTLE INTO EXISTENCE...

CARUMMMMBLLLEEE!

SAVE US, MASTER!

BUT SPELLS OF SUCH MAGNITUDE REQUIRE TIME... *MORE* TIME THAN IT TAKES AN ENTIRE CASTLE TO FALL UPON ITS CREATOR...

RRR-RRUMBLLLEEE!

AS THE FINAL CHUNKS OF STONY DEATH RAIN DOWN, SOMETHING DRIFTS BEFORE DAGAR'S EYES...

A BANNER! WITH THE SIGN OF *SCORPIO!*

SO OSTELLON WAS IN LEAGUE WITH *SCORPIO* ALL ALONG! I COULD HAVE FORCED HIM TO TELL ME WHERE THAT MOST VILE ARCH FIEND IS... BUT NOW IT'S *TOO LATE!*

AND THE MACE OF THE WARRIOR GOD IS LOST... BURIED UNDER ALL THAT TONNAGE! BUT IT DOESN'T MATTER, AS LONG AS ARRANNA IS SAFE!

WHAT—?! *DAGAR!*

"YOU HAVE DONE WELL, NOBLE DAGAR! I HAVE FOUND THE ETERNAL REST... OF DEATH!"

THERE IS NOTHING MORE TO FEAR, ARRANNA! OSTELLON IS DEAD... AND ALL THE EFFECTS OF HIS POWER ARE GONE!

WITHOUT THE POWER OF OSTELLON, THE CASTLE OF THE SKULL NO LONGER HAS REASON TO EXIST!

YOUR FATHER IS AT PEACE, MY LOVE! ALL THAT REMAINS NOW IS OUR WEDDING! THAT IS, IF YOU'LL HAVE DAGAR!

OH, DAGAR... POOR, BELOVED DAGAR... IF ONLY YOU'D HAVE LET ME EXPLAIN!

EXPLAIN? WHAT IS THERE TO EXPLAIN? THE MENACE IS OVER AND WE HAVE EACH OTHER!

TRUE... TRUE...

BUT DID YOU NOT CONSIDER THE FACT THAT OSTELLON KEPT *BOTH* MY FATHER AND ME ALIVE FOR *CENTURIES?* ALIVE ONLY BY HIS EVIL MAGIC?

DID YOU NOT REALIZE THAT ONCE OSTELLON *DIED* AND HIS POWER *ENDED*... JUST AS THE CASTLE OF THE SKULL RETURNED TO ITS RIGHTFUL FORM... SO WOULD *ALL THINGS* PRESERVED BY HIM? THAT I WOULD REVERT TO MY *TRUE AGE?*

ARRANNA!

EYES THAT HAVE SEEN VIOLENCE AND CARNAGE... WITH BUT A GLIMPSE OF BEAUTY AND LOVE... STARE INCREDULOUSLY AS A WORLD SEEMS TO END...

ARRANNA!

DUST! SHE HAS TURNED TO DUST!

DAGAR'S MUSCLES ARE AS STEEL. AS A WARRIOR HE MAY BE INVINCIBLE...BUT EVEN A WARRIOR'S HEART CAN SHATTER. IT TAKES SUCH A WARRIOR TO SUPPRESS EVEN A SINGLE TEAR...

THE GODS MUST BE ENJOYING THEIR JOKE! IN SAVING ARRANNA I DESTROYED THE ONE WHO COULD TELL ME WHERE TO FIND SCORPIO! AND IN DESTROYING OSTELLON, I HAVE DOOMED MY ONLY LOVE!

DARKNESS BEGINS TO APPEAR AND CLOUDS NO LONGER TRY TO BLOT OUT EVIL. AS THE YOUNG WARRIOR SLOWLY RIDES AWAY ON HIS MAGNIFICENT STEED, HE RESOLVES...

NO MORE WILL I LET LOVE INTERFERE WITH MY QUEST! I WILL FIGHT ONLY FOR PAYMENT...EXCEPT IN THAT CONFLICT WITH THE MONSTER KNOWN AS SCORPIO! FOR I AM A MERCENARY WARRIOR,...AND AN AVENGER!

STORY: DON GLUT
ART: JESSE F. SANTOS

MERCENARY AND AVENGER HE MAY BE, BUT THE WORLD WILL SOON KNOW OF HIM AS... DAGAR, THE INVINCIBLE!

the END

GOLD KEY ®

90279-301
JANUARY

TALES OF SWORD
AND SORCERY

DAGAR
THE INVINCIBLE

DAGAR PITS HIS MIGHT AGAINST A NIGHTMARISH
MONSTER...THE BEAST WITHIN

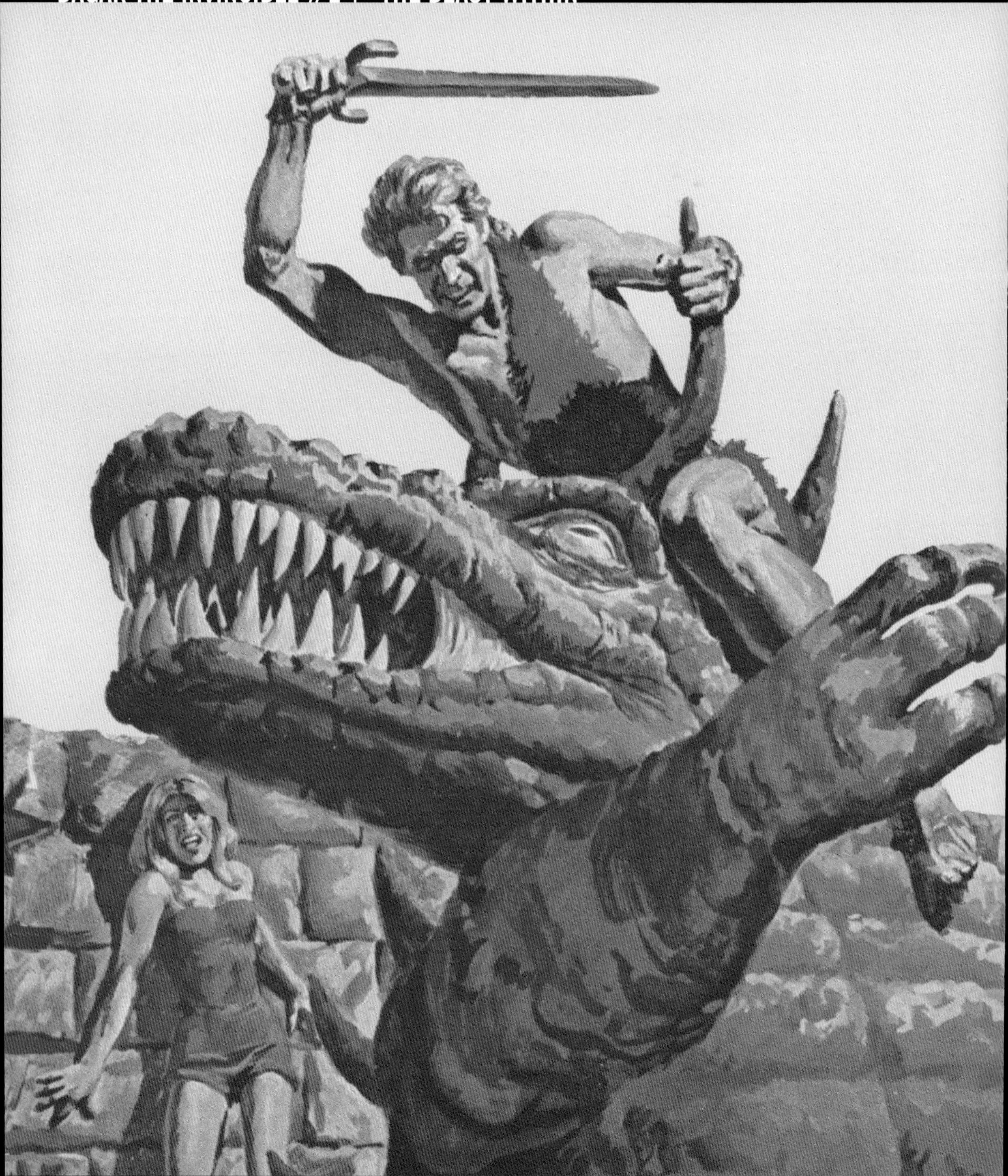

DAGAR THE INVINCIBLE

THE BEAST WITHIN

IN THE TWILIGHT YEARS FOLLOWING THE AGE OF THE CAVEMAN AND THE MASTODON, WHEN THE EARTH IS GOVERNED BY **MAGIC FORCES**, A WARRIOR RIDES INTO A SMALL TOWN. BUT THIS IS NO ORDINARY WARRIOR WHO FIGHTS FOR RIGHTEOUS CAUSES. THIS IS **DAGAR** OF TULGONIA...

PERHAPS WE'LL FIND EXCITEMENT IN THIS TOWN, KASA! THERE ARE WEAK MEN ALL ABOUT THIS LAND WHO CANNOT FIGHT THEIR OWN BRAWLS...MEN WHO WILL SEEK TO PAY DAGAR TO BATTLE FOR THEM!

90279-301
DAGAR THE INVINCIBLE #2-7210

AFTER HALTING HIS STEED, DAGAR OVERHEARS...

NO, LORA-LEI! I **WON'T** GO THROUGH THAT AGAIN! NOT TONIGHT! NOT **EVER**!

BUT, LUPOF...YOU CAN'T DO THIS MAD THING! I AM YOUR SISTER! DOES MY LOVE FOR YOU MEAN NOTHING?

BECAUSE YOU ARE MY SISTER IS EVEN **MORE** REASON FOR WHAT I AM ABOUT TO DO! PLEASE...LEAVE ME ALONE! YOU CANNOT BE SISTER TO A **MURDERER**!

LUPOF!

THIS GIRL CALLED LORA-LEI MIGHT BE NEEDING THE **SERVICES** OF A MERCENARY WARRIOR! THEN WHEN I SHAKE MY FIST IT WILL RING WITH THE SOUND OF GOLD COINS!

YOU SEEM TO BE IN THE NEED OF **AID**, WOMAN! I AM DAGAR! AND I'VE BEEN KNOWN TO FIGHT FOR CAUSES NOT MY OWN...FOR A **PRICE**!

THE COST DOES NOT MATTER, MERCENARY! LUPOF IS ALL THAT I HAVE IN THIS WORLD! YOU **MUST** SAVE HIM! IS THIS AMOUNT SUFFICIENT?

THIS LORA-LEI IS SO BEAUTIFUL, I AM TEMPTED TO RETURN THE GOLD! BUT...NO!

THIS SEEMS TO BE FAIR PAYMENT! BUT FROM **WHAT** MUST I SAVE LUPOF?

FROM **HIMSELF!** MY BROTHER SEEKS TO **DESTROY** HIMSELF THIS NIGHT!

THEN IF I AM TO **EARN** THESE COINS, I MUST **RIDE!**

WITHIN MOMENTS...

THERE HE IS, ASCENDING THE CLIFF! BUT WE CAN OVERTAKE HIM! FASTER, KASA!

HOW I WISH I WERE CLOSING IN ON SCORPIO, THE FIEND THAT I SEARCH FOR, INSTEAD OF THIS TROUBLED LUPOF!

LUPOF! WAIT!

WHOEVER YOU ARE, DON'T TRY TO STOP ME! I'LL NEVER BE **TORTURED** OR FORCED TO KILL AGAIN!

DAGAR RIDES TOWARD THE FIGURE OF LUPOF...WHO PAUSES MOMENTARILY BENEATH THE COLD BLUE RAYS OF THE FULL MOON...HIS FACE TWISTING INTO A LOOK OF HORROR...AND THEN...

HEART RACING... BREATH HEAVY... DAGAR PAUSES AT THE EDGE OF THE CLIFF... GAZING DOWN INTO THE MOON-BATHED WATERS...

THE WATERS HAVE CONSUMED HIM...

IT **MUST** END THIS NIGHT!

LUPOF!

...BUT DAGAR DOES NOT GIVE UP SO EASILY!

THERE HE IS! IF I CAN SEIZE HIM BY SURPRISE, I MAY YET SAVE HIM!

GOT HIM! BUT HIS FACE...NEVER HAVE I SEEN SUCH RAGE! BY THE WAR GODS....HE'S TRYING TO **PULL ME DOWN** WITH HIM!

HIS LUNGS CRAVING AIR, DAGAR BATTLES TURBULENT WATERS...AND A MAN SEEMINGLY **MAD**...TO REACH THE SURFACE...

HIS STRENGTH SEEMS TO BE **INCREASING!**

AS DAGAR STRUGGLES TO BREAK FREE OF LUPOF'S UNBREAKABLE GRIP, HE FEELS THE GROWTH OF SHARP POINTS DIGGING INTO HIS FLESH...

HE HAS THE STRENGTH OF AN ANIMAL...BY THE GODS! HE'S NOT **HUMAN!**

USING ALL HIS STRENGTH TO BURST FROM THE TORTUROUS WATERS, THE MERCENARY WARRIOR IS FACED WITH A STARK REALITY!

YOU'RE...A **WEREWOLF!**

ARRGGRRRR!

THIS WILL NOT DAZE YOU FOR LONG, BUT MY ONLY CHANCE IS TO REACH THE SHORE!

SOCK!

SPLASHING THROUGH THE SHALLOW WATER, DAGAR REACHES HIS DESTINATION.

I NO LONGER HAVE THE WATER TO CONTEND WITH, BUT I'M STILL NOT SAFE! AT LEAST ON LAND I HAVE A BETTER OPPORTUNITY TO FIGHT THAT...THAT **THING!**

MY **SWORD**...IT IS MY ONLY CHANCE! BUT HOW CAN I **SLAY** THAT MONSTER? I WAS PAID TO **SAVE** HIM!

ARRROOOWWWW

DAGAR HAS NO OPPORTUNITY TO MAKE THE DECISION WHETHER THE MONSTER IS TO LIVE OR DIE...FOR AS THE WEREWOLF SPRINGS ON POWERFUL HAUNCHES, HIS SWORD HAND ACTS MECHANICALLY...

GGRRRROOWMMRRR!!!

AND THE BEAST FALLS UPON THE BLADE!

MAY LORA-LEI FORGIVE ME! BUT IT IS HIS LIFE... OR MINE!

OOWWW!!

BY MY GRANDFATHER'S GRAVE! HE PULLED OUT THE SWORD LIKE IT WAS NOTHING!

CAN THE WEREWOLF DIE BY MORTAL MEANS? DAGAR REALIZES THAT THE BEAST-MAN HAS BEEN CAUSED PAIN, WHICH FURTHER AROUSES THE BLOODLUST IN ITS UNHOLY SOUL...

GGRRR--GGAARRRMM--GA-RROOOOOO!!!

AND AS THE WARRIOR SEES THE WET FANGS APPROACH HIS FLESH...

THE FIEND HAS THE STRENGTH OF A DOZEN WARRIORS...

WHILE DAGAR STRUGGLES WITH THE INHUMAN WEREWOLF...ELSEWHERE, TWO TRAVELERS REST BEFORE THE WARMTH OF A CRACKLING CAMPFIRE...

AND WHY ARE YOU SO GLUM?

THE SAME REASON **YOU** ARE! EVEN THE HORSES SENSE THERE IS **EVIL** IN THESE WOODS!

BONNNGGGGGG!!!

DID YOU HEAR THAT GONG?! WHY WOULD A GONG SOUND IN THE WOODS AT NIGHT?

NOW WHAT DO WE DO? WE ARE STRANDED IN THESE DARK WOODS WITHOUT OUR STEEDS!

I TELL YOU IT WASN'T JUST THAT GONG THAT SCARED THEM OFF! THERE IS SOME **TERRIBLE PRESENCE** LURKING HERE! BY THE GODS — DID YOU HEAR **THAT?!**

AND THROUGH THE UNDERBRUSH COMES THE SLITHERING SOUND OF SOMETHING GIGANTIC.

CAR-RRRUNNCH-CHHH!!!

THERE! THE SOUND COMES AGAIN! AND... AND **LOOK!**

I... I SEE IT! AN ENORMOUS **SHADOW**... PUSHING ASIDE **TREES!**

NOW IT LUMBERS INTO THE MOON-LIGHT! I CAN **SEE** IT!

IT'S A **DEMON** FROM THE WORLD OF **NIGHTMARES!** IT **SEES** US! IT'S...IT'S...

HISSSSSS!

AARRRRGHHHH! HISSS! GAAAAH!

SOON THERE IS ONLY THE SILENCE OF THE FOREST...SAVE FOR THE CRUNCHING OF BONES.

BEFORE THE WEREWOLF'S FANGS CAN PENETRATE DAGAR'S SKIN, A SUDDEN APPARITION CAUSES THE BEAST TO PAUSE... RELEASING ITS CRUSHING GRIP...

ARROOORRWFF!

LORA-LEI! SHE SEEMS TO HAVE CAST SOME TYPE OF **SPELL** OVER THE BRUTE!

TELL ME, WOMAN! ARE YOU A **WITCH?** THE WAY HE FLED WHEN HE SAW YOU...

I AM NO WITCH! BUT EVEN IN HIS BEAST FORM, LUPOF CANNOT HARM HIS OWN **SISTER!**

WHY DIDN'T YOU TELL ME THAT YOUR BROTHER WAS A WEREWOLF? YOU HAVE MUCH TO EXPLAIN, LORA-LEI!

I WILL EXPLAIN...

After a long search which mercifully overlaps into the dawn...

THAT MAN! IS HE ONE OF LUPOF'S VICTIMS OR...?

LUPOF! THANK YOUR GODS, LORA-LEI, THAT HE IS A MAN AGAIN!

LUPOF REGAINS CONSCIOUSNESS AND...

WHY DIDN'T YOU LET ME DIE AND FIND PEACE? NOW EVERY NIGHT THE FULL MOON RISES I'LL BE TRANSFORMED INTO A WEREWOLF THIRSTING FOR HUMAN BLOOD! ALL BECAUSE OF THAT MONSTER SCORPIO!

WHAT?! YOU KNOW OF SCORPIO? THEN YOU MUST KNOW WHERE TO FIND HIM! TELL ME!

I WILL TELL YOU WHAT I KNOW ABOUT THIS VERMIN CALLED SCORPIO! YOU SEE, I WAS NOT ALWAYS A MAN-BEAST! ONCE I WAS AS NORMAL AS YOU...

"I WAS A HUNTER... PROUD OF THE SKIN I WORE, TAKEN FROM A **DIRE WOLF** I SLEW! ONE NIGHT I CAME UPON AN ABANDONED FORTRESS.

"THERE WERE LEGENDS ABOUT THE OLD FORTRESS... STORIES OF WEIRD RITES PERFORMED BY THE **CULT OF THE SCORPION**... WHICH THE BRAVEST MEN SPOKE OF ONLY IN WHISPERS...

"I WAS CURIOUS TO SEE THE SO-CALLED FORBIDDEN RITES OF SCORPIO... BUT MY CURIOSITY SEALED MY OWN DOOM..."

AH! THE MASTER WILL BE PLEASED! HE SO LOVES TO DEAL OUT PUNISHMENTS TO SPIES!

"I WAS DRAGGED WITHIN THE FORTRESS, WHERE I BEHELD IN ALL HIS BLASPHEMOUS MAJESTY, **SCORPIO HIMSELF!**"

FOR YOUR INTRUSION, YOU SHALL BECOME THAT WHICH YOU HUNT... THE BEAST WHOSE SKIN YOU WEAR!

"SCORPIO GESTURED... HIS EYES BLAZING... HIS LIPS SILENTLY FORMING OBSCENE SPELLS. I COULD HEAR HIS TERRIBLE LAUGHTER AS MY BODY WAS WRENCHED BY HIS WRETCHED POWERS...

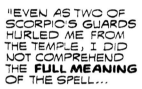

"EVEN AS TWO OF SCORPIO'S GUARDS HURLED ME FROM THE TEMPLE, I DID NOT COMPREHEND THE **FULL MEANING** OF THE SPELL..."

"I RAN AS FAST AS I COULD FROM THAT PLACE OF DEMON RITUALS. NEARLY EXHAUSTED, I STOPPED TO REST...THEN FELT COMPELLED TO GAZE AT THE **FULL MOON**..."

"A SUDDEN CONVULSION SEIZED ME...AND I REALIZED THE TRUE HORROR OF MY FATE. UNDER THE INFLUENCE OF THE MOON, I TRANSFORMED INTO A HIDEOUS **WEREWOLF**..."

...THIRSTING FOR **BLOOD**...AND VULNERABLE ONLY TO A WEAPON OF **SILVER**!"

THAT IS EVERYTHING! BUT YOU ALSO SEEM TO HAVE A PERSONAL GRUDGE AGAINST THIS SCORPIO!

AYE! HIS ARMY MASSACRED ALL THE PEOPLE OF **TULGONIA** EXCEPT ME... DAGAR!

WITHIN ME IS ALL THAT IS LEFT OF AN ENTIRE NATION! I **AM** TULGONIA! AND AS MY GODS DESERTED ME, I RENOUNCED THEM TO BE A **HIRED WARRIOR**! NOW I LIVE TO FIND AND DESTROY SCORPIO AND HIS VICIOUS HORDES!

I DON'T KNOW WHERE SCORPIO'S DOMAIN LIES! BUT I CAN LEAD YOU TO THAT FORTRESS! YOU SEE, I TOO WOULD LIKE TO END SCORPIO'S MISERABLE LIFE!

THEN LEAD THE WAY, MY FRIEND!

SOON...

PERHAPS WE'D BETTER PART COMPANY BEFORE TOO LONG, DAGAR! THE MOON WILL STILL BE FULL TONIGHT!

NO! WE DO THIS **TOGETHER**!

THERE IS THE FORTRESS!

YOU AND I WILL GO THERE, LUPOF, WHILE LORA-LEI STAYS HERE!

NO! MY PLACE IS WITH MY BROTHER! I AM NOT AFRAID TO **FIGHT**!

YOU WILL **STAY HERE**! BESIDES, WE NEED SOMEONE TO WATCH THE HORSES!

DAGAR IS RIGHT, LORA-LEI! DO AS HE SAYS!

I THOUGHT YOU SAID THIS WAS AN OLD FORTRESS! IT APPEARS MORE TO BE A **GRAVEYARD**! THESE ARE **HUMAN** BONES!

I'VE BEEN A HUNTER LONG ENOUGH TO RECOGNIZE **FANG MARKS** WHEN I SEE THEM! THESE POOR MEN WERE **DEVOURED**... BY SOME TYPE OF **MONSTROUS BEAST**!

A BEAST?

I KNOW WHAT YOU'RE THINKING, DAGAR! BUT THIS GRISLY WORK WAS DONE BY SOME... SOME **OTHER** MONSTER!

I AM SORRY! I DID NOT **THINK!**

NO, **I** APOLOGIZE! I CANNOT DENY THAT I HAVE KILLED LIKE AN ANIMAL! COME... NOW WE HAVE MORE IMPORTANT THINGS WITH WHICH TO CONCERN OURSELVES!

LOOK HERE, LUPOF! A GONG BEARING THE SIGN OF **SCORPIO!** AND THESE MANACLES, PROBABLY USED TO RESTRAIN THE FIEND'S PRISONERS!

AND THIS **PIT**...

THIS IS MOST OMINOUS! IS THIS PIT THE FINAL GRAVE OF SCORPIO'S VICTIMS?

PERHAPS! IT IS SO DEEP ALL I CAN SEE IS **BLACKNESS!**

I DON'T LIKE THE **EASE** WITH WHICH WE APPROACH THE FORTRESS! SCORPIO MAY BE **TOYING** WITH US... LETTING US BLUNDER INTO A **TRAP!** WE SHOULD HAVE COME HERE AT NIGHT, WHEN WE'D HAVE THE CONCEALMENT OF SHADOWS!

NIGHT? DON'T TALK FOOLISHNESS, DAGAR! WE'VE ALREADY BEEN THROUGH **THAT!**

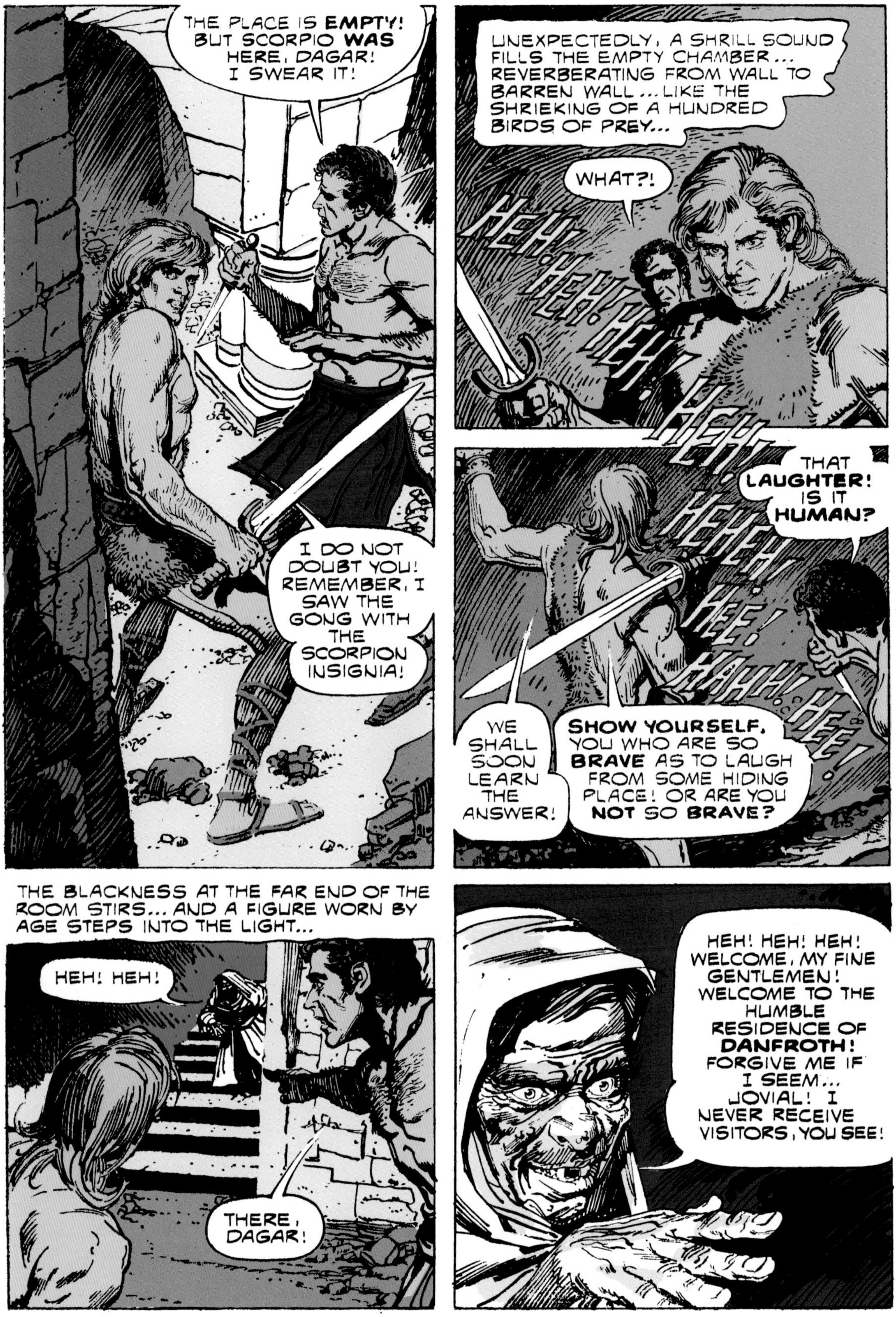
THE PLACE IS EMPTY! BUT SCORPIO WAS HERE, DAGAR! I SWEAR IT!
I DO NOT DOUBT YOU! REMEMBER, I SAW THE GONG WITH THE SCORPION INSIGNIA!
UNEXPECTEDLY, A SHRILL SOUND FILLS THE EMPTY CHAMBER... REVERBERATING FROM WALL TO BARREN WALL... LIKE THE SHRIEKING OF A HUNDRED BIRDS OF PREY...
WHAT?!
HEH! HEH! HEH! HEH! HEH!
THAT LAUGHTER! IS IT HUMAN?
HEHEH! HEE! HAHH! HEE!
WE SHALL SOON LEARN THE ANSWER!
SHOW YOURSELF, YOU WHO ARE SO BRAVE AS TO LAUGH FROM SOME HIDING PLACE! OR ARE YOU NOT SO BRAVE?
THE BLACKNESS AT THE FAR END OF THE ROOM STIRS... AND A FIGURE WORN BY AGE STEPS INTO THE LIGHT...
HEH! HEH!
THERE, DAGAR!
HEH! HEH! HEH! WELCOME, MY FINE GENTLEMEN! WELCOME TO THE HUMBLE RESIDENCE OF DANFROTH! FORGIVE ME IF I SEEM... JOVIAL! I NEVER RECEIVE VISITORS, YOU SEE!

WE WANT NONE OF YOUR SENILE CHATTER, DAN-FROTH! JUST TELL US... WHERE IS THE ARCH-FIEND **SCORPIO?**

SCORPIO? I HAVE NOT HEARD SUCH A NAME BEFORE!

PUT HIM DOWN, DAGAR! HE IS A DEFENSELESS OLD MAN!

HMM... PERHAPS YOU ARE RIGHT, LUPOF! DAGAR DOES NOT FIGHT HELPLESS ANCIENTS!

I HAVE LIVED IN THIS FORTRESS FOR BUT A SHORT TIME! AND DURING THAT TIME NO ONE SAVE YOU HAS PAID ME A VISIT!

PERHAPS HE SPEAKS THE TRUTH! NO ONE COULD LIVE HERE, KNOWING IT WAS USED AS A TEMPLE BY SCORPIO!

PERHAPS...

BUT SINCE YOU ARE MY GUESTS, LET ME OFFER YOU FOOD AND DRINK!

WE HAVEN'T EATEN SINCE LAST NIGHT! NOW THAT WE'RE HERE, IT WON'T MATTER IF WE FILL OUR STOMACHS!

A SHORT WHILE LATER...

HERE IS A MEAL FIT FOR A GOD, DEAR SIRS!

MAYBE I MISJUDGED THE OLD FOOL! I CAN ALREADY TASTE THAT FOOD! WHAT DO YOU SAY WE BRING SOME BACK TO LORA-LEI?

THE FOOD IS INDEED FIT FOR A GOD... BUT THE **DRINK**...

THE **WINE!** SOMETHING IS IN THE WINE! CAN'T... STAY AWA—※

HEH! HEH! A FEW OF THE RIGHT KINDS OF **HERBS** IN YOUR DRINKS, AND YOU SUBMIT TO THE **GOD OF DREAMS!** IF SCORPIO WERE HERE RIGHT NOW, HE WOULD BE PROUD OF HIS FORMER SERVANT! HEH! HEH! HEH!

MEANWHILE, IN THE CLEARING WHERE LORA-LEI WAITS IMPATIENTLY WITH THE HORSES...

I'M WORRIED! LUPOF AND DAGAR HAVE STILL NOT RETURNED! YET I HAVE SEEN NO **CONFLICT**... NO SIGNS OF **ANYONE!**

SOON THE MOON WILL RISE! THEN MY BROTHER WILL NOT BE ABLE TO CONTROL HIMSELF! DAGAR COULD BE HIS FIRST VICTIM...

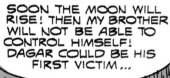

LATER... INSIDE THE FORTRESS...

OOO, MY BRAIN FEELS LIKE A SWORD HAS BEEN RUN THROUGH IT! I CAN STILL HARDLY MOVE! EVERYTHING... SO HAZY...

GLAZED EYES FOCUS ON A FOREBODING SHAPE...

YOU! YOU **DRUGGED** US! I'LL...

BEFORE YOU THREATEN TO DO **ANYTHING**, I SUGGEST YOU TRY TO MOVE YOUR ARMS! HEH! HEH!

WE'RE CHAINED TO THE WALL! AND I'M STILL TOO GROGGY TO PUT TO USE ALL MY STRENGTH... TO...

NEVER MIND BREAKING FREE! LOOK AT THE **SKY!**

IT IS NIGHT... AND THE FULL MOON IS BEGINNING ITS ASCENT INTO THE HEAVENS! DAGAR... PLEASE FORGIVE ME **NOW**... FOR WHAT I CANNOT HELP BUT DO **LATER!**

DANFROTH, I BEG OF YOU! RELEASE ME FROM THESE CHAINS! BEFORE **ALL** OF US SUFFER!

SILENCE, FOOL! FOR YOU ARE TO SERVE SCORPIO! YES, SCORPIO **WAS** HERE... TO SUMMON FORTH A MONSTROUS SLAVE TO SERVE HIM! I, DANFROTH, WAS LEFT HERE TO TEND TO THE CREATURE'S **NEEDS!**

AFTER SCORPIO LEFT FOR THE **NORTH,** I WAS ENTRUSTED WITH THIS GONG... AND THE TASK OF SEEING THAT THE MONSTER BE **FED**... FED ON THOSE WHO HAPPEN BY!

I SUMMON YOU... TO SPREAD THE **EVIL OF SCORPIO!**

CLAAAANNNNNGGGG!

YOU! WHY DO YOU CONTINUE TO STARE AT THE **MOON?** IT IS FROM THE **BLACK PIT** THAT YOUR DOOM WILL ARISE!

BUT LUPOF HAS NOT HEARD THE RAVINGS OF DANFROTH... NOR THE TOLL OF THE SCORPIO GONG...

THE MOON! I CAN'T... HIDE FROM IT! OH, THE **AGONY**... LIKE MY SOUL... BEING RIPPED FROM MY BODY...

...THE **PAIN**...OF MY FLESH REFORMING... MY TEETH...✳ M-M-MFFF...

GRRRR ROOWWW!

YOU! THESE OLD EYES DID NOT RECOGNIZE YOU! YOU ARE THE ONE SCORPIO CHANGED INTO A **BEAST!**

SINEWS BULGE BENEATH MOON-BATHED FUR... AND WITH A DEMONIC BURST OF RAW STRENGTH...

SNAPPP!

THE BEAST-MAN'S NOSTRILS TWITCH... AND SNIFF THE SCENT OF **MAN**...

STILL HAVEN'T OVERCOME THE EFFECTS OF THAT DRINK... CAN'T BUDGE THESE CHAINS!

RRRFFFFF!

HUH? NOW LUPOF STOPS, AS IF HE SCENTS SOME OTHER PREY! WAIT! THAT SOUND FROM BELOW...

Grrr... snff! snifff!

SO CONCERNED WITH THE BEAST THAT HAD BEEN HIS FRIEND, DAGAR HAS MOMENTARILY FORGOTTEN THE STRIKING OF THE **GONG**... BUT NOW A TERRIBLE RUMBLING WITHIN THE EARTH PRODUCES A PORTENTOUS **TREMOR**... AND AN IMAGE OF SCALY ORANGE SLITHERS FROM THE GAPING PIT...

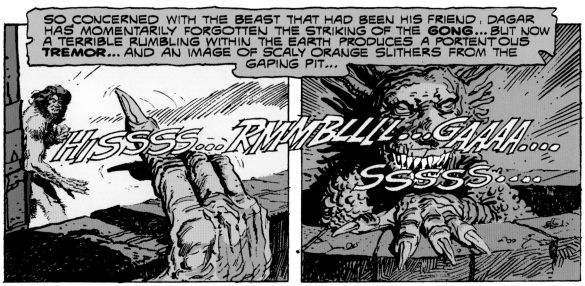

HISSSS... RMMBLLLL... GAAAA.... SSSSS...

DAGAR'S EYES LOOK WITH GRIM FASCINATION ON THE GIANT MONSTER... AND HE RECALLS THAT THE GONG WAS SOUNDED TO HERALD THE REPTILE'S **NEXT MEAL**...

IF I COULD BREAK FREE... REACH MY SWORD... I **MIGHT** HAVE A CHANCE! AT LEAST AGAINST THE **LIZARD**!

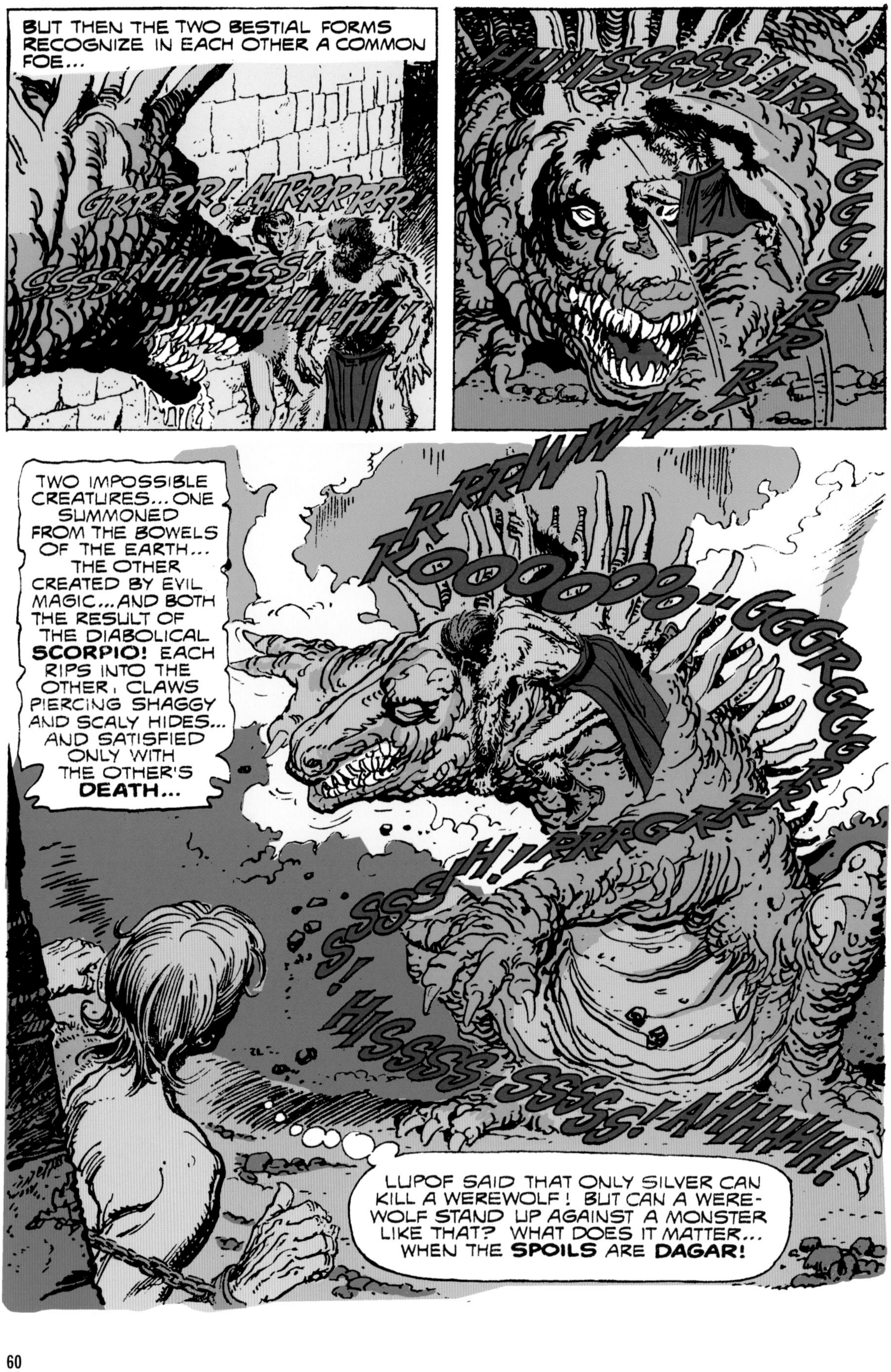
BUT THEN THE TWO BESTIAL FORMS RECOGNIZE IN EACH OTHER A COMMON FOE...
GRRRR! AARRRRRR
SSSS!HHISSSSS!
AAHHHHHHH!
HHHISSSSSS!ARRRRGGGGGRRR!
RRRRWWWWW!
RROOOOOOOB!!GGGRGGGGRRR!
TWO IMPOSSIBLE CREATURES... ONE SUMMONED FROM THE BOWELS OF THE EARTH... THE OTHER CREATED BY EVIL MAGIC... AND BOTH THE RESULT OF THE DIABOLICAL **SCORPIO!** EACH RIPS INTO THE OTHER, CLAWS PIERCING SHAGGY AND SCALY HIDES... AND SATISFIED ONLY WITH THE OTHER'S **DEATH...**
SSSSSH!!RRRRGRR
HISSSSS-SSSSS!AHHHHH!
LUPOF SAID THAT ONLY SILVER CAN KILL A WEREWOLF! BUT CAN A WERE-WOLF STAND UP AGAINST A MONSTER LIKE THAT? WHAT DOES IT MATTER... WHEN THE **SPOILS** ARE **DAGAR!**

YOU HAIRY **FOOL!** IF I CHOSE, I COULD HAVE **CURED** YOU WITH A FRAGMENT OF **LOBROSTONE!** BUT THEN SCORPIO WOULD HAVE FED **ME** TO THE MONSTERS!

B-BUT SCORPIO **ALSO** COMMANDED ME TO FEED ONLY **HUMAN** VICTIMS TO HIS CREATURES! OH, THE **CONFUSION** ...MAKING IT SO HARD TO **THINK!**

UGHHHH!

THE MONSTROSITY IS MOTIVATED ONLY BY **HUNGER.** SLOWLY, THE REPTILIAN HORROR MOVES TOWARD THE UNCONSCIOUS WOLF-MAN...

HHSSS

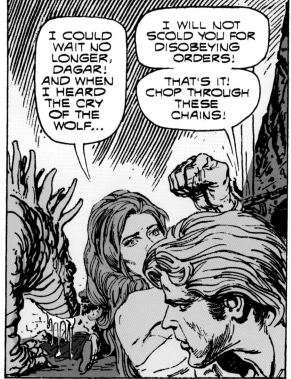

I COULD WAIT NO LONGER, DAGAR! AND WHEN I HEARD THE CRY OF THE WOLF...

I WILL NOT SCOLD YOU FOR DISOBEYING ORDERS!

THAT'S IT! CHOP THROUGH THESE CHAINS!

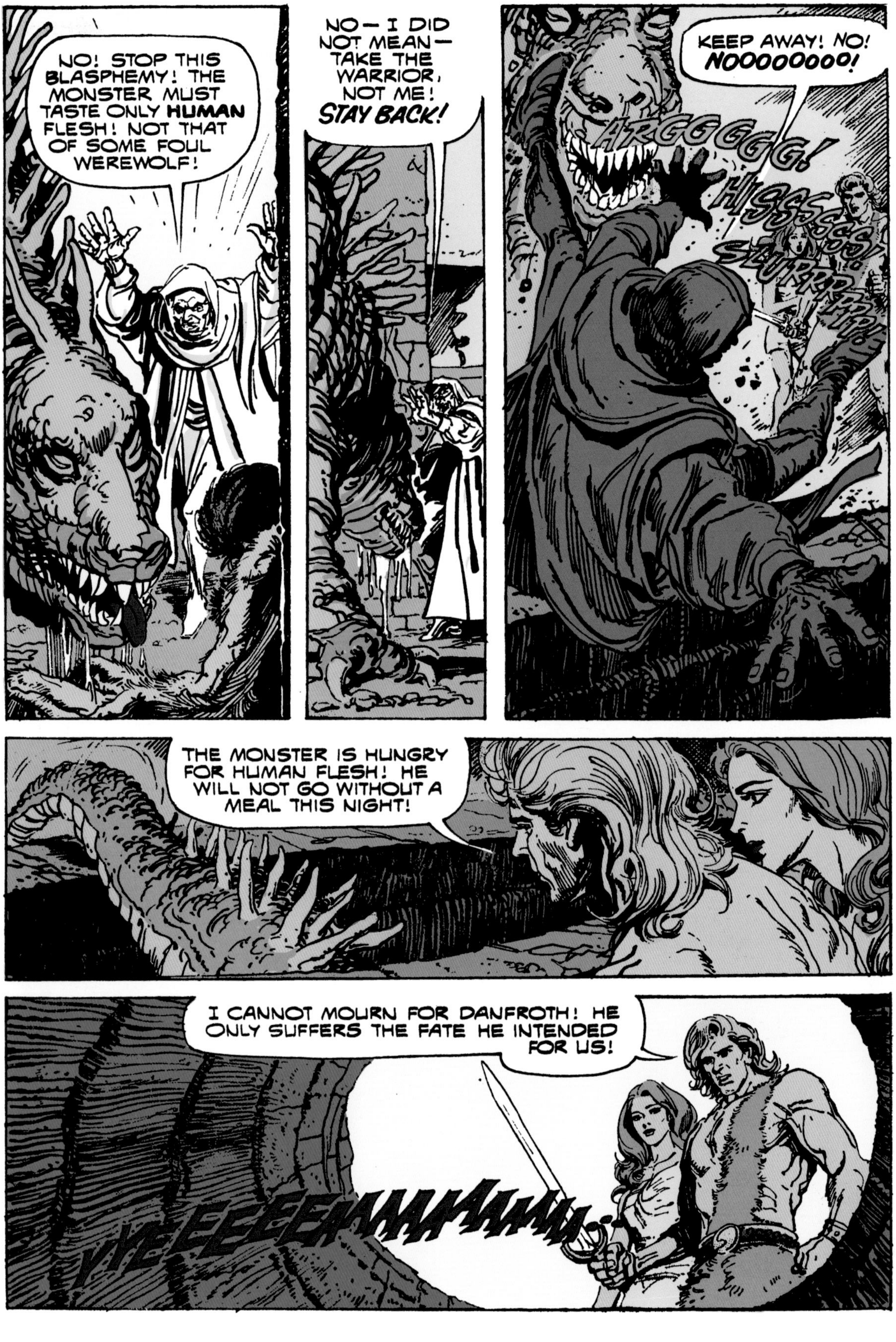
NO! STOP THIS BLASPHEMY! THE MONSTER MUST TASTE ONLY **HUMAN** FLESH! NOT THAT OF SOME FOUL WEREWOLF!
NO—I DID NOT MEAN—TAKE THE WARRIOR, NOT ME! ***STAY BACK!***
KEEP AWAY! NO! ***NOOOOOOOO!***
ARGGGGGG!
HISSSSSS!
THE MONSTER IS HUNGRY FOR HUMAN FLESH! HE WILL NOT GO WITHOUT A MEAL THIS NIGHT!
I CANNOT MOURN FOR DANFROTH! HE ONLY SUFFERS THE FATE HE INTENDED FOR US!

IT IS ALL OVER, LORA-LEI! AND THERE APPEARS TO BE NEW **HOPE** FOR LUPOF!

HOPE? WHAT DO YOU MEAN?

THE OLD MAN SAID SOMETHING BEFORE! HE SPOKE OF A **CURE** FOR A WEREWOLF... WITH SOMETHING CALLED THE **LOBROSTONE!**

PERHAPS IF WE CAN FIND THAT STONE, LUPOF WILL NEVER AGAIN HAVE TO DREAD THE FULL MOONS!

DAGAR! BEHIND YOU!

BY THE GODS AND DEMONS!

GET BACK, LORA-LEI! THE MONSTER IS **STILL HUNGRY!** NOW THAT I AGAIN HAVE MY **STRENGTH** AND MY **SWORD,** I'LL DESTROY THIS FOUL THING FOR ALL TIME!

DON'T **FIGHT** IT, DAGAR! **RUN!** YOU DON'T HAVE A **CHANCE** AGAINST SUCH A MONSTER!

THE COLD HIDE SLIPS BENEATH DAGAR... BUT HIS POWERFUL GRIP DIGS INTO THE GLEAMING SCALES. MEN CALL HIM **DAGAR THE INVINCIBLE**... AND TO RETAIN THAT TITLE HE MUST BATTLE MONSTROUS FOES USUALLY SEEN ONLY IN **NIGHTMARES**...

I DON'T HAVE A CHANCE, LORA-LEI? AND WHAT CHANCE WOULD I HAVE RUNNING LIKE A COWARD FROM SUCH A DEMON? DAGAR MAY DIE... BUT HE **NEVER FLEES!**

ARRRRRRR! HHHISSSSS! HHUUUUINKKKK!

LASHING OUT WITH THE SKILL OF A SUPERBLY TRAINED WARRIOR...

THIS **SPAWN** OF SCORPIO MUST... **DIE!**

AGAIN AND AGAIN, USING ALL OF HIS INCREDIBLE STRENGTH, DAGAR THRUSTS HIS BLADE INTO THE LIZARD'S BRAIN...

THUDDDD-SSHHHH! HHISSS-REEEEK!

THE REPTILE GIVES ONE FINAL, PAIN-RENDING ROAR... WRIGGLES IN A LAST EFFORT TO MAINTAIN ITS GHASTLY EXISTENCE... THEN **DIES**...

THE CREATURE WILL NOT RISE AGAIN, LORA-LEI! NOW ALL THAT REMAINS IS TO TELL YOUR BROTHER THAT THERE IS A CHANCE FOR HIM... AND THEN TO GO OFF IN SEARCH OF **SCORPIO!**

WHEN THE MORNING SUN ERASES THE TERROR OF THE FULL MOON...

...AND THAT IS WHAT HAPPENED, LUPOF! A POSSIBLE **CURE** FOR YOU LIES WITHIN WHAT DANFROTH CALLED... THE **LOBROSTONE!**

I'VE HEARD OF THAT, DAGAR! THE LEGENDARY WOLF-STONE WHICH SUPPOSEDLY HAS MAGICAL PROPERTIES! IT IS FOUND IN THOSE DISTANT MOUNTAINS!

I MUST GO THERE AND FIND A CURE... SO THAT I WON'T ENDANGER ANYONE EVER AGAIN!

AND I MUST GO WITH MY BROTHER!

FAREWELL!

JESSE F. SANTOS

DAGAR PAUSES FOR A MOMENT TO WATCH HIS FRIENDS RIDE OFF... BUT ONLY FOR A MOMENT, FOR HE IS ANXIOUS TO HEAD NORTH... NORTH ON HIS QUEST FOR **SCORPIO!**

the END

GOLD KEY
90279-304
DAGAR
15c
TALES OF SWORD AND SORCERY
DAGAR THE INVINCIBLE
THIRST-CRAZED VAMPIRES SEND DAGAR AGAINST THE FIEND WHO GUARDS THE LIFE-GIVING BLOOD PLANT!
© WESTERN PUBLISHING COMPANY, INC.

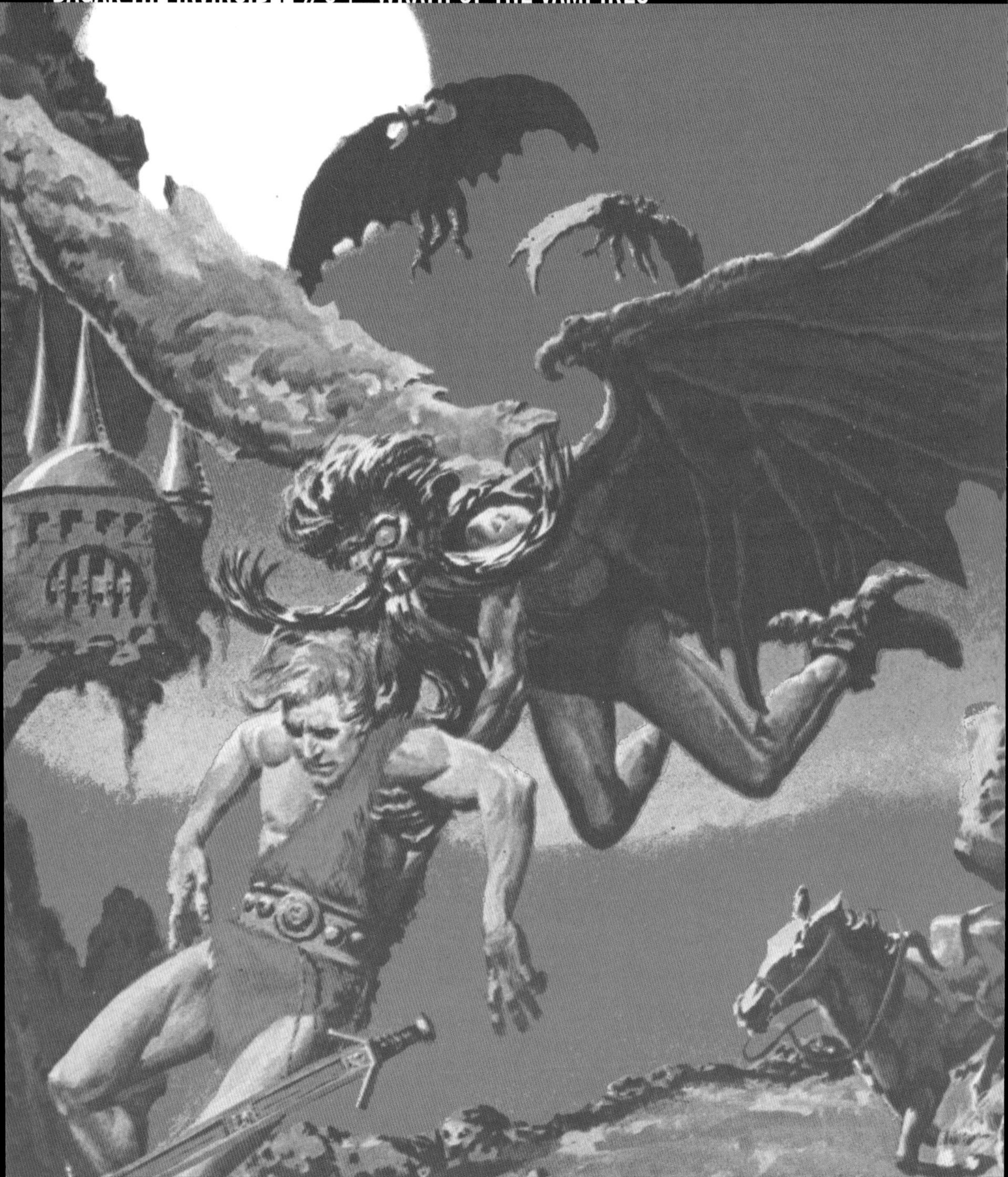

TALES OF SWORD AND SORCERY
DAGAR THE INVINCIBLE
WRATH OF THE VAMPIRES

DAGAR, THE ONLY SURVIVOR OF THE NATION TULGONIA, IS SEARCHING FOR SCORPIO... THE FIEND WHO SLAUGHTERED HIS PEOPLE. THE SUN IS NEARLY BLOOD RED, DIPPING BEHIND THE MOUNTAINS, AS THE YOUNG MERCENARY WARRIOR COMES UPON A STRANGE SCENE...

BY THE GODS! A GIRL— ABOUT TO BE SACRIFICED ON THAT ALTAR!

90279 304
DAGAR #3-731

69

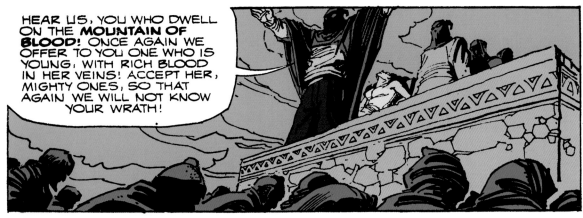

HEAR US, YOU WHO DWELL ON THE **MOUNTAIN OF BLOOD!** ONCE AGAIN WE OFFER TO YOU ONE WHO IS YOUNG, WITH RICH BLOOD IN HER VEINS! ACCEPT HER, MIGHTY ONES, SO THAT AGAIN WE WILL NOT KNOW YOUR WRATH!

THEY ARE ALL **MAD!** BUT WHAT THEY DO IS OF NO CONCERN TO DAGAR!

HUH-?! WHAT IS THAT SOUND?

" THE SOUND OF FLAPPING...AS IF MADE BY LEATHERY WINGS...

"...ENORMOUS **BATS**...OR..."

WHY, THEY'RE NOT BATS...BUT SOME WEIRD COMBINATION OF BAT AND MAN! IT IS TO THEM THAT THE GIRL HAS BEEN SACRIFICED!

SHOULD I UNSHEATH MY SWORD AND GO TO HER AID? **NO!** I DO NOT KNOW THE GIRL... AND I FIGHT ONLY FOR GOLD!

LET THESE FOOLS WORK OUT THEIR **OWN** PROBLEMS!

NOW THAT THOSE MONSTERS HAVE FLOWN TOWARD THE MOUNTAIN, THESE PEOPLE SEEM DEJECTED! WHY HAVE THEY DONE THIS TERRIBLE THING?

YOU, THERE! TELL ME WHY YOU SACRIFICED THAT GIRL!

BELIEVE ME, NONE OF US WANTED TO SACRIFICE POOR GRAYLIN!

A RACE OF **VAMPIRES** EXISTS ON THE MOUNTAIN OF BLOOD! A YEAR AGO THEY BEGAN TO PREY UPON OUR PEOPLE... DEMANDING SACRIFICES LEST WE FEEL THEIR WRATH! WE ALL FEAR THE VAMPIRES...AND DO AS THEY COMMAND!

THE FOLLOWING AFTERNOON, DAGAR'S MIND IS TORMENTED BY THOUGHTS OF THE LOVELY GRAYLIN...

I KEEP REMINDING MYSELF OF HOW I ONLY FIGHT FOR **PAY**! YET I CANNOT ERASE THAT BEAUTIFUL FACE FROM MY MIND!

I **COULD** HAVE SAVED HER IF IT WEREN'T FOR MY PRIDE... MY STUBBORNNESS! NOW I FEEL AS IF IT IS MY FAULT THAT SHE IS IN THE CLUTCHES OF THOSE MONSTERS! NO, THE GIRL **SHALL NOT DIE**... NOT IF SHE STILL LIVES!

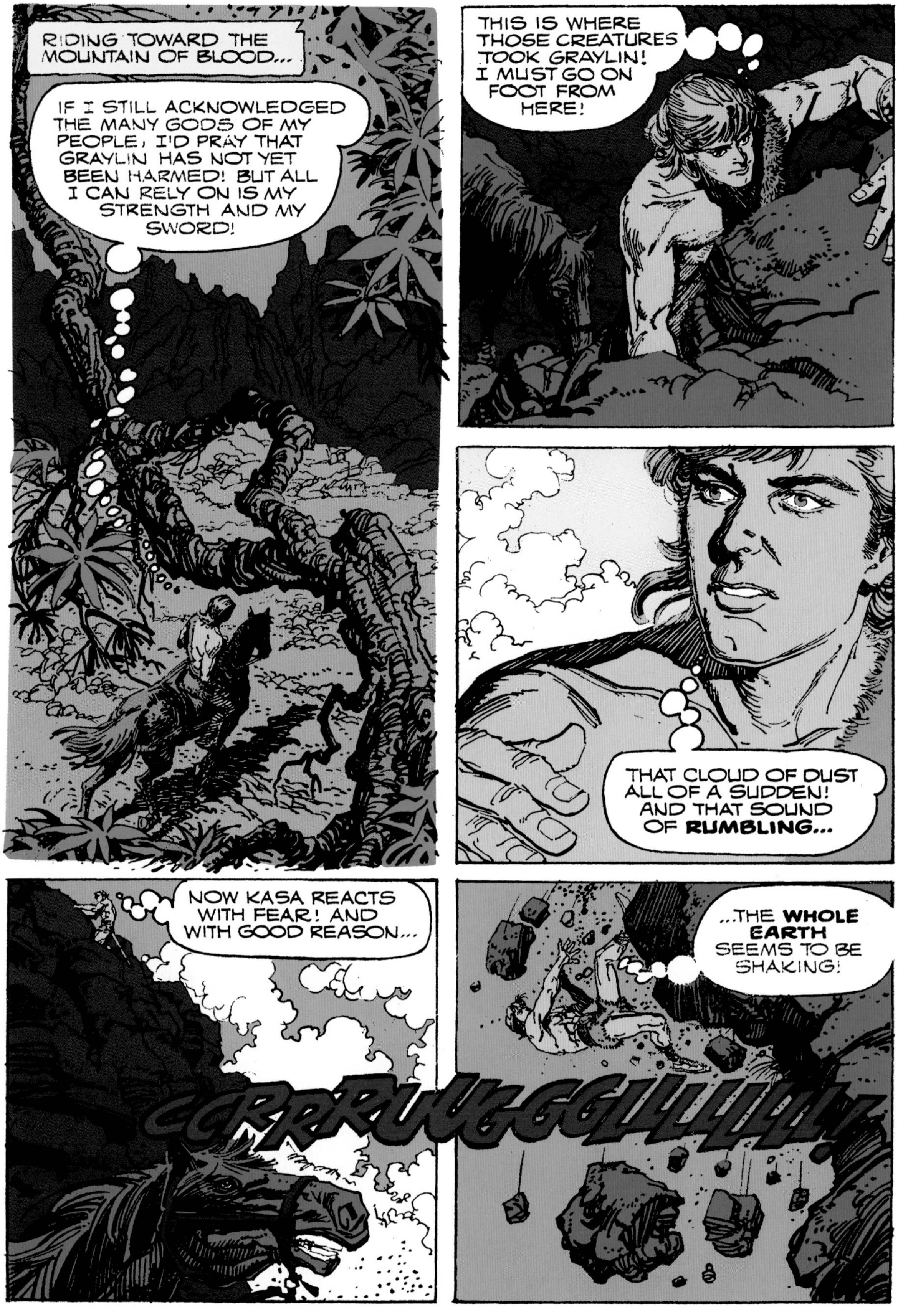
RIDING TOWARD THE MOUNTAIN OF BLOOD...
IF I STILL ACKNOWLEDGED THE MANY GODS OF MY PEOPLE, I'D PRAY THAT GRAYLIN HAS NOT YET BEEN HARMED! BUT ALL I CAN RELY ON IS MY STRENGTH AND MY SWORD!
THIS IS WHERE THOSE CREATURES TOOK GRAYLIN! I MUST GO ON FOOT FROM HERE!
THAT CLOUD OF DUST ALL OF A SUDDEN! AND THAT SOUND OF **RUMBLING...**
NOW KASA REACTS WITH FEAR! AND WITH GOOD REASON...
...THE **WHOLE EARTH** SEEMS TO BE SHAKING!
CCRRRUUGGLLLLLL!

DO ANIMALS SENSE THAT THERE ARE LOATHSOME THINGS LURKING ATOP THE MOUNTAIN OF BLOOD? PERHAPS... FOR SOME UNKNOWN **PRESENCE** CAUSES THE HERD OF THUNDERING **MASTODONS** TO FLEE PAST THE TERRIBLE PLACE...

RRUUMMMBLLL-KRA-CA-LIKRUMMMBLLL!!

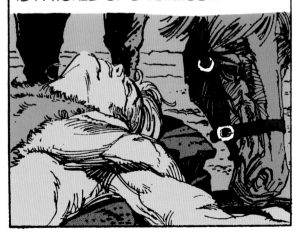

THE DUST REQUIRES A LONG TIME TO DISPERSE. THE SUN IS ALREADY SETTING, BUT ALL THAT DAGAR KNOWS IS A WORLD OF DARKNESS...

THE MAGNIFICENT STALLION REACTS AS THE WIND ABOVE HIM MOVES WITH EACH FLAP OF BAT-WINGS...

THE LOYAL KASA WATCHES HELPLESSLY AS THE FURRY HORRORS FLY OFF WITH HIS MASTER.

WHEN DAGAR AWAKENS, HIS HEAD STILL THROBS WITH THE PAIN FROM THE FALL...

LUCKILY I WASN'T TRAMPLED BY THOSE MASTODONS! BUT—WHERE AM I NOW?

I'VE BEEN THROWN INTO A PRISON CELL!

THEN, FROM ONE OF THE OTHER CELLS...

GOOD! YOU ARE AWAKE! I SAW THEM BRING YOU IN!

THE VOICE OF A YOUNG WOMAN! COULD YOU BE—?

I AM GRAYLIN! MY PEOPLE SACRIFICED ME TO THESE VAMPIRES! BUT THE MONSTERS ARE SAVING ME FOR THE **FEAST OF THE ROYAL NIGHT**...WHICH FALLS ON THE NEXT SUNSET!

IF ONLY WE COULD GET OUTSIDE THE CITY OF VAMPIRES DURING THE **DAY**! THE BAT PEOPLE FEAR SUNLIGHT! BUT THERE IS NOT A WINDOW IN THE PLACE FROM WHICH TO ESCAPE! THE LIGHT HERE IS FROM A MYSTIC AURA ENGULFING THE CITY!

SILENCE IN THERE! COME WITH ME, YOU MALE CREATURE! **KING DESMOS** HAS GIVEN ORDERS THAT YOU APPEAR BEFORE HIM!

SO, MY CAPTORS SHOW THEIR HAIRY FACES! AND THE MONSTERS **SPEAK**!

BE AS INSOLENT AS YOU WANT, YOU HAIRLESS APE! BECAUSE TOMORROW YOU WILL ADD TO THE FEAST OF THE ROYAL NIGHT!

BUT AS THE CELL IS OPENED...

WRONG! TOMORROW DAGAR WILL BE **FREE**!

THUNK!

UGHH!

THUD!

PICK HIM UP!

SOON, IN THE THRONE-ROOM OF THE CITY OF VAMPIRES, DAGAR VIEWS A SCENE OF BIZARRE SPLENDOR...

SO THIS IS THE LATEST VICTIM FOR THE FEAST OF THE ROYAL NIGHT! YOU DID WELL, CHIRRON, TO SUBDUE HIM! HE LOOKS AS IF HE'S A POWERFUL BRUTE!

NEVER HAVE I SEEN SO MAGNIFICENT A CREATURE AS THIS ONE! THE SIGHT OF HIM MAKES ME FEEL... STRANGE!

PRINCESS MYZARR LOOKS AT THIS DAGAR THE WAY I'VE ALWAYS WANTED HER TO LOOK AT ME! BUT AFTER TOMORROW EVENING, SHE'LL LOOK AT HIM AS A VULTURE LOOKS AT A DEAD SABRE-TOOTH!

SO YOU ARE THE MIGHTY POTENTATE OF THIS RACE OF BLOODTHIRSTY MONSTERS!

THEN IF I'M TO DIE ANYWAY, LET ME FIRST SEND YOU TO THE KINGDOM OF THE DEAD!

GUARDS!

ARRGHH!

LET ME SLAY HIM NOW, HIGHNESS!

L/NN... NO! LET HIM LIVE!

I HAVE MY REASONS, CHIRRON! THIS HUMAN MUST NOT DIE—AT LEAST NOT UNTIL HE HAS RESPONDED TO WHAT I HAVE TO SAY!

YOU CALLED US **MONSTERS**... BECAUSE WE ARE A RACE THAT EXISTS BY CONSUMING HUMAN BLOOD! IT IS OUR LOT TO LOOK HIDEOUS IN YOUR EYES!

ONCE WE WERE NOT FORCED TO PREY UPON YOUR KIND! WE THRIVED ON THE SAP OF **BLOOD-PLANTS**! BUT THEN THE DEMON **SCORPIO** DESTROYED ALL THE PLANTS, SAVE **ONE**!

SCORPIO? YOU MEAN THE FIEND WHO KILLED MY COUNTRYMEN HAS ALSO AFFECTED YOU? WHERE IS HE? **TELL ME!**

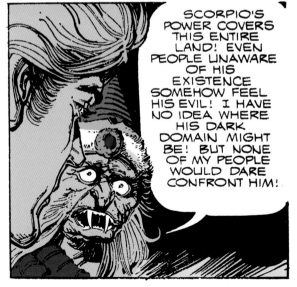

SCORPIO'S POWER COVERS THIS ENTIRE LAND! EVEN PEOPLE UNAWARE OF HIS EXISTENCE SOMEHOW FEEL HIS EVIL! I HAVE NO IDEA WHERE HIS DARK DOMAIN MIGHT BE! BUT NONE OF MY PEOPLE WOULD DARE CONFRONT HIM!

BUT WHAT OF THIS LAST REMAINING BLOOD-PLANT?

THAT COVETED PLANT IS IN THE POSSESSION OF A HIDEOUS FIEND LOYAL TO SCORPIO! BUT NONE OF US DARE FACE HIM... FOR HE WIELDS THE POWER OF **SUNLIGHT**, WHICH NONE OF THE VAMPIRE RACE CAN STAND!

WAIT, YOUR HIGHNESS! PERHAPS THIS **DAGAR** CAN GET THE PLANT!

DAGAR CANNOT SURVIVE SUCH A QUEST! THEN HE WILL NOT BE A RIVAL FOR MYZARR'S AFFECTIONS!

AH, CAPTAIN CHIRRON! NOW YOU KNOW WHY I SPARED DAGAR'S LIFE! HEAR THIS, HUMAN! IF YOU CAN BRING US THE BLOOD-PLANT BEFORE THE FEAST OF THE ROYAL NIGHT, YOU AND THE GIRL SHALL BE **FREE**... AND NONE WILL EVER NEED FEAR US AGAIN!

I FEAR NO ONE! GIVE ME MY SWORD AND YOU SHALL HAVE YOUR BLOOD-PLANT BEFORE ANOTHER SUNSET! OR I'LL DIE IN THE ATTEMPT!

IF IT IS NOT **IN** THE ATTEMPT, IT WILL BE **AFTER** THE ATTEMPT!

LATER, WHEN DAGAR IS GRANTED PRIVACY...

IT IS GOOD TO HAVE MY SWORD BACK IN MY HANDS!

HEARING THE GENTLE RUSTLE OF WINGS, DAGAR TURNS...

PRINCESS MYZARR! WHY ARE YOU HERE?

DAGAR! FORGET THIS MAD QUEST THAT CAN ONLY BRING YOU **DEATH!** STAY HERE AND I SHALL MAKE YOU MY **PRINCE!**

I AM SORRY, PRINCESS! BUT I **WILL** SEE THIS THROUGH TO THE END! IF THE FATES PERMIT, I SHALL LEAVE THE CITY OF VAMPIRES WITH GRAYLIN!

HE SHUNS ME FOR THE WOMAN WITH RAVEN HAIR!

THEN GO TO YOUR **DEATH**, HUMAN! DIE WITH MY CURSE UPON YOU!

TRYING TO FORGET THE ACTIONS OF THE VAMPIRE PRINCESS, DAGAR HURRIES TO THE PLACE DESIGNATED BY KING DESMOS. OVERHEAD FLY GIANT SHAPES THAT MAKE BIZARRE SILHOUETTES AGAINST THE FULL MOON...

DAGAR! IT IS TIME...

AND YOU MAY LEAVE YOUR WEAPON IN ITS SHEATH!

WHAT IN THE NAME OF FORAK'S BONES—!? BUT THAT THING IS SWOOPING DOWN FOR THE KILL, CHIRRON!

CHIRRRRR... CHIRRRRP... CHIRRP...

DO NOT FEAR THIS BAT-MOUNT, DAGAR! IT IS TRAINED TO RESPOND TO A RIDER AS WOULD A PRIZED STALLION IN YOUR WORLD!

I WILL FLY ALONG-SIDE! THE SANCTUARY OF SCORPIO'S SERVANT IS IN A CAVE ON ANOTHER MOUNTAINTOP!

AFTER A WHILE OF FLYING ON THE BAT-MOUNT, DAGAR SEES A MOUNTAIN SHROUDED BY MIST...

I CANNOT FACE THE FIEND'S **LIGHT**, DAGAR! AND SO YOU MUST GO ALONE TO HIS CAVE! JUST FOLLOW THIS PATH!

THERE IS THE MOUNTAIN WE SEEK!

LEAVING THE BAT-MOUNT WITH CHIRRON...

EITHER BY THE **FIEND** OR BY **ME** YOU SHALL DIE, DAGAR! MYZARR WILL NEVER SET EYES ON YOU AGAIN!

PRESENTLY...

BY THE WARRIOR GODS!

THE SIGN OF SCORPIO! THE SAME EMBLEM AS ON THE SHIELDS OF THOSE WHO WIPED OUT MY PEOPLE! IF SCORPIO HIMSELF IS IN THIS CAVE IT WILL MEAN FAR MORE THAN SAVING GRAYLIN OR GETTING THE BLOOD-PLANT!

THE VAMPIRES WERE RIGHT ABOUT SCORPIO'S POWER! THIS CAVERN SEEMS TO HAVE CAPTURED THE **DAYLIGHT** FROM THE SUN!

THE LIGHTS GET BRIGHTER THE FARTHER I GO! I MUST BE NEAR TO THIS SO-CALLED **FIEND!** WAIT! THOSE ARE **VOICES!**

THE VAMPIRES WEREN'T EXAGGERATING WHEN THEY CALLED HIM A **FIEND!** BUT NO ONE TOLD ME OF HIS UGLY ACCOMPLICES! I'LL HAVE THEM TO CONTEND WITH IN ADDITION TO WHATEVER MAGIC HE POSSESSES!

WHAT? SOME- ONE DARES SPY UPON US?!

GURRRFF! NAIPOGAH!

WELL, AN INTENSE CONCEN- TRATION OF **SUNLIGHT** SHOULD MAKE HIM **SEE** HIS ERROR!

SSSSSSS...

ARRGG! IT'S **BLINDING** ME!

SKRAGAHHSSSHH!

NOW THAT HE IS SIGHTLESS, **END** HIS INSIGNIFICANT LIFE!

GRUB- NEERG! GAWWK!

Thudd!

UGHH!

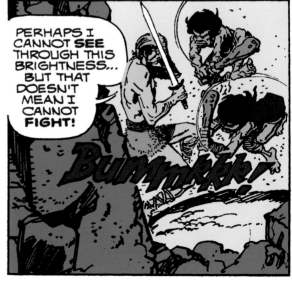

PERHAPS I CANNOT **SEE** THROUGH THIS BRIGHTNESS... BUT THAT DOESN'T MEAN I CANNOT **FIGHT!**

Bummkk!

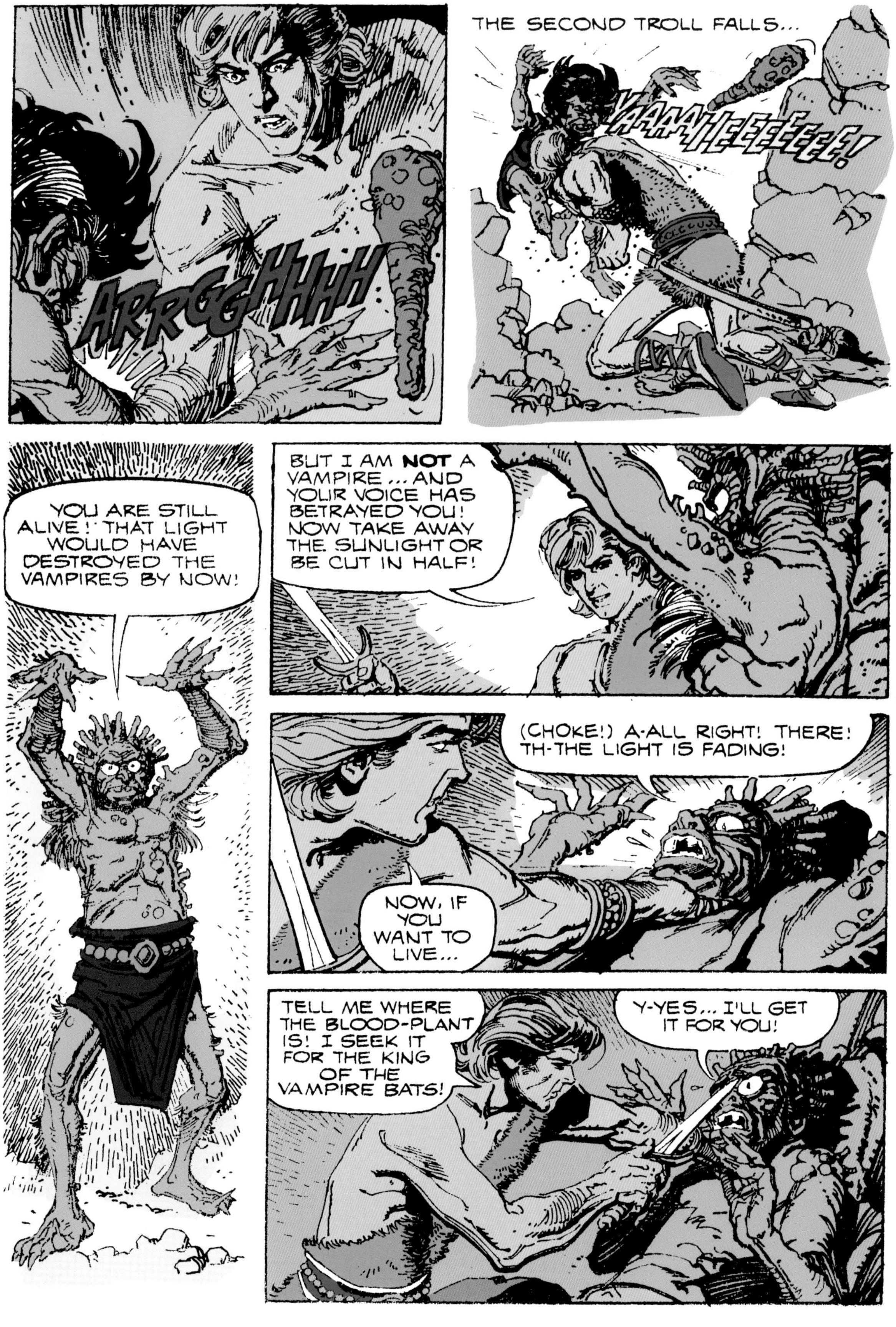
ARRGGHHHH
THE SECOND TROLL FALLS...
YAAAAHEEEEEEE!
YOU ARE STILL ALIVE! THAT LIGHT WOULD HAVE DESTROYED THE VAMPIRES BY NOW!
BUT I AM NOT A VAMPIRE... AND YOUR VOICE HAS BETRAYED YOU! NOW TAKE AWAY THE SUNLIGHT OR BE CUT IN HALF!
(CHOKE!) A-ALL RIGHT! THERE! TH-THE LIGHT IS FADING!
NOW, IF YOU WANT TO LIVE...
TELL ME WHERE THE BLOOD-PLANT IS! I SEEK IT FOR THE KING OF THE VAMPIRE BATS!
Y-YES... I'LL GET IT FOR YOU!

THERE IT IS! THERE IS NO END TO THE PLANT'S BLOOD-LIKE SAP! AND IT READILY PRODUCES SEEDS, SO THAT THE VAMPIRE RACE WILL NEVER AGAIN HAVE TO THIRST!

NOW THERE IS BUT ONE MORE THING FOR US TO SETTLE...

TELL ME... WHERE IS SCORPIO?

SCORPIO? NO! I HAVE ALREADY TOLD YOU TOO MUCH!

WAIT! THAT PARCHMENT!

N-NO! DON'T TOUCH IT!

YOU NEED TELL ME NOTHING, UGLY ONE! THIS IS A MAP WHICH TELLS ME EXACTLY HOW TO FIND YOUR ACCURSED MASTER!

N-NO! I HAVE FAILED THE MASTER!

NOW SCORPIO WILL DESTROY ME...AND THE MOUNTAIN!

RUMMMMMBBBBLLLLLLE!

BAROOM!

THE FIEND AND THE CAVERN ARE GONE... BUT I LIVE... AND I HAVE THE **MAP**!

WHAT?! DAGAR RETURNS WITH THE BLOOD-PLANT! I THOUGHT SURELY THE FIEND WOULD HAVE KILLED HIM!

CHIRRON! THAT **FIEND** WILL NEVER AGAIN PLAGUE THE RACE OF VAMPIRES! SCORPIO HIMSELF HAS SEEN TO THAT!

THEN **I** WILL TAKE THIS PLANT BACK TO DESMOS...AND TELL HIM THAT YOU WERE SLAIN BY THE FIEND! FOR NOW, BY MY SWORD...

...YOU DIE!

CLANNNG!

WHAT HAS GOTTEN INTO YOU? HAVE YOU GONE **MAD**?

MAD? MAD? IS IT MADNESS TO SLAY THE ONE WHO HAS TAKEN THE HEART OF YOUR BELOVED?

YOU MEAN PRINCESS MYZARR?

BAM-nng!

YES, MYZARR... WHOM I HAVE LOVED SINCE I FIRST SAW HER!

SO FILLED WITH THE DESIRE TO KILL IS CHIRRON THAT HE DOES NOT NOTICE THE SKY GROWING STEADILY **BRIGHTER**...

N-NO! THE **SUN**! THE **SUN**! AAIIIEEEEEEEEE!!

I CANNOT SEE! THE SUN HAS **BLINDED** ME!

SHIELD YOUR EYES FROM THE LIGHT! THE TWO OF US WILL RIDE THE BAT-MOUNT BACK TO THE CITY!

YOU ARE NOT GOING TO SLAY ME?

I **COULD**! BUT I WOULD PREFER TO TELL YOU THE **TRUTH** ABOUT THE PRINCESS AND MYSELF!

AS THEY SOAR THROUGH THE MORNING SKY, DAGAR EXPLAINS THAT MYZARR IS NOT IN HIS THOUGHTS, THAT HIS ONLY CONCERN IS SAVING GRAYLIN.

I ACTED LIKE A LOVE-SICK FOOL, DAGAR! I AM SORRY!

THINK NO MORE ABOUT IT, CHIRRON — IT IS OVER!

IMMEDIATELY UPON ARRIVING IN THE LIGHT-SHIELDED CITY, DAGAR HURRIES TO GRAYLIN'S CELL...

GRAYLIN IS NOT HERE! HAS THE KING ALREADY RELEASED HER?

PRINCESS MYZARR CAME HERE WHEN SHE SAW YOU APPROACHING! SHE RELEASED THE PRISONER AND TOOK HER DOWN THOSE STAIRS!

DAGAR! THOSE STAIRS DO **NOT** LEAD TO FREEDOM! THEY HARBOR——

THAT SCREAM! GRAYLIN!

EEEAAAAAAAA!!!

IN A CHAMBER BELOW THE PRISON...

BECAUSE OF YOU AND YOUR HUMAN BEAUTY, DAGAR HAS REJECTED MY LOVE!

I HOPED HE WOULD DIE ON HIS QUEST! BUT NOW THAT HE HAS RETURNED, HE SHALL NOT KNOW HAPPINESS... FOR **YOU** ARE ABOUT TO DIE!

SQUEEAKKK!

AS THE MAMMOTH IRON DOOR RISES...

SCREAM ALL YOU LIKE, GRAYLIN! NO ONE WILL HEAR YOU DOWN HERE! DO YOU FEAR THIS CREATURE? YOU SHOULD, SINCE HE IS THE ONLY BAT-MOUNT IN THE CITY THAT REFUSES TO BE TAMED! AND HE IS **QUITE THIRSTY!**

MY BLADE IS ALSO THIRSTY, MYZARR... FOR THE BLOOD OF THIS MONSTROSITY!

IF THIS BEAST CANNOT BE TAMED, THEN HE MUST **DIE**!

THU-GUSSHH!

AVOIDING THE SHARP FANGS AND TEARING CLAWS, DAGAR THRUSTS HIS BLADE FOR THE CREATURE'S HEART...

RRRRAAGGHH!

THE BAT-BEAST QUIVERS... THEN RELEASES ITS LAST GASP OF LIFE...

IT IS ALL RIGHT, GRAYLIN! THAT MONSTER WILL NOT HURT ANY-ONE AGAIN!

91

I WILL NOT ASK FOR FORGIVENESS, DAGAR! THE MADNESS OF JEALOUSY OVERCAME ME!

AS IT DID CHIRRON! HE LOVES YOU, MYZARR!

WHAT DID YOU SAY? CHIRRON LOVES ME? BUT HE NEVER TOLD ME HOW HIS HEART FELT! **NEVER!**

WHAT HAS HAPPENED TO YOU, CHIRRON? YOUR EYES —

I WAS BLINDED BY THE SUN! MY VISION IS BLURRED, BUT IT WILL RETURN!

PERHAPS I'VE ALWAYS HAD FEELINGS FOR **YOU,** CHIRRON, BUT NEVER EXPRESSED THEM!

THAT NIGHT, IN THE THRONE ROOM OF KING DESMOS...

BECAUSE OF YOUR HEROISM, DAGAR OF TULGONIA, WE WILL NEVER AGAIN BE FORCED TO PREY UPON THE HUMANS! THIS SWEARS DESMOS, KING OF THE **CITY OF VAMPIRES!**

RIDING BAT-MOUNTS, DAGAR AND GRAYLIN LEAVE THE CITY OF VAMPIRES...

KASA! MY FAITHFUL KASA! I KNEW YOU WOULD NOT LEAVE THIS PLACE UNTIL I RETURNED!

A WELCOME SUN ASCENDS OVER THE HORIZON AS TWO WINGED CREATURES RETURN TO THEIR MASTERS... AND DAGAR, HIS BODY LONGING FOR A MOMENT'S REST, CANNOT STOP, FOR DEEP INSIDE HIM IS A GNAWING THAT URGES HIM ON TOWARD HIS QUEST FOR SCORPIO — AND **REVENGE!**

the END

GOLD KEY ®

DAGAR

90279-307

20c

TALES OF SWORD AND SORCERY

DAGAR
THE INVINCIBLE

HIS QUEST ENDED,
DAGAR TESTS HIS
MIGHT AGAINST SCORPIO'S
MIND-SHATTERING MAGIC!

DAGAR THE INVINCIBLE #4 | "VENGEANCE—SWEET VENGEANCE"

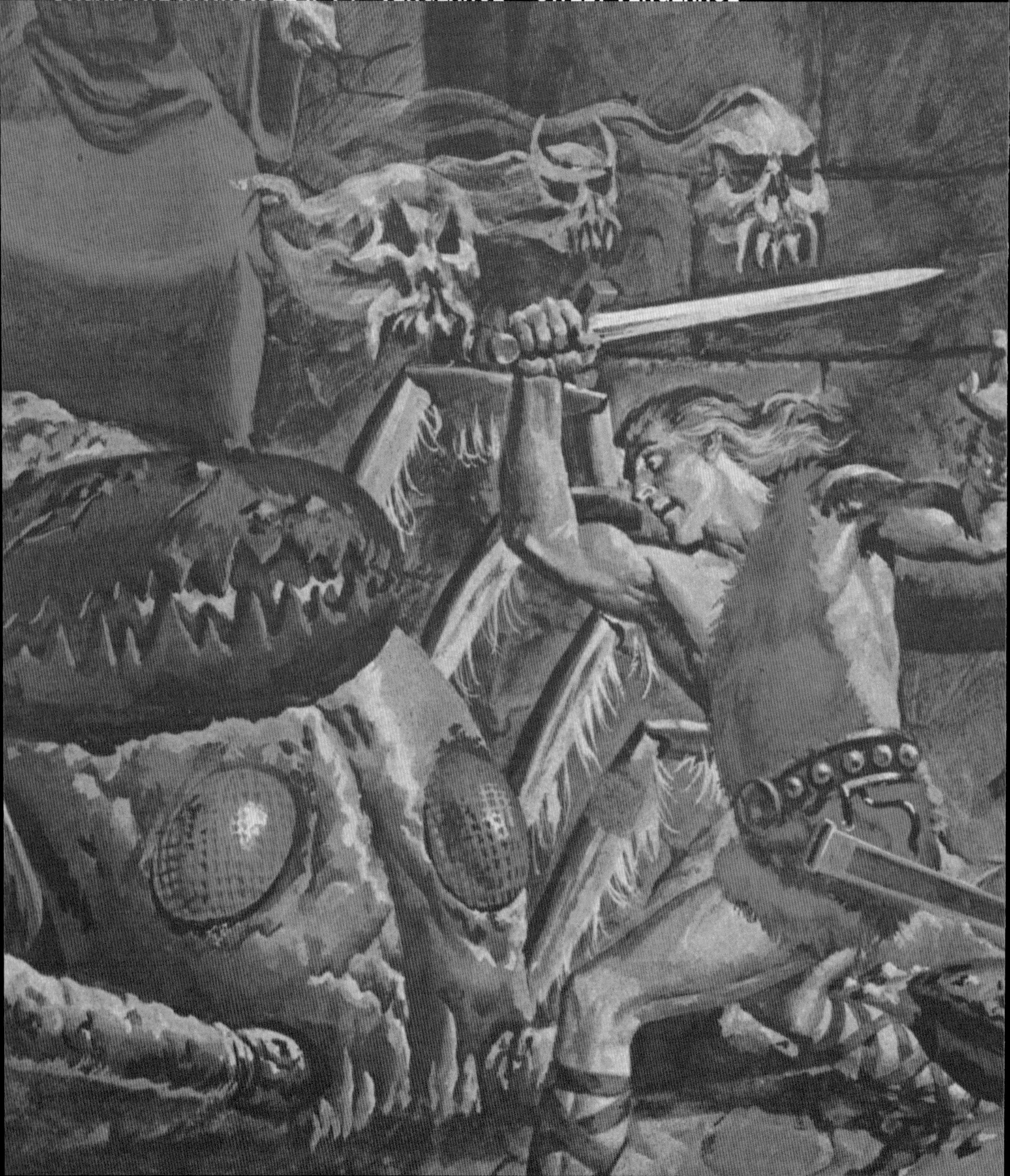

DAGAR THE INVINCIBLE

VENGEANCE—SWEET VENGEANCE

FOLLOWING THE MAP TO THE DOMAIN OF SCORPIO, DAGAR, THE YOUNG MERCENARY WARRIOR, FINDS **NOTHING**... SAVE THE BLEACHED BONES OF CREATURES FOOLISH ENOUGH TO CROSS THE STEAMING DESERT...AND A FLOCK OF HUNGRY VULTURES HOPING TO SEE HIM FALL...

COULD THIS MAP BE A **FRAUD?** ACCORDING TO IT, I AM STANDING RIGHT NOW ON SCORPIO'S KINGDOM! HAVE I COME THIS FAR TO DESTROY THE MASS MURDERER OF MY PEOPLE ONLY TO FAIL? THERE IS NOTHING HERE BUT **DEATH!** AND YET IT SEEMS APPROPRIATE THAT WHERE THERE IS DEATH...THERE IS SCORPIO!

A BEAUTIFUL IMAGE FLASHES ACROSS DAGAR'S MIND...

MAYBE I CAN FIND HAPPINESS WITH **GRAYLIN** SOMEDAY... BUT I COULD NOT LET HER COME WITH ME! DAGAR ALONE MUST BATTLE THE DESTROYER OF HIS NATION!

BUT EVEN AS DAGAR DWELLS UPON THE LOVELY IMAGE...

THAT NOISE! SOUNDS LIKE AN ARMY!

"YES, IT'S ONE OF SCORPIO'S LEGIONS! I RECOGNIZE THE EMBLEMS ON THEIR SHIELDS! SCORPIO'S DOMAIN *IS* HERE!"

IN THE NAME OF SCORPIO, I BECKON YOU TO GIVE US ENTRANCE!

AS THE AIR VIBRATES, IT **PULLS APART** UNDER THE OFFICER'S INVOCATION...

BY MY GRANDFATHER'S BONES... SCORPIO'S KINGDOM IS REALLY A **WORLD WITHIN A WORLD**... BRIDGED BY THAT MAGICAL OPENING! IF I'M TO REACH SCORPIO, I'LL HAVE TO ACT BEFORE THE OPENING CLOSES!

AFTER THE LAST SOLDIER HAS VANISHED THROUGH THE MYSTERIOUS "DOORWAY"...

IT IS A GOOD THING I DIDN'T HESITATE! ALREADY THE ENTRANCEWAY IS SHRINKING!

SO THIS IS SCORPIO'S DOMAIN! THE VERY AIR SEEMS TO VIBRATE WITH A STRANGE FORCE... AND THE SMELLS OF DEATH! FOR A WHILE IT SEEMED AS IF I'D NEVER GET THIS FAR!

THAT MUST BE ONE OF SCORPIO'S GUARDS! IF I'M TO EVER GET TO SCORPIO HIMSELF, I'LL HAVE TO MAKE IT THROUGH THIS CORRIDOR!

IT IS SCORPIO'S LIFE I WANT... AND NOT NECESSARILY YOURS!

UNGHHH!

KA-THAK!

I HAVE NO IDEA WHERE TO GO NEXT! BUT I MIGHT JUST AS WELL FOLLOW THIS PASSAGEWAY!

AND I MIGHT HAVE USE FOR THIS LANCE! WAIT! I'VE BEEN DISCOVERED!

YOU THERE!

MOVE OUT! YOU KNOW HOW THE MASTER DISLIKES BEING KEPT WAITING!

ER...YES! THEY MUST THINK I'M THE ONE FROM WHOM I TOOK THIS LANCE!

I MUST GO ALONG WITH THEM, OR THEY'LL SURELY SLAY ME WHERE I STAND! BUT **WHAT** AM I GETTING MYSELF INTO?

THE HEAVY DOOR CLANGS BEHIND DAGAR... AND AFTER HIS EYES ADJUST TO THE SUNLIGHT, HE REALIZES...

BY THE WARRIOR GODS! THAT MAN I CLOUTED WASN'T A GUARD! HE WAS A **GLADIATOR**! AND I'VE TAKEN HIS PLACE IN THE **ARENA**!

"AND THERE...SEATED LIKE SOME GAPING SCAVENGER OF THE TAR PITS,... IS HE WHOM I'VE DEVOTED MY LIFE TO SLAYING... *SCORPIO!*"

AHH... ANOTHER LOYAL GLADIATOR WHO WILL GLADLY GIVE HIS WRETCHED LIFE FOR THE AMUSEMENT OF HIS MASTER!

HIS EYES ALMOST SEAR MY FLESH! I'LL REMEMBER THAT TERRIBLE STARE LONG AFTER MY LANCE PIERCES SCORPIO'S EVIL HEART!

KNOW YOU THIS, GLADIATOR... THAT ALTHOUGH YOUR LIFE MAY HAVE BEEN INSIGNIFICANT... YOUR **DEATH** WILL HOLD GREAT MEANING IN THE ETERNAL COSMOS! FOR BY DYING, YOU SHALL AFFORD THE IMMORTAL SCORPIO A FEW MOMENTS OF PLEASURE! AND NOW... *LET THE SPORT BEGIN!*

HAIL! HAIL SCORPIO! HAIL THE MASTER OF MASTERS!

THE FIEND MUST DIE! I'D BEST HURL MY LANCE NOW...

BUT A NOISE DISTRACTS DAGAR. HIS EYES WATCH THE IRON DOOR RISE... PULLED BY CLANKING CHAINS TO REVEAL...

SKREEE... EERR!

...A TRIO OF LONG-FANGED MONSTERS THAT DAGAR KNOWS TOO WELL... **SABRE-TOOTHS!**

GRRRAARRRR--ARGGGRRR!!

IT APPEARS AS IF SCORPIO WILL HAVE TO WAIT TO DIE!

ARGGrrrrwwraa...

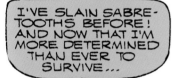

I'VE SLAIN SABRE-TOOTHS BEFORE! AND NOW THAT I'M MORE DETERMINED THAN EVER TO SURVIVE...

...FIGHTING **THREE** WILL NOT BE TOO DIFFICULT!

Agrrrrggrrrrrrawrwu...

YOU WILL HAVE TO FIND ANOTHER MEAL!

thudd! dd!

grrff!

WHAT?! THE GLADIATOR FINDS HIS PERIL TOO EASY, DOES HE?! HIS ANTICS **BORE** ME... AND SO I SHALL TIP THE SCALES IN FAVOR OF HIS LAST LIVING ADVERSARY...AND THUS ENHANCE THE ENTERTAINMENT!

DAGAR GAPES IN ASTONISHMENT AS SCORPIO'S POWERS OF TRANSFORMATION ENLARGE AND DISTORT THE FLESH OF THE REMAINING SABRE-TOOTH CAT...

BY THE GODS—!

HEARING ONLY THE CHEERING OF THE CROWD AND THE DEMONIC ROARS OF THE MONSTER, DAGAR IS HURLED TO THE GROUND...

DAGAR DOES NOT WANT A LIFE-RISKING BATTLE AT THIS TIME... HE WANTS TO BE SURE OF LIVING... AT LEAST LONG ENOUGH TO CARRY OUT HIS REVENGE AGAINST SCORPIO. HIS SPEAR FLIES TRUE...

WREEEAAKKKKKK...

UNNN!

RAAAAGGGGKKK!

DIE, MONSTER... DIE!

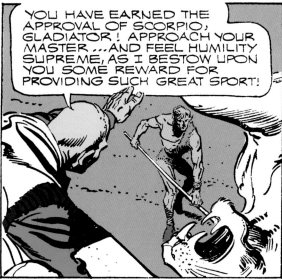

YOU HAVE EARNED THE APPROVAL OF SCORPIO, GLADIATOR! APPROACH YOUR MASTER... AND FEEL HUMILITY SUPREME, AS I BESTOW UPON YOU SOME REWARD FOR PROVIDING SUCH GREAT SPORT!

103

THE ONLY REWARD I DEMAND IS THE **DEATH** OF SCORPIO!

BUT SCORPIO'S REFLEXES ARE QUICK... HIS MAGIC ALWAYS READY. THE DEADLY LANCE BECOMES A HARMLESS FEATHER...

WHAT? ARE YOU **MAD**?!

GUARDS! CAPTURE HIM! BUT DO NOT KILL HIM! THAT PLEASURE WILL BE RESERVED FOR SCORPIO! AND HIS DEATH WILL **NOT** BE **SWIFT!**

IF I'M TO LIVE LONG ENOUGH TO KILL SCORPIO, I'LL HAVE TO RUN... FOR THE PRESENT!

DO NOT FEAR, NOBLE WARRIOR! I SHALL LEAD YOU TO SAFETY!

A **VOICE!** SPEAKING TO MY **BRAIN!**

WHAT?! THE WALL OPENS... A HIDDEN DOOR!

Thunggg!

THE DOOR HAS CLOSED! AM I NOW TRAPPED SOMEWHERE ELSE?

SLOWLY, DAGAR DESCENDS THE STONE STAIRCASE. THE SUBTERRANEAN CHAMBER ECHOES WITH PATHETIC GROWLS MADE BY INHUMAN VOCAL CORDS...AND REEKS WITH THE STENCH OF DECAY...

SO THESE ARE THE PRISONERS OF SCORPIO! IF THESE WERE ONCE **MEN**, I AM GLAD THAT HIS ASSASSINS DID NOT TAKE ANY PRISONERS FROM MY COUNTRY!

AaarrooooEdaahh!

AYE, YOU SEE THE HANDIWORK OF SCORPIO! IF I HAD NOT RESCUED YOU FROM THE ARENA, YOU TOO MIGHT SUFFER THE SAME FATE!

HUH? WHO ARE YOU, OLD ONE?

MY NAME? I'VE ALMOST FORGOTTEN! BUT **WHO** I AM IS OF NO CONCERN! WE BOTH OPPOSE SCORPIO! THAT IS ENOUGH REASON FOR YOU TO FOLLOW ME!

THESE UNDERGROUND CHAMBERS RUN UNDER SCORPIO'S PALACE! HE USES THEM TO HARBOR THESE PRISONERS... CREATURES HIS MAGIC HAS CHANGED INTO MINDLESS ATROCITIES... BETTER OFF DEAD THAN LIVING LIKE THIS!

MANY YEARS AGO I WAS A MAGICIAN WITH FAIRLY STRONG POWERS! BUT WITH THE PASSAGE OF TIME AND THE DOMINATING FORCES OF SCORPIO, MY POWERS HAVE SINCE FADED!

MY PEOPLE WERE AMONG THOSE HERDED INTO THESE CELLS AND CHANGED INTO MONSTERS! I MANAGED TO REMAIN INVISIBLE FOR A WHILE AND THUS ESCAPE SCORPIO'S WRATH!

I MANAGED TO FIND THIS SMALL GROTTO, WHERE I'VE LIVED ALONE EVER SINCE, CONSERVING WHAT REMAINED OF MY POWERS FOR A SPECIAL DAY!

YOU SPOKE TO MY MIND IN THE ARENA!

YES, I RETAINED ENOUGH POWER TO SEND MY THOUGHTS TO YOU! WHEN I "SAW" THAT THERE WAS FINALLY A WARRIOR TO RENOUNCE SCORPIO, I KNEW THE TIME HAD COME! THE TIME OF SCORPIO'S DESTRUCTION!

GRIP MY ARMS AND CONCENTRATE... AND LET WHAT REMAINS OF MY MAGIC FLOW INTO YOUR OWN BODY!

I FEEL...STRANGE! MY LIMBS VIBRATE WITH **POWER!**

"NOW SEE SCORPIO... ENVISION THE FIEND WHO HAS LEARNED THAT THE CONFIGURATION OF THE STARS CAN GIVE GREAT POWERS TO CERTAIN MEN..."

"AND OBSERVE HOW SCORPIO NOW RENEWS HIS POWERS...WHICH HE ACQUIRED SO MANY YEARS AGO BY TAPPING THE CONSTELLATION HE HAS NAMED **SCORPIO**...WATCH HIM BASK IN THE POWERS THAT HAVE MADE HIM IMMORTAL..."

"BUT KNOW THAT SCORPIO IS NOT **ALL**-POWERFUL! FOR IN RETURN FOR THE POWER OF THE CELESTIAL SCORPION, HE RELINQUISHED HIS **SOUL** TO THE EVIL GODS...AND WEARS IT IN THE **JEWEL** AROUND HIS NECK..."

DESTROY THAT JEWEL AND YOU'LL DESTROY SCORPIO...AND ALL HIS DOMAIN! FOR NEITHER MAY SURVIVE WITHOUT IT! YOU NOW HAVE MY MEAGER POWER, WARRIOR! GO—AND SEEK VENGEANCE FOR **BOTH** OF US!

HIS BODY THROBBING WITH ENERGIES HE HAS NEVER KNOWN BEFORE, DAGAR HURRIES THROUGH THE UNDERGROUND PASSAGEWAYS, FOLLOWING THE DIRECTIONS GIVEN BY THE OLD MAN...

BUT...

I DID NOT TELL HIM THAT IN GIVING MY POWER, I ALSO DRAINED OFF MOST OF MY LIFE FORCE! SOON I SHALL BE DEAD!

BUT ENOUGH HUMAN STRENGTH REMAINS IN ME... TO PERFORM ONE FINAL... AND NECESSARY... ACT!

GO, MINDLESS ONES!

cl-ankkkk!

AFTER SMASHING MORE OF THE JAIL CELL LOCKS...

GO! GO! ATTACK THE SOLDIERS SO THAT THE YOUNG WARRIOR MAY CONFRONT SCORPIO ALONE!

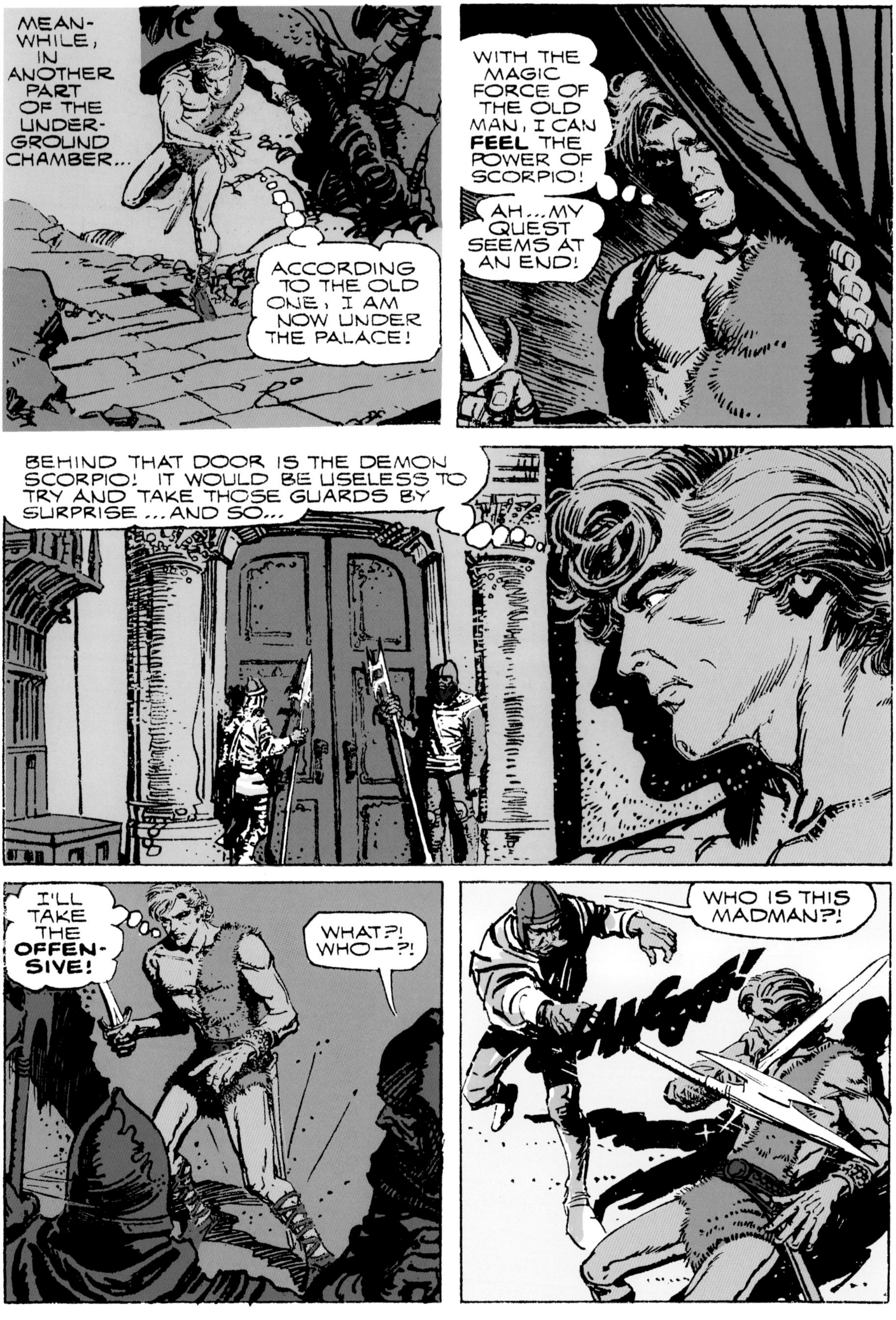
MEAN-WHILE, IN ANOTHER PART OF THE UNDER-GROUND CHAMBER...
ACCORDING TO THE OLD ONE, I AM NOW UNDER THE PALACE!
WITH THE MAGIC FORCE OF THE OLD MAN, I CAN **FEEL** THE POWER OF SCORPIO!
AH... MY QUEST SEEMS AT AN END!
BEHIND THAT DOOR IS THE DEMON SCORPIO! IT WOULD BE USELESS TO TRY AND TAKE THOSE GUARDS BY SURPRISE ...AND SO...
I'LL TAKE THE **OFFEN-SIVE!**
WHAT?! WHO--?!
WHO IS THIS MADMAN?!

I AM NOT SO EASY TO SLAY! UNLESS YOU HAVE SUPERNATURAL POWERS!

BANGG!

UNGH!

THOONK!

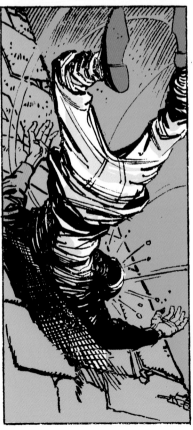

AT LAST, AFTER YEARS OF TRAINING AND SEARCHING, THE DAY OF VENGEANCE IS AT HAND! BEYOND THIS DOOR IS THE FIEND WHO DESTROYED MY ENTIRE NATION!

THE VERY AIR IS ELECTRIFIED WITH STRANGE FORCES! AND THAT VOICE... THE VOICE OF HIM WHO MUST DIE!

LOOKING INTO THE PRIVATE CHAMBER OF SCORPIO, DAGAR SEES THE IMPOSSIBLE... AS THE EVIL SORCERER CONJURES UP VISIONS OF PAST CONQUESTS...THRILLING AT THE SIGHT OF EVERY DESPICABLE ACT... THE SHEDDING OF EVERY DROP OF HUMAN BLOOD...

HAH! HAH! HAH! HOW IT PLEASES ME TO SEE WHOLE NATIONS GROVEL AND DIE BEFORE ME! AT A WHIM, I **DESTROY**...OR IF MERCIFUL, I PROVIDE NEW SPORT FOR THE ARENA...OR CREATE INMATES FOR THE **DUNGEONS**! HAH! HAH! SOON THE ENTIRE WORLD WILL BE DOMINATED BY ME...AND THERE WILL BE NONE TO CHALLENGE MY POWER! NO NATION SHALL ESCAPE THE **WRATH** OF SCORPIO!

111

AS DAGAR WATCHES THE MAGICAL DISPLAY, HE SEES A FLEETING GLIMPSE OF HIS OWN LAND, **TULGONIA**, FALLING TO THE ARMY OF SCORPIO...AND IN THAT INSTANT, HE REALIZES THAT HE CAN RESTRAIN HIS SWORD NO LONGER!

BOAST NO LONGER, SCUM... FOR NOW BY MY SWORD, **SCORPIO** DIES!

WHAT KIND OF FOOL DARES? **YOU!** THE GLADIATOR WHO TURNED ON ME IN THE ARENA! WHO ARE YOU?

TULGONIA? I HAVE CONQUERED SO MANY NATIONS THAT TULGONIA IS NO LONGER IN MY MEMORY!

I AM DAGAR...SOLE SURVIVOR OF TULGONIA, A NATION WHICH YOU ORDERED DESTROYED!

BUT **DAGAR**... I KNOW THAT NAME! YOU ARE THE ONE WHO HAS BEEN INTERFERING WITH MY PLANS FOR SO LONG! NO, DAGAR, IT IS NOT SCORPIO... BUT **YOU**...WHO **DIES!**

I'LL NOT DIE, SCORPIO... NOT AS LONG AS I HAVE MY SWORD... AND AN ENTIRE NATION TO AVENGE!

YOU HOPE TO USE A SWORD AGAINST MAGIC FROM THE **STARS**? YOUR COURAGE AMUSES ME!

I'VE NEVER BEEN ATTACKED WITH SUCH... FORCE! LIKE... MONSTROUS HANDS... TRYING TO BREAK MY BONES... *UGNNNN...*

WHERE IS YOUR NOBLE BLADE NOW, TULGONIAN? CAN YOU NOT MOVE JUST A TRIFLE MORE...SO I MAY BASK IN YOUR AGONY A LITTLE LONGER?

BUT DAGAR'S BODY HAS BEEN ENDOWED WITH MEAGER MAGIC POWER. HE STRAINS TO **BREAK FREE** OF SCORPIO'S SPELL...

IMPOSSIBLE! YOU RESISTED MY MAGIC!

YOU'LL NEED STRONGER MAGIC THAN THAT TO STOP **ME**, SCORPIO!

THAT WOULD HAVE KILLED AN AVERAGE MAN! BUT APPARENTLY I AM DEALING WITH SOMEONE POSSESSING POWERS OF RESISTANCE! THEN FEEL THE SAME SPELL GIVEN TO PRISONERS OF SCORPIO... THE PRISONERS WHO ARE NO LONGER MEN!

KRAKALIK

ARGH!

AT THAT SAME TIME, IN ANOTHER PART OF THE PALACE...

BY SCORPIO! THE CREATURES FROM UNDERGROUND! THEY'RE **HERE**!

ONLY SCORPIO CAN COMMAND THEM! BUT HE ISN'T HERE! WE'LL HAVE TO **FIGHT**!

THE SOLDIERS, SENSING THEY ARE DOOMED, CRY OUT FOR THEIR MASTER... BUT SCORPIO IS NOT ABOUT TO GO TO ANYONE'S AID...

FOR SCORPIO IS SUPREMELY AMUSED...

WH-WHAT'S HAPPEN-NAGRDMMFFPHH.... ARRGHRRRRR...

NOW FEEL THE TRUE MIGHT OF SCORPIO... AS YOUR FLESH TWISTS AND CHANGES INTO THAT OF A MONSTER... AND YOUR MIND BECOMES THAT OF A BEAST!

GRRRR-GRRRRR-RRRRR-OOWWW!

WITH YOUR MIND GONE, DAGAR, YOU EXIST ONLY TO HEAR MY COMMANDS... AND OBEY LIKE THE LOWLY SLAVE YOU ARE!

AND NOW, BRUTE, BEND YOUR KNEES TO SCORPIO, AND MAY YOUR BEASTLY EYES GAZE UPON YOUR MASTER WITH AWE AND REVERENCE!

YOUR ARROGANCE SEEMS TO HAVE LEFT YOU, DAGAR! HEH! HEH! I HAVE THE POWER IN MY FINGERS TO DESTROY YOU IN AN INSTANT, IF I SO CHOOSE...

BUT I CHOOSE A MORE PICTORIAL DEATH FOR YOU... AND ONE BEFITTING THE NAME OF SCORPIO!

LONG AGO I LEARNED OF THE MAGIC IN CERTAIN GROUPINGS OF STARS, DAGAR! AND AS I WAS BORN UNDER THE STARS THAT MAKE UP THE CELESTIAL SCORPION, I AM ABLE TO USE MY OWN ENCHANTMENTS TO CONTROL THOSE STARS FOR MY OWN ENDS! NOW GAZE WITH HORROR AS YOU LEARN THE TRUE ESSENCE OF THE SCORPION CONSTELLATION! HAH! HAH! HAH!

THE SPECTRAL SCORPION DRIFTS INTO THE SORCERER'S CHAMBERS... UNDER THE CONTROL OF ITS MASTER, THE HORROR FROM THE STARS FLOATS TOWARD THE FORMER HUMAN BEING...

OBSERVE, DAGAR... AS THE FORCES FROM THE HEAVENS BECOME A VISIBLE AND LIVING ENTITY... THE NAMESAKE OF **SCORPIO!**

INSTINCTIVELY DAGAR WIELDS HIS SWORD, BUT...

SSWWSSHH!

EVEN WITH THE MIND OF A BEAST YOU TRY TO SURVIVE! YOU NEVER CEASE TO AMAZE ME, DAGAR... EVEN TO YOUR **GRAVE!**

DAGAR'S STRUGGLES ARE MORE THAN MERE ANIMAL INSTINCT...

C-CANNOT... END...LIKE THIS! NOT... **NOW!**

DAGAR'S OWN **WILL** TO SURVIVE AND HAVE REVENGE HAS ALLOWED HIM TO RETAIN HIS **OWN** MIND...

MUST REMEMBER... I AM DAGAR! I AM DAGAR...

WHAT WITCHERY IS **THIS?!** NO ONE CAN SURVIVE THE STELLAR SCORPION! **NO ONE!**

YOU...MADE A GOOD...EFFORT, SCORPIO! BUT DAGAR HAS RETAINED HIS MIND!

WHAT—?

THE SURPRISED SCORPIO DOES NOT SEE THE POWERFUL HAND STREAK TO HIS THROAT, SQUEEZING IT IN AN UNBREAKABLE GRIP...

GAAAH!

I HAVE MY MIND...AND I ALSO HAVE **YOUR SOUL!**

DAGAR! NO-O! WITHOUT THE JEWEL I CAN NO LONGER CONTROL MY POWERS... I WILL BE THE SCORPION'S **VICTIM! SAVE** ME, DAGAR... I'LL GIVE YOU ANYTHING...YOUR OWN KINGDOM....SLAVES... RICHES...**AHHHGGHHH!** KEEP THE MONSTER AWAY....

YEAHHHAAAEEE!

SINCE I HOLD THE JEWEL, SCORPIO CAN NO LONGER MAINTAIN HIS SPELL ON ME! I'M A **MAN** AGAIN!

THERE IS NOTHING TO BE DONE HERE! THOSE MONSTERS THAT ARE STILL ALIVE WILL NEVER AGAIN BE HUMAN!

SOON DAGAR STANDS WHERE HE FIRST ENTERED THE KINGDOM OF SCORPIO... HE SPEAKS THE MYSTIC WORDS...

THE DOOR TO MY WORLD APPEARS!

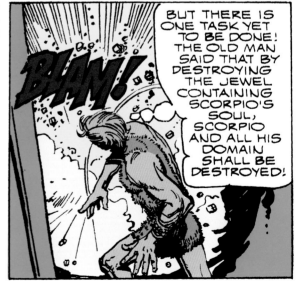

BLAM!

BUT THERE IS ONE TASK YET TO BE DONE! THE OLD MAN SAID THAT BY DESTROYING THE JEWEL CONTAINING SCORPIO'S SOUL, SCORPIO AND ALL HIS DOMAIN SHALL BE DESTROYED!

BUT THE DESTRUCTION OF SCORPIO'S KINGDOM IS SOMETHING WHICH DAGAR DOES NOT WITNESS...

KA-ROOOOMMM!

...FOR ONCE AGAIN HE STANDS IN HIS OWN WORLD...

THE STRANGE POWER HAS LEFT ME...AND THERE IS NO SIGN OF THE KINGDOM OF SCORPIO!

HEAR ME, GODS OF TULGONIA...WITHOUT YOUR AID I HAVE VANQUISHED THE FIEND WHO DESTROYED MY PEOPLE! TODAY DAGAR HAS TASTED SWEET VENGEANCE...FOR HIMSELF...AND FOR HIS PEOPLE!

the END

121

GOLD KEY
DAGAR
90279-310
20c
TALES OF SWORD AND SORCERY
DAGAR
THE INVINCIBLE
A CAVE OF MAGICAL
MISTS LEADS DAGAR INTO
ANOTHER WORLD-ANOTHER TIME
© WESTERN PUBLISHING COMPANY, INC.

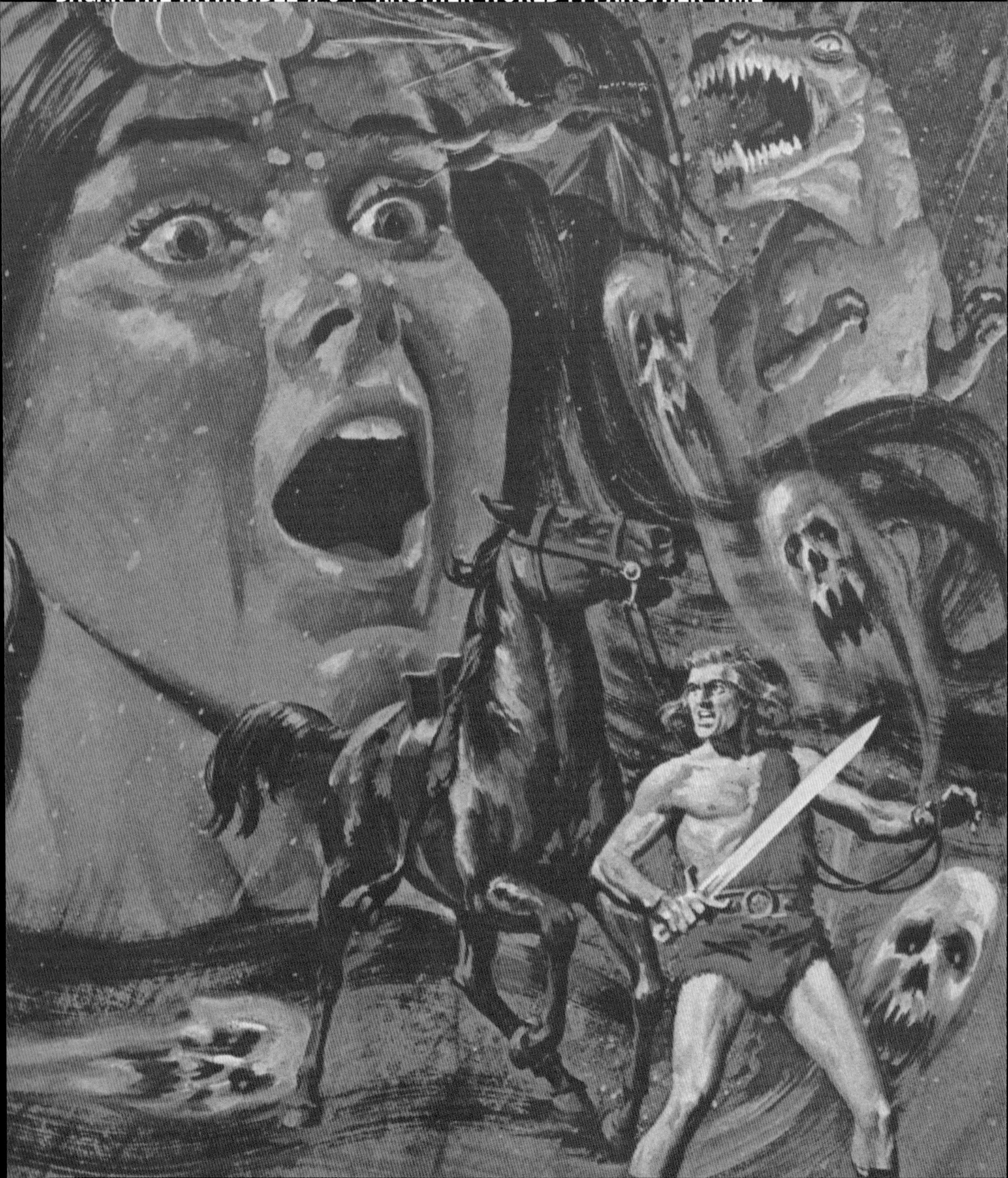

TALES OF SWORD AND SORCERY
DAGAR THE INVINCIBLE

ANOTHER WORLD... ANOTHER TIME

HAVING FINALLY VANQUISHED THE EVIL SORCERER WHO DESTROYED HIS ENTIRE NATION, THE MERCENARY WARRIOR CALLED **DAGAR** SEARCHES FOR **GRAYLIN**... THE RAVEN-HAIRED BEAUTY HE HAD LEFT BEHIND...

IT IS IN THIS STRANGE CAVE, WITH THOSE **MISTS** SWIRLING OUT OF ITS GAPING MOUTH, THAT GRAYLIN SUPPOSEDLY **VANISHED!**

BACK IN THE TOWN WHERE I'D LEFT HER, THE PEOPLE TOLD ME OF THIS CAVE... CALLING IT A **FORBIDDEN ORACLE!**

SUDDENLY...

DON'T BE AFRAID OF THESE VAPORS, KASA! WE'VE ENCOUNTERED STRANGER THINGS BEFORE!

90279-310
DAGAR #5·737

125

BUT THE GREAT STALLION HAS GOOD REASON TO FEAR... AS BOTH HE AND HIS MASTER ARE SWEPT AWAY THROUGH THE STREAMS OF **TIME** BY THE ENCHANTED MISTS...

WHAT MANNER OF ORACLE ARE YOU?! AND THAT IMAGE... THAT VOICE... GRAYLIN, BECKONING TO ME!

DAGAR! DAGAR!

"YES, DAGAR, IT IS GRAYLIN. WHEN YOU DID NOT RETURN FOR ME, I FEARED YOU HAD BEEN SLAIN. ONLY ONE PERSON IN THE TOWN WOULD TELL ME HOW I **MIGHT** FIND YOU...

"THE BOY TOLD ME OF AN **ORACLE CAVE** WHICH MIGHT TELL ME IF YET YOU LIVED...

"THE ORACLE ANSWERED MY QUESTIONS... AND YET I FELT A PECULIAR, **COMPELLING** FORCE TO ENTER THE CAVE...

" ONCE INSIDE THE ORACLE, I WAS ATTACKED BY ITS MYSTIC VAPORS... WHICH SEIZED CONTROL OF MY MIND AND BODY... AND HURLED ME FROM THE WORLD I KNEW... AND INTO ANOTHER..."

THEN...

EVERYTHING IS AS IT WAS... AND GRAYLIN'S VOICE HAS LEFT ME!

AN **EXIT**! HOPEFULLY, IT WILL LEAD ME TO GRAYLIN...AND EXPLAIN WHAT HAS HAPPENED IN THIS CAVE!

DAGAR EMERGES TO SEE A WORLD THAT SEEMS TO BE A NIGHTMARE...A WORLD ADORNED BY THE VERDANT SPLENDOR OF STRANGE TROPICAL FOLIAGE...AND TEEMING WITH CREATURES NEVER BEFORE SEEN BY THIS WARRIOR...A WORLD WHICH HE SOMEHOW KNOWS, BY THE POWER OF THE **ORACLE**, HAS NOT EXISTED FOR COUNTLESS AGES...

BY THE WARRIOR GODS! COULD GRAYLIN HAVE POSSIBLY **SURVIVED** IN THIS SAVAGE WORLD?!

BUT EVEN AS DAGAR PONDERS OVER THE WOMAN HE LOVES, HE HEARS A DEEP MASCULINE **YELL** SOUND ABOVE THE STEADY GROWLS OF THE ANIMALS...

YAAA!

THE MERCENARY WARRIOR TURNS TO SEE...

SSKKRREEEEEEE!!!

SKREEEEEKKK!

UGHNN!

I DON'T KNOW THIS MAN...BUT I CAN'T WATCH HIM DIE! BESIDES, HE MAY HAVE WORD OF GRAYLIN!

AIMING WITH THE SKILL TAUGHT HIM BY HIS GRANDFATHER, DAGAR THROWS HIS WEAPON...

SKEE-EEEKK!

DAGAR RETRIEVES HIS KNIFE AND...

YOU HAVE SAVED MY LIFE! FOR THAT YOU ARE JARN'S FRIEND!

HMM...THE ORACLE MUST HAVE GIVEN ME THE ABILITY TO UNDERSTAND HIS LANGUAGE!

I AM DAGAR, A WARRIOR FROM ANOTHER TIME! I HAVE COME IN SEARCH OF GRAYLIN...A FAIR-SKINNED BEAUTY!

I HAVE SEEN SUCH A ONE!

THERE IS A FEMALE ...WHO LOOKS **DIFFERENT,** AS YOU LOOK DIFFERENT FROM MY PEOPLE! SHE IS AT THE CAVES WHERE WE LIVE!

"IT WAS SOON AFTER OUR CHIEF HAD DIED THAT THE STRANGE WOMAN IN STRANGER ATTIRE EMERGED FROM THE CAVE YOU POINTED OUT TO ME...

"**ZERG,** A WITCH DOCTOR WHO HAD COVETED THE THRONE EVEN WHILE OUR CHIEF LIVED...AND WHO, I SUSPECT, SLEW HIM WITH HIS MAGIC...DECLARED THAT THE WOMAN WAS NOT ORDINARY...

"CLAIMING TO LEARN HER REAL IDENTITY THROUGH HIS MYSTIC POWERS, ZERG TOOK POSSESSION OF THE STRANGER AND LED HER BACK TO THE CAVES..."

SOON AFTER, ZERG PUT HER UPON THE THRONE, DECLARING HER TO BE A **GODDESS** OUT OF OUR LEGENDS! GODDESS, BAH! SHE IS MORTAL! ZERG MUST BE PLANNING SOMETHING FOR WHICH HE **NEEDS** A GODDESS!

THEN WE MUST GO TO YOUR GODDESS! **KASA!**

WHAT KIND OF BEAST OBEYS YOU LIKE THAT?

YOU HAVE NOTHING TO FEAR, JARN! MY HORSE WILL LET US BOTH RIDE HIM! COME... I'LL HELP YOU ON!

THIS KASA SOMEHOW **REMINDS** ME OF THOSE SMALL BEASTS! BUT **THEY** WILL NEVER GROW INTO SUCH A CREATURE!

ALL RIGHT, I'LL TRUST A MAN WHO SAVED MY LIFE...AND MOUNT THIS STRANGE ANIMAL!

MUST YOU RIDE SO FAST, DAGAR? I AM NOT USED TO THIS!

IF GRAYLIN IS THE WOMAN AT YOUR CAVES, I CAN'T MAKE KASA RUN FAST ENOUGH!

SOON AFTER, AT THE CAVES...

LOOK! IT IS JARN...RETURNING WITH A STRANGER ON THAT **BEAST!**

I WAS INTERRUPTED IN THE MIDDLE OF MY HUNT...BUT DAGAR, HERE, SAVED ME FROM A **FLYING DRAGON!**

AFTER BEING LED THROUGH THE MOB OF GAPING CAVE PEOPLE, DAGAR STOPS... HIS EYES FOCUSING UPON A FAMILIAR FACE... HIS MIND REFUSING TO BELIEVE...

GRAYLIN! I HAVE FOUND YOU AT LAST!

WHO IS THIS **STRANGE MAN** WHO DARES APPROACH A **GODDESS?**

SHE DOESN'T KNOW ME! SHE IS **BEWITCHED!**

STEADY, DAGAR! SHE SITS BESIDE **ZERG,** THE WITCH DOCTOR! AND THE TRIBE OBEYS HIS EVERY COMMAND!

LISTEN, PEOPLE, TO ZERG! THE **SECOND STRANGER** HAS COME TO OUR TRIBE! NOW BEHOLD, AS I REVEAL HIS IDENTITY TO YOU!

THE CROWD OF CAVE PEOPLE GROWS SILENT, AS ZERG GESTURES...AND PRODUCES A MYSTIC SMOKE, WHICH WRITHES AND TAKES ON FLEETING, YET DISCERNIBLE SHAPES...

SEE THE ANCIENT **PROPHECY** APPEAR ONCE MORE...TELLING OF THE TWO **STRANGERS** WHO WILL SOMEDAY COME TO OUR LAND! A BEAUTIFUL **GODDESS** TO **COMMAND** US...AND A **DEMON** TO **CONQUER** US!

HE IS THE DEMON WHO WOULD DESTROY US! I COMMAND YOU TO DESTROY *HIM!*

WITHOUT QUESTION, THE LOYAL CAVEMEN RESPOND...

THERE MAY STILL BE A WAY TO SAVE MY FRIEND!

KASA!

SUDDENLY, A STREAK OF BLACK-NESS MOVES INTO THE MIDST OF THE CONFLICT...

Y//////! IT IS THE DEMON'S **BEAST!**

GET OUT OF ITS PATH!

KASA!

SECONDS LATER...

THE DEMON ESCAPES!

NO! LISTEN TO ME! DAGAR IS NO DEMON... BUT A **FRIEND!** HE SAVED MY LIFE!

ZERG MURDERED OUR CHIEF, STOLE THE THRONE, AND HAS CREATED THIS "GODDESS" FOR HIS OWN PLANS!

YOU HAVE DEFIED ME THE FINAL TIME! LET JARN JOIN HIS DEMON FRIEND!

THE MISSILES HURLED AT JARN'S BODY HURT HIM, BUT NOT AS MUCH AS THE THOUGHT OF THE TERRIBLE **MADNESS** THAT HAS BEFALLEN HIS PEOPLE...

THIK!

SPAK!

THUNK!

133

AT THAT MOMENT, BACK AT THE THRONE OF THE LEGENDARY GODDESS...

WHO WAS THAT STRANGE MAN? SOMEHOW I...REMEMBER SOMEONE...

HE WAS AN EVIL DEMON...ONE BEST FORGOTTEN!

MY PEOPLE...THE GODDESS AND I MUST DEPART...BUT ONLY FOR A WHILE! BOW TO HER AS SHE RISES FROM HER THRONE!

THE "GODDESS" WAS BEGINNING TO REMEMBER THINGS! IT IS GOOD WE DIDN'T STAY OUT THERE A MOMENT LONGER! SHE MIGHT HAVE RECALLED TOO MUCH!

IT WAS FORTUNATE FOR ME WHEN BOTH STRANGERS ARRIVED! HOW NICELY THEY FIT THE OLD LEGEND...AND MY PLANS!

SOON WE SHALL WED, MY LOVE! FOR ONLY ONE WITH THE POWERS OF THE WITCH DOCTOR DESERVES A GODDESS! AND AS MATE OF A GODDESS, ZERG SHALL BE KNOWN AS...A GOD!

SOON, THE SUN BECOMES A DEEP ORANGE... AND SLOWLY CRAWLS BEHIND THE DISTANT MOUNTAIN PEAKS. ALONE IN A STRANGE WORLD, DAGAR SITS BEFORE A CAMPFIRE... AND LISTENS TO THE BELLOWS OF THE GREAT REPTILES THAT, EVEN THROUGH THE NIGHT, SEEM TO STRUGGLE FOR SURVIVAL...

HE COOKS THE LEG OF A SMALL SAURIAN SLAIN BY HIS SWORD...

RESCUING GRAYLIN FROM THAT FANATICAL GROUP SEEMS IMPOSSIBLE!

BUT I HAVE FACED **WORSE** ODDS BEFORE! AT DAWN I WILL RETURN TO THE CAVE!

A WARRIOR SUCH AS DAGAR IS TRAINED TO REQUIRE LITTLE SLEEP... BUT EVEN SUCH BRIEF PERIODS OF REPOSE ARE UTILIZED TO THEIR FULLEST...

HOWEVER, EVEN AS DAGAR SLEEPS, THE SMELL OF HIS ROASTED KILL DRIFTS WITH THE EVENING AIR... UNTIL ENTERING THE NOSTRILS OF A HUNGRY CREATURE...

DAGAR AWAKENS AT THE SOUND OF FOLIAGE RIPPED ASUNDER... AND SEES THE SCALY HORROR WINGING FORWARD, HUNGRY JAWS GAPING...

BY ANDO'S BONES! THE MONSTER HAS TAKEN ME OFF GUARD! IN ANOTHER MOMENT IT WILL —

HHIISSSSS-GA-HONK!!

BUT SUDDENLY, THE DIMETRODON STOPS...

HEEEE-AAAAA!

YES, LOOK AT **ME**, FIN-BACK! **AT ME!**

GGRRAAARRGGG!

IN A WORLD WHERE SUCH MONSTERS ARE COMMONPLACE, THE CAVEMAN KNOWS WHERE TO AIM HIS SPEAR...

ERRRR-GGG!!

YOU WILL NEVER HAVE TO WORRY ABOUT HUNTING ANOTHER MEAL, FIN-BACK!

VVAAARRRRRRGGG! THGG-GUSHH!!

THE MONSTER WRITHES CONVULSIVELY... THEN DIES.

JARN!

YES, DAGAR! PERHAPS I HAVE PAID YOU BACK FOR SAVING ME FROM THE FLYING DRAGON!

JARN EXPLAINS HOW HE WAS OUSTED FROM THE TRIBE BY ZERG...

...AND NOW BOTH OF US ARE OUTCASTS!

BUT THERE IS STILL GRAYLIN, THE WOMAN OF MY HEART!

GRAYLIN WAS NOT IN HER RIGHT MIND! OTHERWISE, SHE WOULD HAVE KNOWN ME! I TELL YOU THAT WITCH DOCTOR PUT HER UNDER A SPELL WHICH ROBBED HER MIND AND WILL!

I'VE FOUGHT WORSE VILLAINS THAN THIS ZERG! BUT STILL, TO GET PAST HIS HORDES AND RESCUE GRAYLIN REQUIRES PLANNING!

THEN WE'LL BOTH TRY TO FORM A PLAN...AND SAVE THE WOMAN YOU LOVE! WE ARE IN THIS... TOGETHER!

BY THE GODS, WE **STILL** HAVE NO IDEA HOW TO GET BY ZERG'S SENTRIES!

IF ONLY — WHAT'S THAT NOISE?

GRREERRAAAARRGG!

THE VERY GROUND SEEMS TO QUAKE UNDER THE FEET OF MONSTERS FLEEING FROM A MUTUAL, AND USUALLY HUNGRY, ENEMY... THE **TYRANNOSAURUS!**

IT IS THE BIGGEST FLESH-EATER... THE **TYRANT LIZARD!** THE STAMPEDE WILL **GROW** AS THE MONSTERS FLEE ACROSS THE PLAINS!

GAA-HONNNKK! ISSS-SSSS! GRRRRRRR SKREEKK!

THEY ARE RUNNING IN THE DIRECTION OF THE **CAVES!**

THE CAVES! THEN GRAYLIN IS IN EVEN **MORE** DANGER!

TELL ME, JARN... HOW DOES ONE STOP A STAMPEDE OF SUCH HORRORS?

I FEAR THERE IS **NO WAY,** DAGAR! MANY AT THE CAVES WILL SURELY DIE!

AT THE CAVES, GRAYLIN HAS NOT YET WAKENED FROM HER NIGHT'S SLEEP... AND FINDS HERSELF **HAUNTED** BY GRADUALLY RETURNING MEMORIES...

D-DAGAR?

BUT AS HER EYES SNAP OPEN, THE IMAGE OF THE WARRIOR VANISHES...

DAGAR! WHAT? I WAS **DREAMING!** BUT NOW MY MIND IS CLEAR! I REMEMBER **ALL!**

DAGAR HAS COME BACK FOR ME... EVEN IN THIS NIGHTMARE WORLD! I MUST **FIND** HIM!

A MOMENT LATER, AS ZERG ENTERS GRAYLIN'S CHAMBERS TO AWAKEN HER...

WHAT'S THIS? SHE'S NOT **HERE!**

BUT THEN...

THERE SHE IS! YOUR GODDESS IS NOT WELL, THIS MORNING! **STOP HER!** DON'T LET HER RUN AWAY, UNLESS YOU WANT TO DIE BY ZERG'S MAGIC!

GRAYLIN LOOKS WITH TERROR UPON THE SAVAGE HORDE THAT SURROUNDS HER...THEIR SWEATY FACES GAWKING AT HER PERFECT BEAUTY...

N-NO! PL- PLEASE...

IRON GRIPS LOCK AROUND HER ARMS... AND GRAYLIN IS FORCED TO WALK BACK TOWARD THE CAVES...

DON'T TAKE ME BACK THERE! **DON'T!**

YOU **FIEND!**

FIEND, AM I? YOU ALL CAN SEE HOW A TERRIBLE **SPELL** HAS STOLEN OUR DEITY'S SENSE OF **JUDGMENT!**

I ALONE HAVE THE MAGIC TO LIFT THAT SPELL! TAKE HER TO MY PRIVATE QUARTERS!

SHORTLY, GRAYLIN AND ZERG ARE ALONE IN HIS CHAMBERS...

SO YOUR **MEMORY** HAS RETURNED, HAS IT?!

I'LL HAVE TO DO SOMETHING ABOUT THAT...WITH THE AID OF THIS RARE POTION! I HAVE ENOUGH OF IT YET TO BEND YOU TO MY WILL BEFORE OUR MARRIAGE!

SSSSSSTTT...TTT!

THERE! BREATHE THE FUMES DEEPLY... AND TELL ME WHO YOU ARE!

(COUGH!) I AM... (CHOKE!) I AM... GR... G...

I... AM... THE GODDESS OF LEGEND!

SOON AFTER, THERE IS MUCH EXCITEMENT OUTSIDE THE CAVES... AS THE WITCH DOCTOR AND THE BEAUTEOUS "GODDESS" STAND BEFORE THE PEOPLE...

MY PEOPLE! THIS IS A JOYOUS DAY FOR ALL OF US! OUR GODDESS HAS CONSENTED TO TAKE ME FOR HER MATE... AND IN SO DOING, MAKE ME YOUR GOD!

HAIL OUR GODDESS! PRAISE TO ZERG!

LET THE WEDDING CEREMONY COMMENCE!

TODAY WE SEE A MIRACLE... A MAN REBORN AS A GOD!

BUT EVEN AS THE WEDDING CEREMONY BEGINS, THE TRIBAL SENTRIES PERCEIVE "SOMETHING" MOVING ACROSS THE PLAINS...

IT LOOKS LIKE A MOUNTAIN OF DUST! NO! IT'S...

141

...AND AS THE DUST CLEARS, MONSTERS WITH SCALY HIDES THUNDER TOWARD THE CAVES. WITH THEIR MINISCULE BRAINS, THE GIANT BEASTS ARE AS FRIGHTENED OF ONE ANOTHER AS THEY ARE OF THE APPROACHING FLESH-EATER...

WEE-HORK! GA-HONK! REEEUUNK!

A STAMPEDE! ONLY ZERG'S MAGIC CAN SAVE US!

USE YOUR MAGIC! SAVE US!

WHAT CAN I DO? I HAVE NO POWER TO HALT A STAMPEDE!

AT THAT MOMENT, THE FLEEING PEOPLE SEE TWO FAMILIAR FORMS... RIDING HARD UPON THE BACK OF THE STRANGE, BLACK BEAST...

I HOPE YOUR PLAN WORKS, DAGAR!

IT MUST...IF WE ARE TO SAVE GRAYLIN! NO MATTER IN WHAT WORLD OR TIME, BRUTE ANIMALS HAVE A COMMON FOE...FIRE!

LOOK! THE STRANGER THAT WE CALLED A DEMON IS MAKING A WALL OF FIRE! HE'S DRIVING THOSE MONSTERS AWAY FROM THE CAVES!

HE AND JARN ARE RISKING THEIR LIVES OUT THERE...FOR **US!**

HONK! REEUNK! SNORT! SKREE!

AS THE WALL OF BLAZING DEATH GROWS STEADILY TALLER, THE REPTILES BEGIN TO TURN... HARDLY NOTICING THE MINIATURE CREATURE WHO RIDES AMONGST THEM WITH HIS CRACKLING TORCH!

BUT ONE OF THE GIANT REPTILES IS NOT TIMID LIKE THE OTHERS... AND STILL SEARCHES FOR A PREY TO SATISFY ITS CONSTANT **HUNGER**...

GORRK!

IT SEES ME!

KEEP DRIVING THE OTHER MONSTERS AWAY FROM THE CAVES, JARN! I'LL DEAL WITH THE FLESH-EATER!

RIDING FURIOUSLY, DAGAR SETS HIS TORCH TO THE DRY GRASS... PRODUCING A **CIRCLE OF FIRE** AROUND THE CONFUSED DINOSAUR. THE AIR WAVERS FROM THE HEAT AND DAGAR IS NEARLY **BLINDED** BY THE FLAMES AS HE CHARGES ON KASA...

GAAA-HONK!

IF MY PLAN SUCCEEDS, THE TRIBE WILL SOON FEAST ON THE BEAST'S ROASTED FLESH!

CRAKK

THEN, AS HIS EYES CLEAR, DAGAR REALIZES THAT HE HAS STEPPED **INTO** THE BURNING RING OF FIRE!

BY THE GODS! I AM **TRAPPED!**

THE REPTILE, BELLOWING WITH RAGE AS THE FLAMES CONTINUE TO GROW, **CHARGES...**

I KEEP HACKING AWAY WITH MY SWORD... BUT THE LIZARD WILL NOT DIE! ITS THROAT IS BEYOND MY REACH!

HISSSS!

BUT JARN HAS SEEN HIS FRIEND'S PERIL... AND HAS ALREADY ACQUIRED AN ARMFUL OF SPEARS FROM HIS NOW GRATEFUL TRIBESMEN...

DAGAR!

TAKE THESE SPEARS! USE **ALL** OF THEM!

ON THE OTHER SIDE OF THE RING OF FLAMES, DAGAR SEES THE SPEARS IMPALE THE GROUND...AND INSTANTLY HE KNOWS WHAT TO DO...

Thik-Siiii-thunt

WITH DEADLY ACCURACY, DAGAR RELEASES HIS MISSILE...

GAAAAA!

THAT'S THE FIRST SPEAR! NOW TO KEEP CIRCLING THE BRUTE...KEEP IT CONFUSED...

MOVING AROUND THE MONSTER, DAGAR CONTINUES TO HURL THE PRIMITIVE WEAPONS...UNTIL THE TYRANNOSAURUS, WRITHING FROM THE AGONY OF SO MANY WOUNDS, BEGINS TO SWAY FROM SIDE TO SIDE...

THERE, MEAT-EATER! THIS FINAL SPEAR SHOULD FINISH YOU OFF!

REEEEUUUNNNKKKK!

AND AS THE ONCE MIGHTY REPTILE TOPPLES LIFELESSLY, IT PROVIDES DAGAR WITH A MEANS TO ESCAPE THE APPROACHING FLAMES...

KA-THUDDDDDD!

HURRY, KASA! UNLESS YOU WISH US TO PROVIDE **FOOD** FOR THE SCAVENGERS!

ZERG HAS BETRAYED US! HE...AND NOT THE STRANGER... IS OUR ENEMY!

YES! DAGAR SAVED US! ZERG IS THE ONE WE MUST DESTROY!

MY POTIONS ARE NOT STRONG ENOUGH TO HOLD BACK THAT **MOB!** BUT I DO KNOW OF HIDDEN TUNNELS IN THESE CAVES! IF I CAN ONLY REACH MY QUARTERS FIRST...

AND AS ZERG ATTEMPTS HIS ESCAPE...

I SAW ZERG ENTER THE CAVE WITH GRAYLIN!

IF I DON'T GET THERE FIRST, THAT MOB WILL ALSO ATTACK HER!

LEAVING KASA WITH JARN, DAGAR BOLTS INSIDE THE CAVE. HIS HEART POUNDS FURIOUSLY...AND HIS HAND SWEATS AS IT GRIPS HIS **SWORD**...

BUT AS DAGAR ENTERS THE CHAMBER OF THE WITCH DOCTOR, ZERG HURLS A POTION AND...

THERE! NOW I CAN MAKE MY ESCAPE THROUGH THE SECRET TUNNELS!

BA-KOOFF! SSSSSSS

(COUGH!) UGGHH! FEELS AS IF MY **LUNGS** ARE ON FIRE! C-CAN'T BREATHE... B-BURNING UP!

GRAYLIN! NO! I WON'T LET THE MAGIC STOP ME! NOT NOW, WHEN I'VE COME SO CLOSE!

AND NO WITCH DOCTOR OF A TRIBE OF **SAVAGES** WILL DEFEAT A TRAINED WARRIOR... WITH A PUFF OF SMOKE!

THIK!

UHH!

NOW WILL YOU RELEASE GRAYLIN FROM YOUR SPELL... OR DO I USE THIS BLADE AS IT WAS **MEANT** TO BE USED?

N-NO... I'LL DO WHATEVER YOU WANT!

WITH DAGAR'S SWORD AS A PERSUADER, ZERG PERFORMS THE **REVERSAL** OF THE SPELL WHICH BOUND GRAYLIN'S MIND...

I...I...

HER BEAUTIFUL EYES BLINK SEVERAL TIMES...AND SHE BEHOLDS IN THE TORCHLIGHT...

DAGAR! IT'S REALLY YOU!

YES, I'VE CROSSED THE BARRIERS OF TIME TO FIND YOU! AND NO VILLAIN OR MONSTER WILL EVER SEPARATE US AGAIN!

AFTER JARN HAS TAKEN CUSTODY OF THE WITCH DOCTOR, DAGAR TELLS THE PEOPLE WHAT HAS HAPPENED...

...THE EVIL ZERG HAS CONFESSED TO SLAYING YOUR CHIEF! HE IS IN THE HANDS OF JARN, WHO WILL SEE THAT JUSTICE IS DONE ACCORDING TO YOUR CUSTOMS! AND ALTHOUGH GRAYLIN AND I MAY HAVE COME HERE IN YOUR EYES AS GODDESS AND DEMON, WE LEAVE AS FRIENDS!

LATER THAT DAY, AT THE MOUTH OF THE STRANGE CAVE THAT BROUGHT THEM TO THE PREHISTORIC WORLD...

EXCHANGING THE WARRIOR'S GRIP WHICH HAS EXISTED SINCE MAN'S BEGINNINGS...

DAGAR, YOU HELPED MY TRIBE!

BUT WITHOUT YOUR HELP, JARN, I'D HAVE LOST GRAYLIN! THANK YOU... AND FAREWELL! FOR WE WISH NOW TO RETURN TO OUR OWN WORLD!

AS THEY LEAVE THE STRANGE CAVE, DAGAR AND GRAYLIN LOOK FOR A FINAL TIME UPON THEIR FRIEND OF THE PAST...

BUT NOW THEY MUST CONSIDER THE FUTURE... THE FUTURE WHICH BEGINS TO EXIST AS THEY ARE AGAIN TOSSED BY THE ENCHANTED MISTS OF THE ORACLE...

AS KASA EMERGES FROM THE FORBIDDEN ORACLE WITH HIS TWO RIDERS, THERE IS A SMILE UPON THE LIPS OF DAGAR. THOUGH HE IS STILL A MAN WITHOUT A NATION, HE IS NO LONGER ALONE IN A WORLD OF EVIL MAGIC.

AS HE EXPERIENCES THE WARMTH OF A SMOOTH CHEEK CARESSING HIS HERCULEAN SHOULDER, DAGAR FEELS TRULY INVINCIBLE! FOR NOT EVEN MAGIC MOST FOUL CAN DEFEAT ONE WHO LOVES... AND WHO IS LOVED IN RETURN.

the END

GOLD KEY ®

90279-401

TALES OF SWORD AND SORCERY

DAGAR

THE INVINCIBLE

DAGAR RENEWS AN ANCIENT BATTLE BETWEEN
A WARRIOR GOD AND MONSTROUS DEMON!

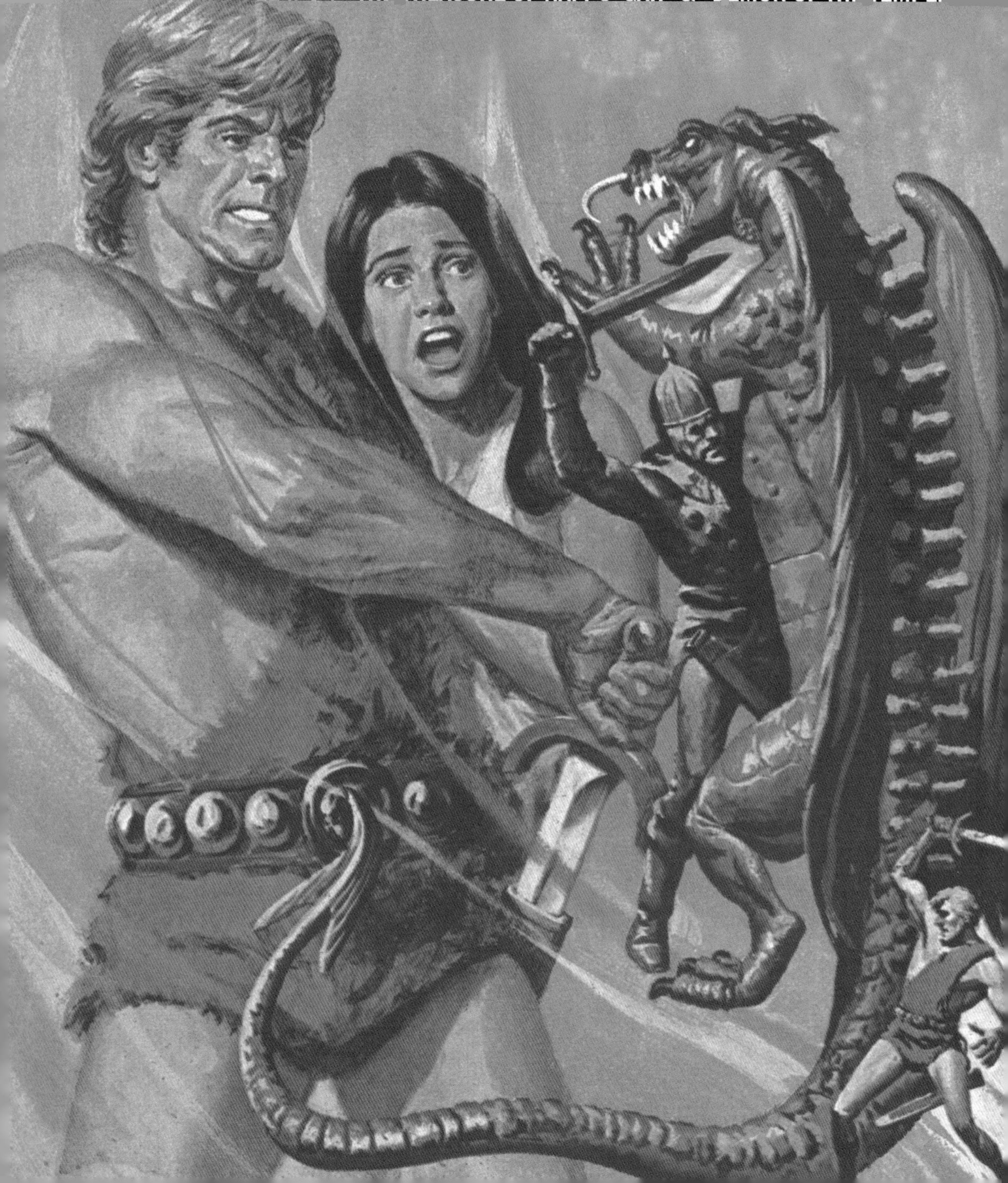

TALES OF SWORD AND SORCERY
DAGAR
THE INVINCIBLE

TREASURE of NAI-PO-GAH

ON THE OUTSKIRTS OF THE ANCIENT RUINS OF THE CITY OF **NAI-PO-GAH** STAND TWO OUTCASTS. THE FIRST IS **DAGAR**, LAST MEMBER OF THE MASSACRED **TULGONIAN** NATION... A BITTER MAN WHO EARNS HIS LIVING BY THE SWORD. WITH HIM IS **GRAYLIN**, BEAUTEOUS VOLUNTARY EXILE OF A PEOPLE WHO SOUGHT TO USE HER AS THE VICTIM OF A BIZARRE SACRIFICE...

THERE IS **NAI-PO-GAH**, THE SO-CALLED **FORBIDDEN CITY**! ACCORDING TO THE **LEGENDS**, THE CITY WAS ABANDONED AGES AGO... BUT STILL CONTAINS A VAST TREASURE, JUST FOR THE **TAKING!**

30279-401
DAGAR #6-7310

BUT UNEXPECTEDLY...

HOLD, THERE, YOU TWO! WHO ARE YOU AND WHY ARE YOU STANDING ON THE BORDER OF NAI-PO-GAH?

WE ARE A PAIR OF **ADVENTURERS**, HERE ONLY TO EXPLORE THE FORBIDDEN CITY! WHO WANTS TO KNOW?

WE ARE THE SENTRIES WHO GUARD THESE RUINS AND KEEP CURIOSITY SEEKERS LIKE YOU **OUT**! THERE IS ONLY **EVIL** IN NAI-PO-GAH! SO IF YOU VALUE YOUR LIVES, GET ON YOUR HORSES AND RIDE!

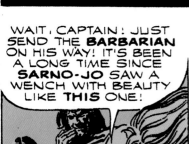

WAIT, CAPTAIN! JUST SEND THE **BARBARIAN** ON HIS WAY! IT'S BEEN A LONG TIME SINCE **SARNO-JO** SAW A WENCH WITH BEAUTY LIKE **THIS** ONE!

DAGAR IS NO BARBARIAN! AND I AM NO **WENCH**! BUT **YOU**...?!

UGHH!

Slapp!

NO ONE SLAPS SARNO-JO AND LIVES! START PRAYING TO WHATEVER GODS YOU WORSHIP, WOMAN!

154

BUT IT'S **DAGAR** AND NOT HER THAT YOU MUST FACE!

HAH! HE IS **MAD** TO THINK HE CAN FIGHT **ALL** OF US!

THEN IF HE IS SO BRAVE, LET'S GIVE HIM A WORK-OUT!

BUT DON'T SLAY HIM **TOO** SWIFTLY! LET'S PROLONG OUR ENJOYMENT! HAH! HAHH!

THOUGH THE **SENTRIES** DESCEND UPON HIM LIKE A SMALL ARMY, DAGAR FIGHTS WITH DETERMINATION FOR THE WOMAN HE LOVES...

Clang! Klang! Klakk!

OOPHFF!

YOU'LL NEVER TOUCH GRAYLIN AGAIN, SARNO-JO! AND YOU'D BETTER START PRAYING TO **YOUR** GODS...UNLESS IT IS ALREADY TOO LATE!

ARRGHHH!

GRAYLIN! I'LL FIGHT THEM OFF! BUT YOU'D BETTER MOUNT **TARNU!**

MOMENTS LATER, MOUNTED UPON THEIR STEEDS **KASA** AND **TARNU**....

RIDE HARD AND FAST, GRAYLIN, UNLESS YOU WANT ONE OF THOSE MISSILES TO STRIKE US!

NIGHT BLACKENS THE SKY, AS IF IT IS SPREADING THE SHADOW OF **EVIL** ACROSS THE FOREST NEAR THE FORBIDDEN CITY. AND IN A CAMP IN THOSE WOODS, A MERCENARY SOLDIER AND THE WOMAN HE LOVES WARM THEM-SELVES BY A FIRE...

DAGAR, YOU MUST **FORGET** THE TREASURE OF NAI-PO-GAH! IT IS BEYOND OUR REACH!

I CAN'T FORGET IT!

IT HAS BEEN **TOO LONG** SINCE I HAVE BEEN PAID FOR THE USE OF MY SWORD! SEE, MY PURSE IS **EMPTY!**

OH, DAGAR! WHY MUST YOU BE A HIRED WARRIOR? THERE MUST BE SOME OTHER LINE OF WORK YOU COULD DO! SOMEHOW, FIGHTING FOR MONEY DOESN'T SEEM RIGHT!

PERHAPS NOT!

BUT WHEN ALL MY GODS PERMITTED THE **SLAUGHTER** OF THE PEOPLE OF TULGONIA, I LOST ALL LOVE FOR MY FELLOW MEN! BUT I DO FIGHT WELL... AND THAT IS THE ONLY WORK I KNOW!

BUT TONIGHT I WILL NOT **HAVE** TO USE MY SWORD! TONIGHT ALL WE'LL NEED TO ACQUIRE GOLD IS OUR **HANDS**... AND WE'LL CARRY AWAY PLENTY OF TREASURE FROM NAI-PO-GAH!

156

THE FORBIDDEN CITY WAITS SILENTLY IN A CLEARING BEYOND THE WOODS. UNSIGHTLY VINES TWIST ABOUT THE ERODED AND CRACKED BUILDINGS AS IF TO SMOTHER SOME UNSEEN **PRESENCE** STILL LIVING THERE. THEN THERE IS MOVEMENT... OF TWO FIGURES STEALING THROUGH THE DARKNESS...

GOOD THING WE LEFT OUR HORSES TIED UP! THE SENTRIES WILL NEVER SEE US IN THESE SHADOWS!

WHAT RUINS! AND LOOK AT THOSE VINES!

SUPPOSEDLY, SOME TERRIBLE **EVIL** BEFELL THE CITY... AND DROVE AWAY ALL OF ITS INHABITANTS MANY YEARS AGO!

THIS SEEMS TO BE WHAT ONCE WAS A GREAT PALACE! AND IT SEEMS TO ME THAT A **TREASURE** WOULD BE KEPT IN SUCH A PLACE! COME ON!

BUT AFTER MUCH SEARCHING IN THE PALACE...

STILL WE FIND NO TREASURE! PERHAPS IN **THIS** ROOM...

DAGAR! LOOK AT THIS **GLOBE**!

BEFORE REACHING GRAYLIN, SOMETHING ELSE CATCHES DAGAR'S EYE...

BY THE WARRIOR GODS!

TOWERING ABOVE THEM, THE MASSIVE CARVED EFFIGY STANDS... WAITING LIKE SOME LIFELESS SOLDIER OF **STONE**...

DAGAR, WHAT—?

IT IS THE STATUE OF... A **WARRIOR GOD!**

AND LOOK AT THE SIZE OF THAT **JEWEL** IN ITS **STONE** HEAD! MAYBE THAT IS THE SO-CALLED **TREASURE** OF NAI-PO-GAM!

BUT I THOUGHT THAT A WARRIOR GOD WAS JUST PART OF AN **EXPRESSION!** I'VE HEARD YOU SAY "BY THE **WARRIOR GODS**" MANY TIMES...BUT DIDN'T KNOW IT REALLY **MEANT** SOMETHING!

BUT IT **DOES!**

"BEFORE THE COMING OF **MAN**...OR SO THE LEGENDS SAY...TWO IMMORTAL RACES INHABITED THE EARTH. THE FIRST, THE **WARRIOR GODS**, WERE **NOBLE** CREATURES...WHILE THE **DARK GODS** WERE TOTALLY **EVIL**...

"NATURALLY, THE TWO RACES OF GODS BATTLED EACH OTHER CONSTANTLY, THE WARRIOR GODS TRYING TO KEEP THEIR ENEMIES FROM SPREADING THEIR EVIL THROUGHOUT THE WORLD. FINALLY, THE TWO RACES **DESTROYED** ONE ANOTHER DURING A TERRIBLE AND FINAL ENCOUNTER..."

BUT SINCE THE WARRIOR GODS HAVE LONG BEEN GONE FROM THIS WORLD, THEY WON'T MIND IT IF WE HELP OURSELVES TO THE JEWEL ON THIS EFFIGY!

WAIT, DAGAR! I CAN READ THE INSCRIPTION ON THIS PEDESTAL! IT SAYS, "IF ANY MAN POSSESSES THE **SACRED JEWEL** LET HIM SUFFER THE WRATH OF THE WARRIOR GOD!"

BAH! THIS IS A FIGURE OF LIFELESS STONE... AND NOTHING MORE! AND THIS JEWEL WILL DO **US** A LOT BETTER THAN IT'S DOING OUR WARRIOR GOD!

DAGAR! THE STATUE IS... **MOVING!** PLEASE, PUT THE JEWEL BACK! YOU CANNOT SPEND IT IF YOU ARE **DEAD!**

IT SEEMS AS IF YOU'RE **RIGHT!**

THERE! THE JEWEL IS BACK IN PLACE AND THE STATUE IS AGAIN WITHOUT MOVEMENT! BUT I FEEL LIKE A **FOOL** LEAVING A JEWEL OF SUCH MAGNITUDE!

A **LIVE** FOOL, AT LEAST!

BUT AFTER DAGAR LEAPS FROM THE STATUE...

PLEASE...HELP ME...

THAT VOICE, COMING FROM THE **GLOBE!** AND THE SPHERE IS **GLOWING** NOW!

LOOK! NOW THERE IS SOMETHING WITHIN THE GLOWING SPHERE! IT LOOKS LIKE A SWIRLING CLOUD!

BUT THERE SEEMS TO BE SOMETHING FORMING INSIDE!

BY ANDO'S SWORD! THERE'S A TINY MAN INSIDE!

NO, THIS IS BUT AN IMAGE! I AM TRAPPED... OUTSIDE THE PALACE! PLEASE HELP ME!

SOON...

DAGAR... OVER HERE!

HURRYING TO GRAYLIN'S SIDE, DAGAR PEERS DOWN INTO A DEEP PIT...

THANK THE GODS I WAS ABLE TO CONTACT YOU THROUGH THE MYSTIC GLOBE!

WHO ARE YOU? AND WHAT ARE YOU DOING IN THAT PIT?

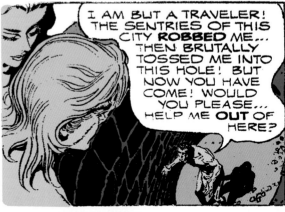

I AM BUT A TRAVELER! THE SENTRIES OF THIS CITY ROBBED ME... THEN BRUTALLY TOSSED ME INTO THIS HOLE! BUT NOW YOU HAVE COME! WOULD YOU PLEASE... HELP ME OUT OF HERE?

DAGAR! YOU CANNOT BE SERIOUS!

NO!

I HAVE LEARNED FROM EXPERIENCE NOT TO TRUST **STRANGERS**, GRAYLIN! THIS ONE COULD BE SOME CONNIVING **WIZARD** IN DISGUISE, WHO WOULD TURN ON US ONCE SET FREE!

BUT DAGAR, HE IS STILL A **MAN!** YOU CANNOT JUST LET HIM **DIE** DOWN THERE!

DAGAR HELPS STRANGERS ONLY FOR **PAYMENT!**

THEN IF IT'S PAYMENT YOU WANT, PAYMENT YOU'LL GET! FREE ME FROM THIS PIT AND I SHALL SHOW YOU WHERE THE **REAL** TREASURE OF NAI-PO-GAH IS HIDDEN!

PLEASE, DAGAR!

I DON'T KNOW IF IT IS HIS PROMISE OF TREASURE... OR YOUR **OWN** METHOD OF PERSUASION, GRAYLIN...

...BUT I **WILL** SAVE THE MAN! YET I STILL HAVE THIS FEELING OF FORBODING THAT I MAY **REGRET** IT AFTERWARDS!

THERE, NOW! TAKE A FIRM GRIP ON THE VINE AND I'LL HOIST YOU OUT OF THERE!

I HAVE IT!

161

AH! I AM **FREE!** AND HOW GOOD IT FEELS TO BE OUT OF THAT ACCURSED HOLE IN THE GROUND!

AND DON'T FORGET **YOUR** SIDE OF THE BARGAIN!

YES, YOUR **REWARD!** THEN FOLLOW ME, DAGAR, BACK INTO THE PALACE!

I'LL FOLLOW! BUT I STILL HAVE MY **DOUBTS** ABOUT HIM!

THE **MYSTIC GLOBE!** IT IS **MINE** AGAIN... AT LAST!

WHERE IS THIS REWARD? IF YOU **LIED** TO ME ABOUT THAT, YOU'LL FEEL THE BLADE OF MY BROADSWORD!

YOU SHALL **HAVE** YOUR REWARD, WITLESS MORTAL! FOR NOW THAT I AM AGAIN IN POSSESSION OF THE GLOBE, MY **FULL POWERS** RETURN!

IN HIS BRIEF CAREER, DAGAR HAS FACED DEATH MANY TIMES... DEFEATING SEEMINGLY UNBEATABLE FOES. AND THOUGH HE BE THUS FAR AN INVINCIBLE WARRIOR, DAGAR IS STILL A **MAN**... AND A MAN WHO DOES NOT ADMIT FEAR IN THE FACE OF DEATH IS A FOOL!

BY THE GODS—!

NOW I CAN SCRAP THIS FOUL MORTAL **GUISE** AND REGAIN MY **TRUE SHAPE**... THAT OF **ZU-BORR**, DEMON OF MY MASTERS, THE **DARK GODS!**

IT WAS **I**, A SURVIVOR OF THE WAR BETWEEN THE WARRIOR GODS AND DARK GODS, WHO DROVE THE PEOPLE FROM NAI-PO-GAH! THEN THOSE MEN WHO GUARD THE CITY CAME AND SEPARATED ME FROM THE MYSTIC GLOBE...WHICH TRANSFORMED ME INTO THE INEFFECTUAL CREATURE YOU RESCUED FROM THE **PIT**!

THE SENTRIES **TRAPPED** ME IN THAT HOLE, THEN STATIONED THEMSELVES ABOUT THE FORBIDDEN CITY, SO THAT STRANGERS WOULD NOT UNWITTINGLY SET ME FREE AGAIN!

BUT NOW ZU-BORR **IS** FREE AGAIN, THANKS TO THE BLIND BENEVOLENCE OF A MORTAL! AND THE **REWARD** FOR SUCH AN ACT, ACCORDING TO THE WILL OF THE **DARK GODS**, IS A MOST UNPLEASANT **DEATH**!

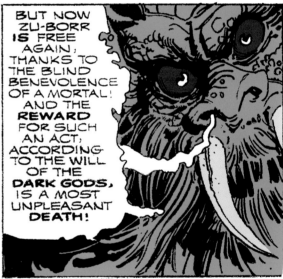

I WILL NOT DIE UNLESS IT IS WHILE HACKING AT YOUR SCALY HIDE, DEMON! GRAYLIN, GET AWAY FROM HERE!

RELUCTANTLY, GRAYLIN DASHES ACROSS THE ROOM. BUT THE DEMON'S TAIL IS SWIFT...AND POWERFUL...

SWI-THAK-K!

UHGH-NNN!

GRAYLIN! YOU'VE **KILLED** HER! YOU'VE SLAIN THE WOMAN I LOVE! FOR **THAT** YOU'LL **PAY**, MONSTER! PAY WITH YOUR **LIFE**!

BUT THE DEMON MOVES FIRST...

SPLAKK!

NOW TO **SQUASH** YOU!

WHAT?! SO, IT SEEMS AS IF YOUR STAMINA AND REFLEXES ARE BETTER THAN I THOUGHT!

STOMMPPP!

AFTER REPEATED STABS...

I KEEP **STABBING** THE DEMON, BUT NOTHING HAPPENS! NO **BLOOD**! NOTHING!

STUPID HUMAN! DID YOU **REALLY** EXPECT THAT MAN-FORGED **STEEL** WOULD HAVE ANY EFFECT ON A **SUPER-NATURAL** SPAWN OF THE DARK GODS? AND NOW, MORTAL, I GROW WEARY OF THIS CHARADE! THUS, YOU **DIE**!

BUT EVEN AS DAGAR WATCHES THE BLASPHEMOUS CREATURE APPROACH FOR THE KILL, HE DETECTS **MOVE-MENT** FROM THE CORNER OF HIS EYE...

DAGAR! I AM ALL RIGHT! DON'T FIGHT THAT THING! **RUN!**

YES, **RUN**, MORTAL! SEE HOW **FAR** YOU CAN RUN FROM SOMETHING THAT IS NOT HUMAN!

ALTHOUGH HE STEPS BACKWARDS, DAGAR DOES NOT FLEE...

AND AS THE MERCENARY MOVES, HE INADVERTENTLY COLLIDES WITH A THICK SLAB OF COLD STONE...

UNGH!

THE STATUE OF THE WARRIOR GOD! BY ANDO, THIS MAY BE THE **ANSWER!**

MOVING WITH THE AGILITY OF A SABRE-TOOTHED CAT, DAGAR CLIMBS THE MONO-LITHIC FIGURE...

DAGAR, WHAT ARE YOU DOING?! THIS ISN'T ANY TIME FOR...

PATIENCE, GRAYLIN!

FOR IF MY PLAN SUCCEEDS, WE'LL BOTH BE RICH **AND** ALIVE THIS DAY!

AS DAGAR CLUTCHES THE SACRED JEWEL AND FEELS ITS MAGICAL WARMTH TINGLE HIS FLESH, HE WITNESSES THE IMPOSSIBLE. STONE... LIFELESS, UNFEELING STONE... CREAKS, MOVES, AND AN ARM OF SOLID ROCK REACHES UPWARD...

KrEEEaaakKK!

I'VE DONE IT! THE **WARRIOR GOD** LIVES!

THEN THE HUGE STONE HEAD OF THE GIANT TURNS ...ITS ANGERED EYES PERCEIVING THE GLOWING JEWEL IN DAGAR'S HAND...

THE STATUE IS COMING FOR US!

BUT NOW WHAT WILL HAPPEN THAT YOU'VE UNLEASHED A **SECOND** MONSTER AFTER US?

JUST WAIT! AND YOU'LL SEE THAT I HAVE **NOT** LOST MY MIND!

IN THE INSTANT THAT DAGAR AND GRAYLIN SEEMINGLY VANISH FROM THE STATUE'S SIGHT, IT NOTICES SOMETHING ELSE MOVING IN THE PALACE...SOMETHING **HUGE**... OBSCENE...

AND FOR A MOMENT, THE **PAST** SEEMS TO LIVE AGAIN—THE PAST, WHEN WARRIOR GOD AND DARK GOD SOUGHT TO WIPE EACH OTHER'S SPECIES FROM THE SPHERE CALLED EARTH...

THEN, IN THE MINDS OF TWO BEINGS FROM THE TIME-BEFORE-MAN, THE TWO PUNY MORTALS CEASE TO EXIST. THERE IS ONLY **ONE** PURPOSE FOR EITHER OF THE TWO IMMORTALS... THE DESTRUCTION OF THE OTHER. THE WARRIOR GOD LUMBERS FORWARD ON PILLAR-LIKE LEGS. ZU-BORR, DEMON OF THE DARK GODS, **HISSES**... SLITHERING TOWARD HIS ANCIENT FOE... AND THE TWO BEHEMOTHS LASH OUT AT ONE ANOTHER WITH A FORCE UNKNOWN FOR CENTURIES ON THIS WORLD...

ARRGHHHHH! HHISSSSS! CRUMMMBLLL!

NOW YOU SEE, GRAYLIN! DAGAR WAS NOT SO MAD AFTER ALL!

NOW WE CAN LET THE MONSTERS DESTROY EACH OTHER... WHILE WE ABSCOND WITH THE SACRED JEWEL AND THINK OF THE MANY WAYS TO SPEND IT!

NO, DAGAR!

WE CANNOT TAKE THE JEWEL WITH US! FOR TO DO SO WOULD MEAN OUR DEATHS!

BUT YOU CANNOT **MEAN** THAT! NOT AFTER ALL WE WENT THROUGH TO GET THE JEWEL!

BUT THINK OF THE **INSCRIPTION** ON THE PEDESTAL! IF THE **WARRIOR GOD** TRIUMPHS IN THIS BATTLE, HE'LL **STILL** BE COMING TO SLAY US!

YOU DON'T HAVE TO FINISH! IF THE **DEMON** WINS, THEN **HE** WILL DESTROY US! THE GLOBE GIVES ZU-BORR HIS POWER! SO... THERE SEEMS BUT **ONE** SOLUTION TO OUR DILEMMA!

THERE IS NO FURTHER NEED FOR DELIBERATION. GRAYLIN HURLS THE MYSTIC GLOBE OF ZU-BORR... WHILE DAGAR THRUSTS THE SACRED JEWEL OF THE WARRIOR GOD AT THE TWO STRUGGLING CREATURES, THEN...

THAT DID IT, GRAYLIN! BUT NOW THE **MAGIC FORCES** IN THOSE OBJECTS ARE BEING **UNLEASHED** UPON THE PALACE!

Barrroo-ommmm!

THEN, A PORTENTIOUS RUMBLING FROM ABOVE...

AND NOW THOSE FORCES ARE PULLING THE ENTIRE BUILDING **DOWN** ON US!

R-RMMBLL-KRA-CA-LIK!

WE'LL BE KILLED, DAGAR!

NOT IF OUR LEGS ARE **SWIFT**!

HAVING BARELY ESCAPED THE CRUSHING WALLS AND CEILINGS OF THE PALACE OF NAI-PO-GAH, DAGAR AND HIS BELOVED WATCH THE FINAL TONS OF DEBRIS PILE UPON ONE ENORMOUS HEAP...

ARE THEY DEAD, DAGAR?

I CANNOT SEE HOW THEY **COULD** LIVE AGAIN, WITH THE JEWEL AND GLOBE DESTROYED! OR SO I **HOPE**...

KRUMMMBLL-CRAS-HHHH--KRRNKKK-LLL!!!

WHERE SHALL WE GO **NOW**, DAGAR?

TO THE NEAREST TOWN... A TOWN POPULATED BY **MEN** AND NOT **MONSTERS!**

AND **THERE** I SHALL AGAIN PUT MY **SWORD** UP FOR HIRE! FOR THAT SEEMS TO BE THE **ONLY** WAY WE'LL EVER AGAIN FEEL THE TOUCH OF **GOLD!**

DAGAR! DO YOU **HEAR** THAT?

IT IS THE **SENTRIES,** AROUSED BY THE SOUNDS OF DESTRUCTION! WE MUST LEAVE THIS PLACE!

WE HAVE FACED **ENOUGH** DANGER THIS NIGHT!

RIDING SLOWLY, QUIETLY, DAGAR AND GRAYLIN BLEND AMID THE SHADOWS, LEAVING BEHIND THE FORBIDDEN CITY... NAI-PO-GAH.

the END

DAGAR THE INVINCIBLE

DEMON OF THE TEMPLE

ALTHOUGH HE HAS BEEN A PROFESSIONAL SOLDIER FOR ONLY A SHORT WHILE, DAGAR'S REPUTATION HAS SPREAD TO SOME AREAS OF THE TERRIBLE WORLD IN WHICH HE LIVES. CONFIDENT IN THE KNOWLEDGE THAT HIS SKILL WITH THE SWORD IS UNMATCHED, THE WARRIOR BOLDLY STRIDES WITH THE BEAUTEOUS GRAYLIN THROUGH THE TOWN OF BARGOLL, WHICH SEEMS IMPRISONED IN THE GRIP OF SUSPICION... AND EVIL...

I DON'T LIKE THIS BARGOLL, DAGAR! HAVE YOU NOTICED?

YOU MEAN THE PEOPLE? YES! WHEREVER I LOOK I SEE ONLY SORROW... LONG FACES...TEARS! I HAVE BECOME ACCUSTOMED TO TERROR, MY LOVE... AND, BY ANDO'S GRAVE, TERROR CERTAINLY EXISTS HERE!

FROM THE LOOKS OF THEM, I'D SAY THAT SOMETHING TERRIBLE HAS HAPPENED HERE, OR IS ABOUT TO HAPPEN!

I KNOW...BUT THEIR PLIGHT IS OF NO CONCERN TO US, UNLESS THEY ARE WILLING TO PAY ME! I FIGHT FOR **GOLD**, NOT TEARS!

DAGAR AND GRAYLIN HAVE JOURNEYED FAR TO REACH THIS TOWN... AND AS THEY EAT AND DRINK AT AN INN, THEY OVERHEAR WHISPERED VOICES...

I TELL YOU HE **IS** A MERCENARY! I'M CERTAIN THAT I RECOGNIZE HIM!

THEN PERHAPS HE'LL FIGHT THE BATTLE THAT WE CANNOT! ASK HIM!

WHY DO LOOK AT ME AND WHISPER? I DISLIKE SECRETS AROUND ME, SO **SPEAK!**

WE KNOW YOU ARE A PROFESSIONAL WARRIOR! AND WE WISH TO TAKE ADVANTAGE OF YOUR SERVICES! WILL YOU **FIGHT** FOR US?

IF THE PAY IS ENOUGH ... BUT WHO IS IT I AM SUPPOSED TO FIGHT?

HE IS **VOGTVAN**... AN EVIL HIGH PRIEST WITH VAST POWERS... POWERS WHICH HE USES TO KEEP THIS TOWN IN A CONSTANT STATE OF TERROR AND MISERY!

VOGTVAN DEMANDS CONSTANT TRIBUTE PAID HIM...OR ELSE HE WILL UNLEASH THE TERRIBLE **DEMON** OF HIS TEMPLE TO DESTROY US ALL! AND VOGTVAN IS THE ONLY LAW IN THIS TOWN!

AFTER TELLING THEM HIS **PRICE**...

FOR **THIS** MUCH GOLD, I'LL SLAY YOUR DEMON AND YOUR OPPRESSOR!

I'M GOING WITH YOU, DAGAR!

NOT UNTIL YOU'VE LEARNED TO **BETTER** HANDLE A SWORD, GRAYLIN! NO, YOU STAY HERE!

SOON, DAGAR REACHES THE TEMPLE...

IT SURELY APPEARS TO BE AN OMINOUS PLACE! BUT I'VE BEEN IN OMINOUS PLACES BEFORE... AND FOR **LESS** PAYMENT!

THEN, WITHIN THE AWESOME BUILDING...

IF ALL OF VOGTVAN'S GUARDS ARE EQUALLY CLUMSY SWORDSMEN, I HAVE LITTLE TO FEAR OF THEM!

CLANGG!

VOGTVAN'S HENCHMEN ARE NO MATCH FOR DAGAR'S SWORDS-MANSHIP...

NOW TO FIND THIS DEMON AND... WHAT IS THAT STRANGE SOUND?!

TRILLLLLLLLLLLLLLL

THE **TRILLING NOISE** GETS LOUDER AS THE MERCENARY REACHES THE END OF THE PASSAGEWAY... AND THRUSTS OPEN THE DOOR...

WHAT?!

DAGAR HAS FACED MONSTERS IN THE PAST... BUT NEVER ONE SUCH AS THE ANTHROPOID HORROR THAT GAPES AT HIM THROUGH ITS ICY PRISON...

BY THE GODS! IT SEEMS TO BE SOME MONSTROUS HORNED **APE**... LIKE SOMETHING FROM THE REALM OF NIGHTMARES! AND THAT MAN IN THE TRANCE, MAKING THAT SOUND... **HE** MUST BE VOGTVAN!

TRRRRIILLLLLLLL

IF I AM TO DEFEAT VOGTVAN, IT WILL BE MAN-TO-MAN...WHEN HE'S **AWAKE!**

HUH? N-NO... Y-YOU DON'T KNOW WHAT YOU ARE DOING...

YOU HAVE **RUINED EVERY-THING!**

YOU **FOOL! THAT WAS NOT VOGTVAN!** AND IN FREEING HIM FROM THE TRANCE YOU HAVE SEALED YOUR OWN **DOOM!**

I AM VOGTVAN! THE MAGE WAS A MERE LACKEY WHOSE POWER OF TRANCE I USED... TO FORM A PRISON OF **MYSTIC ICE** BY THE STRENGTH OF HIS **MIND**... TO IMPRISON THAT BEAST!

EVEN AS VOGTVAN SPEAKS, THE CHANGE IN THE MAGIC ICE BECOMES APPARENT...

AND IN BREAKING THE TRANCE, YOU HAVE MADE HIM STOP **CONCENTRATING** ON THE MYSTIC ICE...AND HAVE **FREED THE MONSTER!**

GGRRRRRRAAAAARRRRROGGARRRRR!!

YIIII!

QUICKLY! GET BACK INTO YOUR TRANCE...FORM THE ICE! MY SWORD IS USELESS AGAINST THAT HORROR!

I CAN'T...M-MY MIND IS TOO SHAKEN...

I MUST **FLEE**!

NO, YOU FOOL! COME BACK HERE! WITHOUT YOU TO CONTROL THE CREATURE, WE'RE **ALL** AS GOOD AS DEAD!

THE MAGE IS DOOMED, FOR THERE IS NO HELP FOR ONE WHO IS PURSUED BY **DEATH**!

RROARRRRRRR...!

NOOOOO...

...AND THERE IS NO STOPPING **DEATH ITSELF** WHEN IN THE GUISE OF A MONSTROUS, HUNGRY BEAST, ENRAGED FOR ITS LONG CONFINEMENT IN THE ENCHANTED ICE...

AIIIEEEEE AAAAAAAAA

AS DAGAR SEES THE BEHEMOTH UNLEASH ITS VENGEANCE, A TERRIBLE PREMONITION FLASHES BEFORE HIM ...AND HE "SEES" WHAT WILL HAPPEN UNLESS THE DEMON OF THE TEMPLE IS DESTROYED...

AAARRRRRGGGGGRRRR...

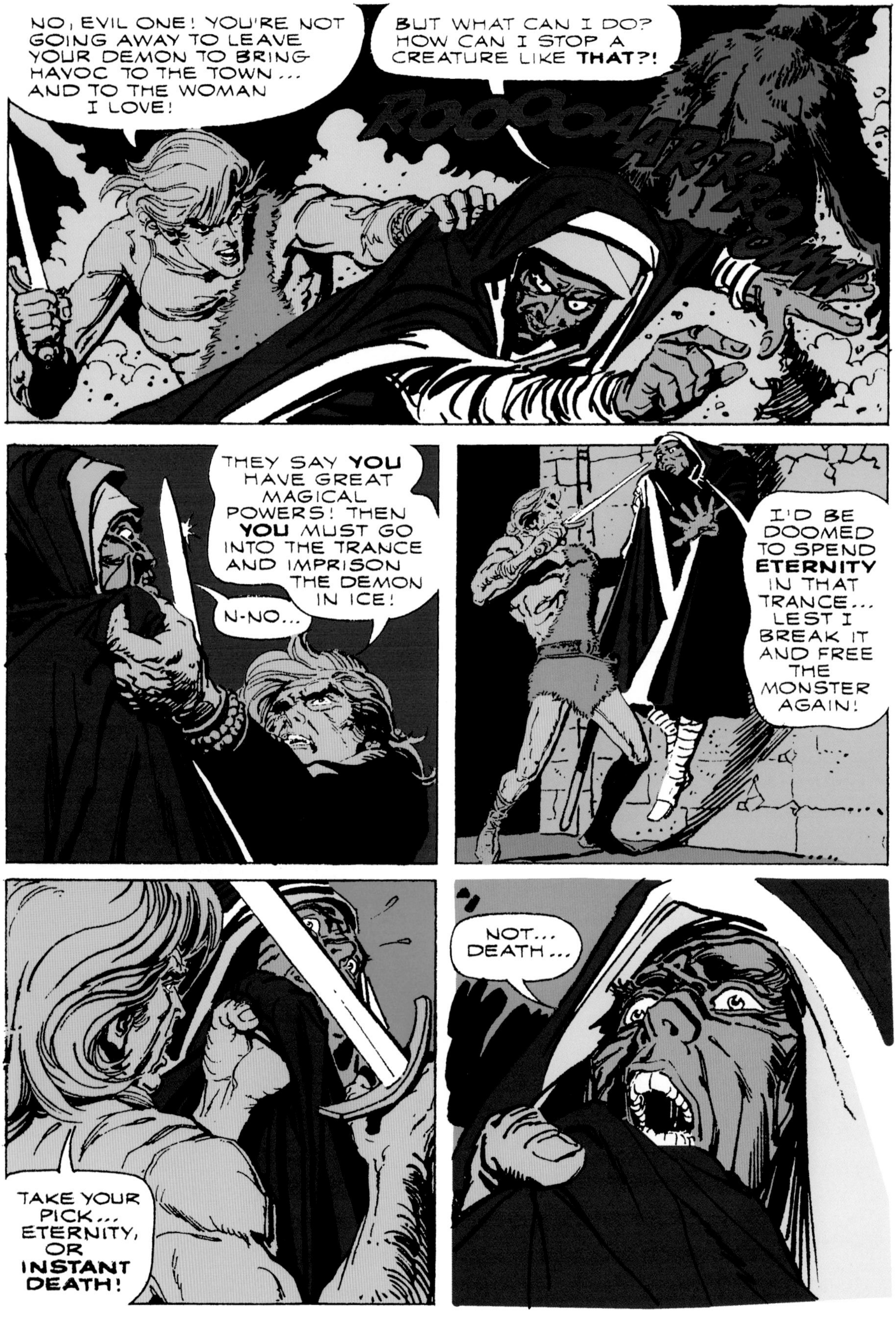
NO, EVIL ONE! YOU'RE NOT GOING AWAY TO LEAVE YOUR DEMON TO BRING HAVOC TO THE TOWN... AND TO THE WOMAN I LOVE!
BUT WHAT CAN I DO? HOW CAN I STOP A CREATURE LIKE THAT?!
ROOOOAARRROWW
THEY SAY YOU HAVE GREAT MAGICAL POWERS! THEN YOU MUST GO INTO THE TRANCE AND IMPRISON THE DEMON IN ICE!
N-NO...
I'D BE DOOMED TO SPEND ETERNITY IN THAT TRANCE... LEST I BREAK IT AND FREE THE MONSTER AGAIN!
TAKE YOUR PICK... ETERNITY, OR INSTANT DEATH!
NOT... DEATH...

THE EMANATIONS FROM VOGTVAN'S POWERFUL BRAIN PERMEATE THE ROOM ...PRODUCE A CHILL... AND SOLIDIFY INTO A BLOCK OF ICE... AGAIN IMPRISONING THE MONSTER OF THE TEMPLE...

THE ACT COMPLETED, DAGAR TURNS AWAY FROM THE TWO MOTIONLESS FIGURES...

TRILLL...

THE MONSTER WILL BE TRAPPED AS LONG AS THE **TRANCE** REMAINS...AND IT **SHALL** REMAIN, FOR VOGTVAN DOES NOT WISH TO SATISFY THE DEMON'S HUNGER!

LATER, AS DAGAR AND GRAYLIN PASS THROUGH THE TOWN, THEY SEE THE SMILES ON THE FACES OF THOSE PEOPLE NO LONGER LIVING IN FEAR OF VOGTVAN'S DEMON. BUT WHAT PLEASES DAGAR EVEN MORE IS THE SMILE ON GRAYLIN'S FACE... AND HIS BAG OF CLINKING GOLD COINS.

the END

GOLD KEY®

90279-404

DAGAR

20c

TALES OF SWORD AND SORCERY

DAGAR
THE INVINCIBLE

Dagar is captive of a
beautiful Queen and her
scheming sorcerer....
**TWO SWORDS
AGAINST ZORA-ZAL!**

DAGAR THE INVINCIBLE #7 | "TWO SWORDS AGAINST ZORA-ZAL"

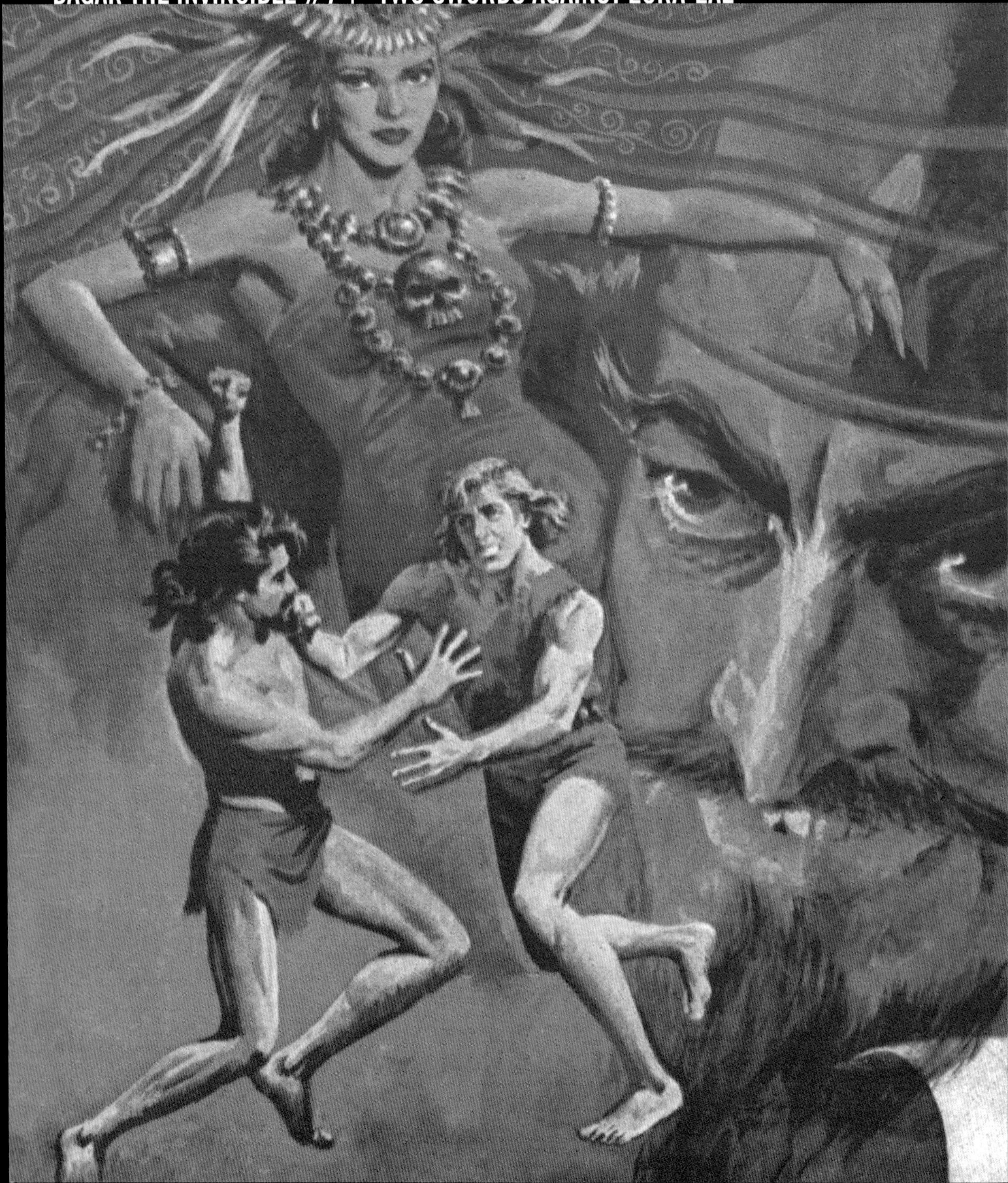

TALES OF SWORD AND SORCERY

DAGAR
THE INVINCIBLE

TWO SWORDS AGAINST
ZORA-ZAL

HAVING BRIEFLY LEFT GRAYLIN, HIS FEMALE COMPANION, IN THE TOWN WHERE LAST HE EARNED MONEY BY HIS SWORD, DAGAR HAS VENTURED TO THE SEASHORE... IN HOPES OF BRINGING GRAYLIN BACK A FINE CATCH OF FISH. INSTEAD, DAGAR IS ATTACKED BY SWARTHY SAILORS FROM A DISTANT LAND...

DON'T LET THIS PRIZED ONE ESCAPE, MATES! OR IT'LL MEAN YOUR *SKINS!*

90279-404
DAGAR #7-741

181

THERE ARE SO *MANY* OF THEM! AND THE MORE I FIGHT, THE *WORSE* I GET TANGLED IN THEIR ACCURSED *NET!*

BATTLING HOPELESSLY AGAINST THE BLUDGEONING SEAMEN, DAGAR'S THOUGHTS MOMENTARILY ENVISION THE BEAUTEOUS FEATURES OF ONE WHOM HE MIGHT NEVER SEE AGAIN...

GRAYLIN!

HERE! LET IT BE YOUR *CAPTAIN'S* SWORD THAT KNOCKS THE SENSE OUT OF HIM!

WAKK!

UHHNN!

THERE! ANOTHER ONE "ENLISTED" IN THE SERVICE OF *ZORA-ZAL!* TAKE HIM TO THE *LEENA*, MEN!

YES, CAPTAIN SEI-SOL!

DAGAR'S CONSCIOUSNESS DRIFTS AS IF IN A VACUUM. HE DOES NOT HEAR THE ONE CALLED CAPTAIN SEI-SOL GIVE THE ORDER THAT SENDS THE MIGHTY CRAFT AWAY FROM THE SUN-BLEACHED SHORE. HE DOES NOT FEEL THE COOLING SPRAY OF THE SEA... OR THE BOISTEROUS TOSSING OF THE WAVES...

DAGAR FEELS NOTHING, UNTIL...

THE WORLD SEEMINGLY RETURNS IN THE FORM OF A HARD FLOOD OF COLD WATER...

WAKE UP! THESE ARE NOT SLEEPING QUARTERS!

HUH ?!

SPLSHHH!

HEY, YOU DID NOT HAVE TO AWAKEN *ME*, SEI-SOL!

SILENCE, BARBARIAN, UNLESS YOU'D LIKE TO TASTE THE *WHIP*!

MANACLES! I'M A *GALLEY* SLAVE ABOARD A SHIP!

HOW *OBSERVANT* YOU ARE!

WELCOME ABOARD THE *LEENA*! I AM CAPTAIN SEI-SOL! AND IF YOU KNOW WHAT IS GOOD FOR YOU, YOU'LL JUST *ROW*...AND NOT MAKE TROUBLE LIKE YOUR *PARTNER*, HERE!

AN *OVEN*, DAGAR THINKS, COULD NOT BE MORE INTENSE THAN THE RELENTLESS SUN...AS HE PULLS A HEAVY OAR...

COME ON, YOU *SLAVES*! PULL *HARDER*!

I'D LIKE TO GET THAT CAPTAIN'S *THROAT* AT THE POINT OF A BROADSWORD!

183

YOUR JOB IS TO *ROW*... AND NOT MAKE *CONVERSATION*, BARBARIAN!

KRA'SNAP!

Y////!

I MAY BE A BAR-BARIAN, SEI-SOL! BUT I AM NO CRUEL *SAVAGE* SUCH AS YOU! WHEN *I* KILL... IT IS WITH *GOOD REASON!*

ARGHH! (CHOKE!)

SECONDS LATER, A LOYAL CREW RESPONDS TO THE VIOLENCE AGAINST THEIR CAPTAIN, AND...

Thud! Crakk!

UHH!

LET THAT BE A *LESSON* TO *ALL* OF YOU SLAVES! LET THERE BE ANOTHER SUCH OUTBURST, AND YOU'LL BE FED TO THE DEMONS OF THE SEA!

AS CAPTAIN SEI-SOL RETURNS TO HIS QUARTERS TO NURSE HIS THROBBING THROAT...

YOU ARE *BRAVE,* BARBARIAN! BUT WE MUST WAIT UNTIL WE TOUCH SHORE AGAIN BEFORE TRYING TO ESCAPE!

DO YOU KNOW WHERE THEY'RE TAKING US?

TO THE ISLAND OF THE GODDESS-QUEEN *ZORA-ZAL,* WHOSE *DIVINE BEAUTY* IS LEGENDARY! AH, IT WILL BE A PLEASURE CONFRONTING A COMELY OPPONENT FOR ONCE!

I AM *DAGAR*, THE LAST OF THE *TULGONIAN* NATION, AND A MERCENARY WARRIOR!

AND I AM *DURAK*... ONCE A MERCENARY, BUT NO LONGER!

SOMEHOW, IT SEEMS *INDECENT* TO FIGHT FOR PAY! I FIGHT SIMPLY FOR THE THRILL OF *ADVENTURE!* I LEFT MY TRIBE IN ORDER TO ROAM THE WORLD IN SEARCH OF *EXCITEMENT* AND *DANGER!*

IT APPEARS THAT YOU'VE *FOUND* IT, DURAK!

BUT EVEN AS THEY BECOME ACQUAINTED, DAGAR AND DURAK ARE *OBSERVED* SOME MILES AWAY...

YOUR *MYSTIC POOL* REVEALS THAT THE SHIP *LEENA* IS NOT FAR AWAY, MOGRA!

AND LOOK AT THOSE TWO SLAVES, MY MAGE! THIS DAGAR AND THIS DURAK! THEY ARE *UNLIKE* THE OTHERS... SO *STRONG*, SO *HANDSOME!*

HMM... PERHAPS THEY SHOULD *NOT* ACCOMPANY THE OTHER SLAVES TO THE *TOWER!* PERHAPS THEY SHOULD BE SAVED FOR... *OTHER* THINGS!

DAYS LATER, THE LEENA REACHES ITS DESTINATION... THE *ISLAND OF QUEEN ZORA-ZAL*...

185

MOVE ALONG, SLAVES! YOUR STRENGTH IS NEEDED AT THE *TOWER!*

SOMEDAY YOU SHALL *PAY* FOR YOUR CRUELTIES, SEA DOG!

AFTER A LENGTHY WALK ACROSS THE HILLS...

I WONDER WHAT THIS *TOWER* IS THAT SEI-SOL MENTIONED!

THERE, DURAK... BEHIND THOSE MISTS! LOOK!

AS DURAK'S EYES FOCUS UPON THE SWIRLING VAPORS, THE NUBILOUS TRAILS PART, REVEALING IN ALL ITS AWESOME SPLENDOR A FOREBODING *TOWER...* AND THE MYRIAD SHAPES OF SUN-BROWNED WORKERS, WHO LONG AGO HAVE CEASED UTTERING INEFFECTUAL COMPLAINTS... AND WHOSE BLOOD AND SWEAT HAVE MIXED WITH MORTAR IN THE TOWER'S CONSTRUCTION...

BEHOLD, NEWCOMERS! THE *TOWER* OF *ZORA-ZAL,* THE GODDESS-QUEEN! THE TOWER WHICH WILL GIVE HER PASSAGE TO HER RIGHTFUL THRONE AMONG THE GODS!

AS DAGAR, DURAK AND THE OTHER NEW SLAVES JOIN THE RANKS AT THE TOWER...

THEY ARE BEING PUT TO WORK WITH THE OTHERS! THIS MUST NOT BE! MAGE, CREATE A *DUPLICATE IMAGE* OF ME!

MOGRA WORKS HIS SPELL AND...

A *PERFECT LIKENESS!* NOW SEND THE ILLUSION TO THE TOWER AND LET ME *SPEAK* THROUGH HER!

YES, MY QUEEN!

AND AT THE TOWER SITE...

I CANNOT HELP THINKING OF HOW MUCH THIS TOWER RESEMBLES A ...(OOPHF!)...GIANT *ANT HILL*, DURAK! AND *WE* ARE THE WORKER ANTS!

THINK NOT OF *ANTS*, DAGAR...BUT HOW WE'LL *ESCAPE*, AND HAVE VENGEANCE ON THAT SLIMY *CAPTAIN* WHO CAPTURED US!

YOU, THERE! CAN YOU TELL US *WHY* WE ARE BUILDING SUCH A TOWER?

I'LL TELL WHAT I KNOW! QUEEN ZORA-ZAL HAS *NO* RECALL OF HER LIFE AS ANYTHING. BUT AN *ADULT!*

SHE BELIEVES SHE IS A TRUE *GODDESS*, BORN AS AN ADULT, WHOSE BEAUTY CAN *ONLY* BE ATTRIBUTED TO ONE *DIVINE!* SHE HOPES THIS TOWER WILL LEAD HER TO THE *HEAVENS*, WHERE SHE'LL ASCEND TO HER RIGHTFUL THRONE!

BUT AS DAGAR RESUMES HIS WORK, HE PERCEIVES THE LIGHT OF AN *APPARITION*, WHICH FOCUSES TO BECOME AN IMAGE OF PERFECT BEAUTY...

ALL *KNEEL* IN THE PRESENCE OF THE GODDESS-QUEEN, ZORA-ZAL!

THE SLAVES CALLED *DAGAR* AND *DURAK* ARE TO BE BROUGHT TO MY THRONE ROOM IMMEDIATELY!

AS YOU COMMAND, O QUEEN OF BEAUTY!

HMM... I THINK I WOULD *LIKE* TO MEET ZORA-ZAL! NEVER HAVE I BEHELD SUCH *BEAUTY* AS HERS!

I TOO WOULD LIKE TO MEET THIS *VILLAINESS* WHO MAKES MEN SLAVES!

AFTER BEING ESCORTED TO THE PALACE...

THE TULGONIAN MERCENARY AND THE BARBARIAN ADVENTURER!

THE WAY SHE LOOKS AT THEM IS HOW SHE SHOULD BE SEEING *ME!* MAY THE DARK GODS *CURSE* THESE TWO!

AH, *DURAK!* HOW GLADLY I'D SHARE MY RULE WITH ONE SUCH AS YOU!

AND *YOU,* DAGAR! YOU COULD ALSO RULE WITH ME, SHARING EQUAL POWER WITH DURAK!

AND NOW I PLAN TO *LEAVE* THIS EVIL PLACE, AND *RETURN* TO THAT WOMAN I LOVE!

WHAT?! YOU *DARE?*

KA-POW

UGH!

AND HOW READILY I THINK I'D *ACCEPT* SUCH AN OFFER, YOUR HIGHNESS!

I ALREADY HAVE A WOMAN...AND WOULD *DIE* BEFORE TAKING A *SHE-DEMON* FOR A WIFE!

HE HAS INSULTED ME *SUPREMELY!* FOR THAT, DAGAR MUST *DIE!* GUARDS, *SLAY* THE TULGONIAN!

A *PLEASURE,* YOUR HIGHNESS!

HOW DAGAR WISHES TO HAVE HIS BROADSWORD, WHICH STILL LIES IN THE HOLD OF THE SHIP *LEENA.* YET HE HAS HIS *FISTS...*

IT SEEMS AN ILL-FATED BATTLE! FOR EVERY ONE I DEFEAT, *MORE* TAKE HIS PLACE!

GIVE UP, DAGAR! CAN'T YOU SEE THAT IT IS *HOPELESS* TO FIGHT THEM ALL?

AS THE THRONE ROOM ECHOES WITH THE SOUNDS OF GROANS, AND FISTS SLAMMING AGAINST HARD FLESH, A CRAFTY SMILE DISTORTS THE FEATURES OF MOGRA...

IF THEY DESTROY *EACH OTHER,* ZORA-ZAL MAY YET FAVOR ME!

SO CONCERNED IS EVERY-ONE WITH THE CONFLICT, THAT NO ONE NOTICES THE MAGE'S *GESTURE...* OR THE WHISPERED WORDS WHICH PRODUCE AN *INVISIBLE AURA* ABOUT THE BARBARIAN...

DURAK! YOU'VE COME TO *HELP* ME!

BUT WITHOUT WARNING...

UGHH!

AND BEFORE THE STUNNED DAGAR CAN FIGHT BACK...

THEN, ACTING AS ONE *ENTRANCED,* DURAK MOVES LIKE LIGHTNING... HIS HAND A BLUR AS IT REACHES FOR A PALACE GUARD'S *SWORD...*

HUH ?!

EYES GLASSY WITH *MADNESS,* DURAK'S HANDS SWEAT UPON HIS BORROWED WEAPON AND...

YOU HAVE INSULTED MY *QUEEN,* TULGONIAN! AND FOR THAT...YOU *DIE!*

NO, DURAK! PUT *DOWN* THE SWORD!

BUT, ZORA-ZAL... DAGAR HAS WRONGED A *GODDESS!*

DAGAR WILL DIE, ALL RIGHT, BUT NOT SO *SWIFTLY!* HIS DEATH MUST BE SLOW...AGONIZING... SO THAT HE WILL BE AN *EXAMPLE* TO ANY OTHERS FOOLISH ENOUGH TO *DEFY* ME!

GUARDS, GET THE MERCENARY OUT OF MY PRESENCE...AND CAST HIM INTO OUR DARKEST, COLDEST *DUNGEON*, WHERE HE CAN AWAIT HIS *DOOM!*

IT SHALL BE DONE, HIGHNESS!

AND WHAT OF *US*, MY QUEEN?

WE SHALL GO TO MY PRIVATE CHAMBERS, DURAK! THERE WE CAN BE ALONE...AND AWAY FROM *PRYING EYES!*

THUS, DAGAR IS BRUTALLY HURLED INTO A DANK-SMELLING DUNGEON CELL...

THERE IS *NO WAY* OUT OF THIS CELL! NO WAY...

AND WHILE DAGAR, LOCKED AWAY FROM FROM THE WORLD OF LIGHT AND FRESH AIR, AWAITING HIS UNKNOWN FATE, DURAK BASKS IN THE DELIGHTS OFFERED BY ZORA-ZAL...

TO THINK I USED TO SEEK OUT *DRAGONS*... AND HAVE BEEN MISSING THIS *GOOD LIFE* ALL ALONG!

YOU HAND-MAIDENS MAY LEAVE US NOW!

NOW THAT WE ARE ALONE, HOW DO YOU FEEL, DURAK?

FROM SLAVERY TO *HEAVEN*, I FEEL LIKE A *GOD*, ZORA-ZAL!

THEN I SHALL *MAKE* YOU A GOD, THROUGH YOUR MARRIAGE TO THE GODDESS-QUEEN!

ER...YOUR HIGHNESS...

WHAT?! *MOGRA!* WHAT IS THE MEANING FOR THIS UNTIMELY *INTRUSION?*

YOU HAVE GIVEN *ME* THE TASK OF DESTROYING THIS DAGAR THROUGH *MAGIC!* BUT I WISH TO ASK YOU WHAT *TYPE* OF DEATH YOU WOULD PREFER I CREATE FOR HIM!

WHAT?!

FOR SUCH *TRIVIA* YOU HAVE DARED INTERRUPT YOUR QUEEN AND HER HUSBAND-TO-BE?

HUSBAND? THEN THEY *ARE* GOING TO BE MARRIED!

IF HE DISTURBS YOU, ZORA-ZAL...

NO, DURAK! I STILL HAVE *NEED* OF HIS MYSTIC SERVICES!

DREAM UP *ANY* TYPE OF DEATH TO WORK ON DAGAR, MAGE! BUT FOR YOUR *OWN* GOOD IT HAD BETTER BE *SPECTACULAR* ENOUGH TO PLEASE *ME*... AND THE MULTITUDE OF *SPECTATORS* WHO WILL COME TO SEE HIM DIE!

NOW *GO!*

I'LL *GO*...BUT BEFORE LONG YOU MIGHT *PAY* FOR REJECTING AND HUMILIATING MOGRA! THIS I SWEAR BY THE *DARK GODS!*

MORNING... AND THE CROWDS COME TO THE SMALL AMPHITHEATRE NEAR THE PALACE. THE WIND IS FRAGRANT WITH THE DRIFTING TRAILS OF INCENSE...AND ALIVE WITH THE CADENT SOUNDS OF MUSIC. THEN, FOLLOWING THE SONOROUS BLARE OF TRUMPETS...

ALL *RISE* IN THE PRESENCE OF *ZORA-ZAL*, THE *GODDESS-QUEEN!*

193

LISTEN TO THE CROWD *CHEER* FOR YOU, MY LOVE!

YES! BUT THEY ALSO CHEER IN ANTICIPATION OF THE COMING *FESTIVITIES!*

AND I TOO WILL BE GLAD TO WITNESS THE DEATH OF DAGAR FOR THE GRAVE *INSULT* HE COMMITTED AGAINST YOU!

THERE, DURAK! THERE HE IS!

BELOW THE SEATS OF THE ANXIOUS SPECTATORS, A LONE WARRIOR IS SHOVED INTO THE ARENA. THE AIR IS ELECTRIFIED WITH THEIR JEERS... THEIR CRIES OF ANTICIPATION OF THE SLAUGHTER, YET DAGAR *IGNORES* THEIR SHOUTS... FOR IF HE IS TO *DIE*, IT MUST BE WITH THE *DIGNITY* OF A BORN *WARRIOR...*

HIS COLD BLUE EYES NARROW UPON THE VISION OF *ONE* MAN AND *ONE* WOMAN... AND HE MUST WAGE AN INTERNAL BATTLE TO CONFINE THE *HATRED* IN HIS WARRIOR'S HEART...

AGAIN, TRUMPETS SILENCE THE CROWD AND...

DAGAR OF *TULGONIA*, YOU ARE CONDEMNED TO *DIE!* THUS, LET THERE BE NO MORE *DELAY!* INTO THE *PIT* WITH YOU!

DAGAR RESISTS... BUT HIS HANDS ARE HELPLESSLY *TIED* BEHIND HIS BACK... AND THERE ARE *TWO* GUARDS WHO THRUST HIM FORWARD INTO THE GAPING, FOUL-SMELLING PIT...

HARRR! *IN* WITH YOU, SLAVE!

BUT THE PIT IS ONLY THE *BEGINNING* OF DAGAR'S HORROR...

BEHOLD, QUEEN ZORA-ZAL! I HOLD IN MY HANDS A *SOLDIER ANT* AND A *SNAKE*... SIMPLE CREATURES IN THEM-SELVES!

BUT OBSERVE WHAT HAPPENS WHEN I TOSS THE INSECT AND THE REPTILE INTO THE *PIT* WITH THE MERCENARY!

WATCH THE UNEARTHLY *MIRACLE* THAT TAKES PLACE WHEN I WORK MY MAGIC *SPELL*... AND SPEAK THE ANCIENT WORDS KNOWN ONLY TO MYSELF AND THE ALL-POWERFUL GODS OF DARKNESS!

THE STAGNANT AIR IN THE PIT WHIRLS AS THE MAGE'S SPELL TAKES ITS GRIM EFFECT. AND DAGAR'S FEATURES TWIST PATHETICALLY AS HE OBSERVES THE AWESOME *HORROR* TRANSPIRING BEFORE HIM...

THE *HORROR*...OF TWO NATURAL CREATURES, TWISTED BY MOGRA'S UNEARTHLY MAGIC WHICH MERGES THEM INTO A SINGLE, HORRENDOUS ENTITY...

EVEN THE *BRAVEST* OF MEN WOULD *SCREAM* IF THEIR LIVES WERE TO BE EXTINGUISHED BY A MONSTER. YET DAGAR CLENCHES HIS TEETH, REFUSING TO ISSUE THE SLIGHTEST MOAN OF ANGUISH FROM HIS MOUTH, AS THE CRAWLING, SLITHERING SHAPE HURRIES TOWARD HIM...

BUT DAGAR DOES NOT GIVE UP. HIS SINEWS BULGE... HIS BLOOD VESSELS NEARLY EXPLODE... AS TWO POWERFUL HANDS PULL AT THE BINDING ROPE...

BY THE WARRIOR GODS!

AT LAST, ONE STRAND OF ROPE BREAKS LOOSE... THEN A SECOND... AND *MORE,* UNTIL IN A TITANIC SURGE OF *RAW STRENGTH*...

I'M *FREE!*

THERE IS *NO TIME* TO SCALE THE HIGH WALLS OF THE PIT...NOR IS THERE ANY OTHER MEANS OF *ESCAPE*. AND SO, DAGAR DOES ALL THAT HE *CAN* DO...

BARE-HANDED, THE MERCENARY WARRIOR COMBATS THE UNEARTHLY CREATURE...

BUT IT TAKES *WEAPONS OF STEEL* TO VANQUISH SUCH A BEAST!

BY ANDO'S GRAVE! MY ONLY CHANCE IS TO TAKE THE *OFFENSIVE!*

ARGGGGG-HISSTT- GRRAAAGGG..

WHILE OUTSIDE THE PIT, DURAK AND HIS QUEEN, INCITED BY THE GRUESOME *SPECTACLE,* EMBRACE...

AND NOW SHE *KISSES* THE BARBARIAN AGAIN! NO LONGER CAN MY HEART *ENDURE* SUCH BREAKING! AND AFTER I *GAVE* HER SUCH GODLY BEAUTY SO THAT SHE WOULD LOVE *ME!*

197

I SAID SHE MIGHT *PAY*... AND SO SHE *SHALL*! I WILL *LIFT* MY ENCHANTMENT FROM DURAK... AND LET ONLY *HIS* EYES SEE ZORA-ZAL AS SHE *TRULY IS*!

SUDDENLY...

HUH? I FEEL SO *STRANGE*, ALL OF A SUDDEN, AS IF SOME VEIL HAS BEEN LIFTED FROM ME! *GAHHH*! ZORA-ZAL... YOU'RE... YOU'RE...

WHAT IS *WRONG*, DURAK?

TO THINK THAT I DID NOT SEE YOU LIKE *THAT* BEFORE! BUT NOW THAT THE *BEWITCHMENT* HAS LEFT ME, I SEE THE *TRUTH*!

AND ONE TRUTH IS THAT MY FRIEND *DAGAR* IS IN THAT PIT *DYING*... BECAUSE OF THAT SHE-MONSTER!

A SWIFT LEAP INTO THE PIT, AND...

DURAK!

BUT I THOUGHT...

IT WAS FOUL *MAGIC* THAT MADE ME FIGHT YOU, DAGAR!

BUT THERE IS NO TIME TO TALK ABOUT THAT NOW! HERE! TAKE MY DAGGER AND WE'LL FINISH OFF THIS HORROR *TOGETHER*!

ONCE DEAD, THE CREATURE RETURNS TO ITS ORIGINAL FORMS...

BY THE GODS...IT'S CHANGING BACK TO A SNAKE AND SOLDIER ANT!

DAGAR! DURAK! YOU MUST *TRUST* ME! I CAN *SAVE* YOU FROM ZORAZAL!

IT IS THAT CRAFTY *MAGE!* BUT WE HAVE NO CHOICE OTHER THAN *TRUSTING* HIM!

THEN...

GUARDS! SLAY THE TRAITORS WHERE THEY STAND!

SOLDIERS DESCEND UPON THE TWO FIGURES, BUT NO MERCENARY FALLS THAT DAY TO A SWINGING SWORD! NO BARBARIAN DIES BENEATH A CHOPPING AXE ...

THEY ARE ONLY *IMAGES,* CONJURED UP BY MAGIC! THAT MEANS THAT MOGRA IS ALSO A TRAITOR! *SLAY ALL THREE OF THEM!*

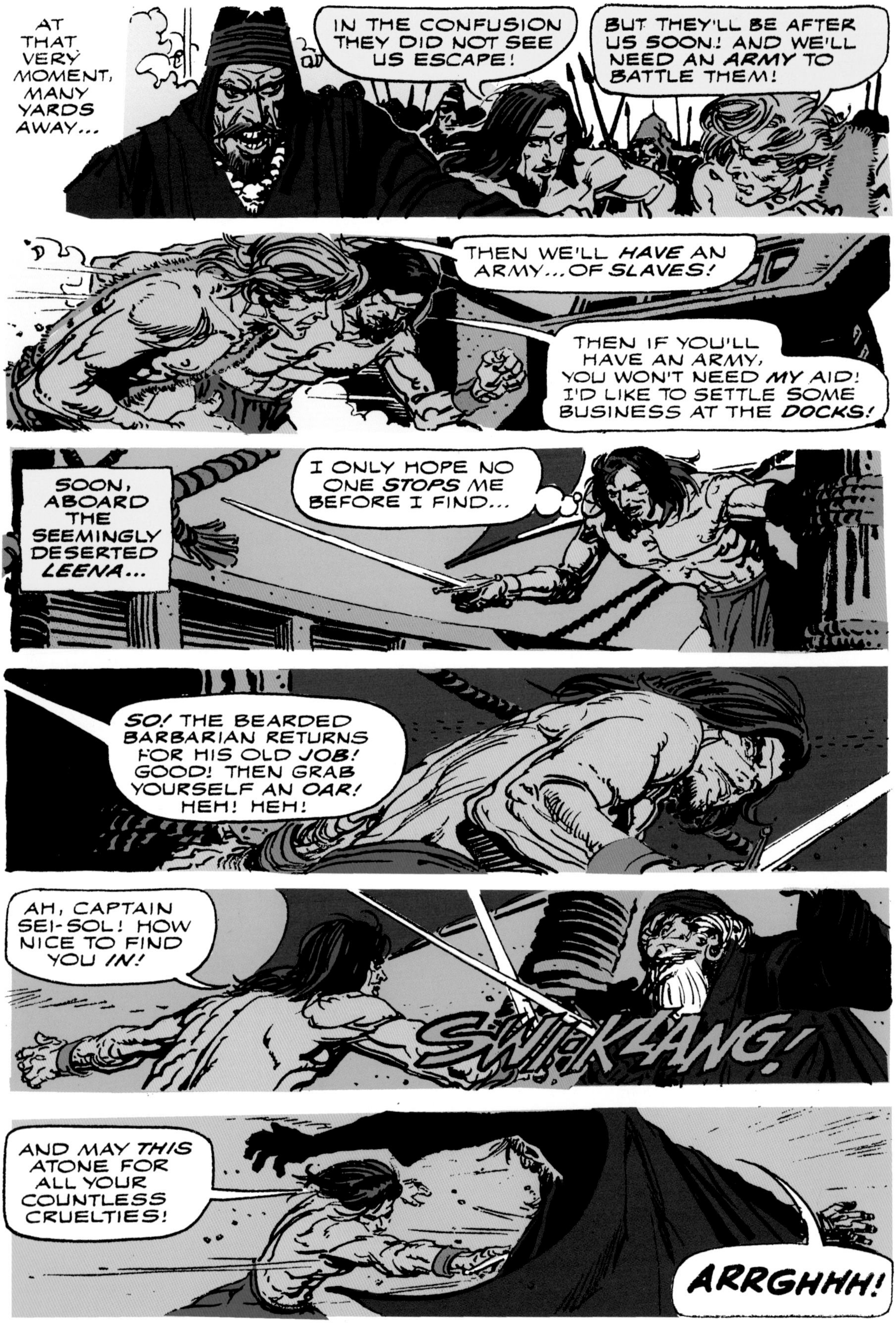
AT THAT VERY MOMENT, MANY YARDS AWAY...
IN THE CONFUSION THEY DID NOT SEE US ESCAPE!
BUT THEY'LL BE AFTER US SOON! AND WE'LL NEED AN ARMY TO BATTLE THEM!
THEN WE'LL HAVE AN ARMY...OF SLAVES!
THEN IF YOU'LL HAVE AN ARMY, YOU WON'T NEED MY AID! I'D LIKE TO SETTLE SOME BUSINESS AT THE DOCKS!
SOON, ABOARD THE SEEMINGLY DESERTED LEENA...
I ONLY HOPE NO ONE STOPS ME BEFORE I FIND...
SO! THE BEARDED BARBARIAN RETURNS FOR HIS OLD JOB! GOOD! THEN GRAB YOURSELF AN OAR! HEH! HEH!
AH, CAPTAIN SEI-SOL! HOW NICE TO FIND YOU IN!
SWIKKLANG!
AND MAY THIS ATONE FOR ALL YOUR COUNTLESS CRUELTIES!
ARRGHHH!

HE HAS SLAIN OUR CAPTAIN—*UGHH!*

SNIKAK! *a-Thudd!*

SO THERE ARE *MORE* OF YOU WHO DIDN'T ATTEND THE *FESTIVITIES* THIS MORNING!

DURAK HASTILY DISPOSES OF THE FEW REMAINING CREW MEMBERS...

I TRUST *DAGAR* IS DOING ALL RIGHT!

THAT PRECISE MOMENT, AT THE *TOWER OF ZORA-ZAL*...

THERE IS OUR ENSLAVED ARMY! BUT HOW DO THE TWO OF US OVERCOME THE SLAVE-DRIVERS?

ONLY *ZORA-ZAL* HERSELF COULD FREE THE SLAVES! AND SO, WE SHALL *PRODUCE* A ZORA-ZAL!

AND...

I WISH THE SLAVES TO BE *SET FREE!*

AS YOU COMMAND, QUEEN ZORA-ZAL! IT SHALL BE DONE!

AFTER HEAVY MANACLES ARE REMOVED FROM SWOLLEN WRISTS... AND THE SLAVE-DRIVERS ARE DISPOSED OF...

RALLY TO ME, MY SLAVE-BROTHERS! FIGHT, IF NEED BE, AT MY SIDE... AND I'LL LEAD YOU TO *TRUE FREEDOM!*

MOMENTS LATER, A DISTANT CLOUD OF DUST REVEALS ZORA-ZAL LEADING HER SWORD-SWINGING ARMY!

IT'S ZORA-ZAL!

THEY ALL MUST DIE! TAKE NO PRISONERS!

AS THE MOUNTED HORDE THUNDERS TOWARD THEM, MOGRA STARES UPON THE UNFINISHED *TOWER OF ZORA-ZAL*... AND HE CONCENTRATES...

KRA-CA-LK!

APPROACH, ZORA-ZAL! FOR IT IS HERE, AT YOUR OWN *TOWER*, THAT YOUR BEAUTY-CURSED FORM WILL MEET ITS *DOOM!* BUT FIRST I MUST SUMMON VIRTUALLY *ALL* OF MY POWER... FOCUS IT... *STRAIN* UNTIL...

THE SOLDIERS HEAR A FOREBODING *RUMBLE* OVERHEAD, AND ALL HOPE OF BATTLE DISINTEGRATES AS THEY BEHOLD THEIR CRUSHING FATE...

KRUMMBMMM!

AIIEEEAA!

THE TOWER IS FALLING!

AND WHILE TONS OF STONE, THE WORK OF SLAVE SWEAT AND BLOOD, RAIN DOWN UPON THE SCREAMING WARRIORS...

I CANNOT ESCAPE, BUT MY SPELL WAS SUCCESSFUL!

BUT I SHALL DIE GLADLY, KNOWING THAT ZORA-ZAL SHALL ALSO BE DESTROYED!

WHILE ON THE FIELD OF BATTLE, DAGAR AND HIS SLAVE ARMY FIGHT THOSE SOLDIERS WHO ESCAPED THE FALLING TOWER. AND WHAT DAGAR'S MEN LACK IN *WEAPONRY*, THEY MAKE UP FOR IN RAW *COURAGE* AND DETERMINATION TO BE VICTORIOUS...

KEEP FIGHTING, MY BROTHERS! BEFORE THIS MORNING IS OVER, WE'LL ALL BE FREE!

AND AS THE BATTLE RAGES...

MOGRA! BUT I SAW YOU *CRUSHED!*

I AM *DYING*, ZORA-ZAL! BUT I'VE RESERVED ENOUGH MEAGER POWER TO PROJECT MY *IMAGE!*

203

INSTEAD OF USING MY POWER TO RULE, I *CREATED* YOU, ZORA-ZAL, HOPING THAT YOU WOULD *LOVE* ME! BUT NOW I REALIZE THAT LOVE CANNOT BE MANUFACTURED LIKE BEAUTY!

THUS, NO LONGER ABLE TO ENDURE YOUR SPURNING AND USING ME, I *REMOVE* MY SPELL OVER YOU! ZORA-ZAL, RETURN TO YOUR *ORIGINAL FORM!*

AS MOGRA'S IMAGE FADES TO NOTHINGNESS AND HIS SPELL DIES WITH HIS CRUSHED BODY, THE GODDESS-QUEEN'S FLAWLESS FLESH *TRANSFORMS...* BECOMES HARD AND CHITINOUS, UNTIL HER ONCE DIVINE BEAUTY IS NO MORE... AND ZOR-ZAL APPEARS AS SHE TRULY IS...

N-NOOO!

EEAAAA!!

...A HIDEOUS *QUEEN ANT!*

AND AS THE FINAL SOLDIERS OF ZORA-ZAL FALL...

WE HAVE *WON!* NOW LET US LEAVE THIS EVIL PLACE!

DAGAR AND HIS MEN HEAD FOR THE HARBOR...

THERE IS THE *LEENA!* AND *DURAK!* ARE YOU ALL RIGHT?

NATURALLY! WHAT TROUBLE COULD I GET INTO AMONG A HANDFUL OF MOTLEY SAILORS! HAH!

THESE, I BELIEVE, ARE YOURS!

AH, MY OWN SWORD AND DAGGER! THEY ONCE BELONGED TO MY GRANDFATHER, SO YOU CAN SEE THAT I'D HATE TO *LOSE* THEM!

DAGAR, IT WAS A JOY HAVING YOU AS AN ALLY! WHERE WILL YOU GO FROM HERE?

BACK TO THE SHORE WHERE I WAS ORIGINALLY TAKEN CAPTIVE... BACK TO MY WOMAN! AND YOU, DURAK?

I CRAVE *ADVENTURE,* DAGAR! AND THIS SHIP CAN TAKE ME TO MANY LANDS WHERE THERE ARE THRILLS TO BE HAD!

A STRONG WIND FILLS THE SAILS OF THE *LEENA.* A BAND OF MEN NOW WILLINGLY TAKE TO THE OARS AND JOIN IN JOYOUS *SONG* WHERE ONCE THERE HAD BEEN ANGUISHED MOANS. AND WHILE THE AFTERNOON SUN BEGINS ITS DOWNWARD JOURNEY, THE GREAT CRAFT PULLS AWAY FROM THE ISLAND OF ZORA-ZAL.

the END

DAGAR

20c

TALES OF SWORD
AND SORCERY

DAGAR
THE INVINCIBLE

A FIERY EARTH MONSTER CHALLENGES THE SWORD OF DAGAR!
...The Red Ruby of Garloth

DAGAR
THE INVINCIBLE

The RED RUBY of GARLOTH

AFTER COMPLETING HIS PERILOUS ADVENTURE WITH THE BARBARIAN **DURAK**, THE TULGONIAN NAMED **DAGAR** RETURNS TO THE MYSTERY-SHROUDED TOWN OF **BARGOLL.** HIS WARRIOR HEART BEATS FIERCELY AS HE ENTERS THE HOUSE WHERE HE HAD LEFT **GRAYLIN,** HIS BELOVED. BUT WHERE HE HAS EXPECTED TO FIND A BLACK-HAIRED BEAUTY, HE FINDS ONLY THE RESULT OF CONFLICT...

GRAYLIN... SHE'S GONE!

90279-407
DAGAR #8-744

THERE HAS OBVIOUSLY BEEN **VIOLENCE** COMMITTED HERE! AND... WHAT IS THIS? A PIECE OF **VOLCANIC LAVA!**

WHO ARE YOU? IF YOU'VE DONE ANYTHING TO MY WOMAN, I'LL...

STAY YOUR SWORD, MERCENARY! FOR WE HAVE ALSO LOST LOVED ONES! HEAR MY WOEFUL STORY...

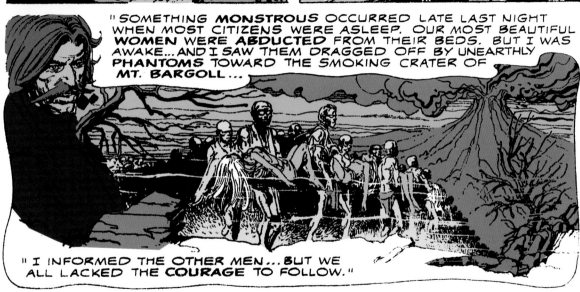

"SOMETHING **MONSTROUS** OCCURRED LATE LAST NIGHT WHEN MOST CITIZENS WERE ASLEEP. OUR MOST BEAUTIFUL **WOMEN** WERE **ABDUCTED** FROM THEIR BEDS. BUT I WAS AWAKE... AND I SAW THEM DRAGGED OFF BY UNEARTHLY PHANTOMS TOWARD THE SMOKING CRATER OF MT. BARGOLL..."

"I INFORMED THE OTHER MEN... BUT WE ALL LACKED THE **COURAGE** TO FOLLOW."

THEN IF I AM TO SAVE GRAYLIN I MUST GO TO YOUR MT. BARGOLL!

WAIT! **OUR** WOMEN WERE ALSO TAKEN BY THOSE PHANTOMS!

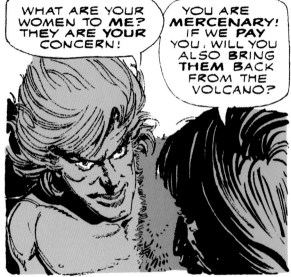

WHAT ARE YOUR WOMEN TO ME? THEY ARE YOUR CONCERN!

YOU ARE **MERCENARY!** IF WE **PAY** YOU, WILL YOU ALSO BRING **THEM** BACK FROM THE VOLCANO?

DAGAR'S REPLY IS LACONIC...AND MINUTES LATER IN THE STREET...

CONTRIBUTE **MORE** GOLD, IF WE ARE TO MEET DAGAR'S PRICE!

BUT DAGAR DOES **NOT SMILE** OVER HIS NEWLY ACQUIRED WEALTH...

SIR... MAY I SPEAK WITH YOU?

I DON'T HAVE GOLD LIKE THE OTHERS! BUT I DO HAVE THIS **NECKLACE** OF PRETTY SHELLS! IF I GIVE IT TO YOU WILL YOU BRING BACK MY MOTHER, TOO?

DON'T YOU WORRY, CHILD! DAGAR SWEARS THAT YOUR MOTHER WILL SOON BE BACK WITH YOU! AND HERE... KEEP YOUR NECKLACE!

THE SUN SETS BEHIND THE MIST-ENVELOPED MOUNTAINS. A DETER-MINED WARRIOR, MOUNTED UPON A STEED AS PITCH BLACK AS THE RISING SMOKE OF THE VOLCANO, PAUSES BEFORE THE FORBODING MT. BARGOLL...

HOLD, KASA! ALREADY YOU GROW UNSTEADY! PERHAPS YOU KNOW THAT ANY MAN WHO VENTURES INTO SUCH A PLACE MUST SURELY BE A MADMAN OR A FOOL!

YET DAGAR IS NEITHER MADMAN NOR FOOL... BUT SIMPLY A **MAN** WHO HAS ENDURED TOO MUCH HARDSHIP, FOUGHT TOO MANY **EVILS** FOR THE WOMAN HE LOVES...ONLY TO LOSE HER NOW...

IF I AM TO SUCCEED IN MY MISSION, I MUST BE MORE CAREFUL THAN I'VE EVER BEEN BEFORE! FOR ONE SLIP AND I'D BE AS MUCH USE TO GRAYLIN AS A ROASTED GROUND SLOTH!

SSSSSSSTTTTT!

I'VE BEEN IN MANY A SORCERER'S CASTLE BEFORE! BUT NONE HAVE **REEKED** WITH THE STENCH OF **DEATH** LIKE THESE **CAVERNS**!

NOT ONLY THE **SMELL** OF DEATH... BUT THE **SOUNDS** AND **SIGHTS** AS WELL!

BY THE WARRIOR GODS—!

GRRRRRRAAARGHHH!!!

THE THING IS ENORMOUS... **HISSING** MONSTROUS SOUNDS FROM ITS CAVERNOUS THROAT. THEN IT SLITHERS FROM THE CONCEALING SHADOWS...

HIIISSSS! GAAAAHHRRRR!

AN EARTH-LIZARD, THE TYPE THAT I'VE SEEN SCAVENGING BURIAL GROUNDS! AND THOUGH IT **MOVES**, IT HAS ALL THE APPEARANCES OF SOMETHING **DEAD!**

THE CREATURE CREEPS **SLOWLY**... YET ITS STRIDE IS **GREAT...**

UGHH!

AS STEELY MUSCLES STRAIN AGAINST THE DRY SCALY HIDE...

Thishhbbb!

THREE... FOUR TIMES, THE SWORD PIERCES THE EARTH-LIZARD'S VITALS, BUT...

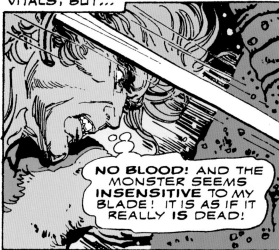

NO BLOOD! AND THE MONSTER SEEMS **INSENSITIVE** TO MY BLADE! IT IS AS IF IT REALLY **IS** DEAD!

UNABLE TO EVEN **HARM** THE REPTILE, DAGAR IS PRESSED HARD AGAINST THE JAGGED ROCK. FROM **BELOW** HE FEELS UNBEARABLE HEAT...

THOUGH HE CANNOT **SLAY** THE CRAWLING **DEAD** THING, DAGAR CAN **FIGHT** IT. WITH SINEWS BULGING BENEATH TANNED SKIN, THE TULGONIAN WARRIOR **PULLS** THE SCALY HORROR ALONG... UNTIL, INADVERTENTLY...

RRRAAAGHHSSSS!!

BbbLLLL...SSSS!

IN THE PIT BELOW, THERE IS A BRIEF ERUPTION AS **SOMETHING** SPLASHES INTO THE SCALDING HEART OF MT. BARGOLL...

SPLOOSHH...HHHSSSS!

BUT ONLY **ONE** CREATURE HAS BEEN INCINERATED IN THE BUBBLING CRATER...

WHAT MANNER OF PLACE **IS** THIS... WHERE THE **DEAD** WALK AS IF ALIVE?

IT SOUNDS LIKE **MEN** TALKING!

WHAT WAS ALL THAT **NOISE?**

FANG OF A SABRE-TOOTH! THEY'RE **ALSO** WALKING DEAD!

IT SOUNDED AS IF AN EARTH-LIZARD WERE FIGHTING WITH **SOMETHING!**

I DOUBT IT'S REALLY IMPORTANT, NORTZA!

JUDGING FROM THE **SMOKE** I WOULD SAY THAT THE EARTH-LIZARD AND ITS FOE WERE DESTROYED IN THE **PIT!**

THEN THERE IS NO POINT IN STANDING HERE! LET US RETURN TO THE **MASTER!**

THE LIVING DEAD DEPART THE CHAMBER...

ALL SAVE **ONE!**

MMMPHF!

DAGAR WAITS UNTIL THE CADAVEROUS GROUP HAS LEFT...

NOW, DEAD-MAN, TELL ME WHERE THE WOMEN ARE, OR ELSE...

YOU MUST REALIZE THAT A SWORD CANNOT SLAY ONE WHO IS **ALREADY DEAD!**

PERHAPS... BUT MY SWORD CAN STILL SEVER THAT SKULL-LIKE HEAD FROM ITS SKINNY NECK!

W-WAIT! I WILL SAY WHAT YOU WANT! BUT DO NOT STRIKE!

 "WE WERE ONCE AS ALIVE AS YOU... A BAND OF **THIEVES** WHO WERE FINALLY **SLAIN** BY VILLAGERS FROM A TOWN WE HOPED TO PILLAGE..."

"OUR CORPSES WERE STRIPPED OF WEAPONS AND BURIED IN UNMARKED GRAVES. BUT OUR BRIEF REST WAS **DISTURBED** WHEN THE EARTH **QUAKED** AS A RESULT OF THE VOLCANO'S **RUMBLING**..."

"THE EARTHQUAKE HAD THROWN OUR DETERIORATING BODIES INTO THE BOWELS OF MT. BARGOLL... IN THE PROXIMITY OF A STRANGE, GLOWING **RUBY**. AND AS THE JEWEL BATHED OUR GRUESOME FORMS IN ITS POTENT **LIGHT**..."

"...WE BEGAN TO **RISE!** BUT WE WERE NOT **TRULY ALIVE**... JUST WALKING, THINKING **CORPSES!**"

"**KAGRA**, OUR LEADER, EVENTUALLY LEARNED THAT THE JEWEL IMPRISONED **GARLOTH**, A DEMON OF THE **DARK GODS**... AND THAT HE COULD COMMUNICATE WITH THE DEMON THROUGH THE POWER OF HIS **MIND**."

KAGRA DISCOVERED THAT WE COULD BECOME **TRULY ALIVE!** BUT FOR EACH ONE OF US THAT LIVED AGAIN, WE FIRST HAD TO **SACRIFICE** A BEAUTIFUL WOMAN TO **GARLOTH!**

NO! GRAYLIN...!

DON'T WEEP, **SARY!** AT LEAST WE ARE STILL **ALIVE!**

QUIET, YOU TWO! AND SHOW YOUR **RESPECT!** THE **MASTER** COMES!

HE WALKS SLOWLY YET PROUDLY INTO THE DEATH-SMELLING CHAMBER. HIS TATTERED **ROBE** AND SMILE OF **ARROGANCE** BRAND HIM AS A **LEADER**... BUT HIS WITHERED FACE STILL BETRAYS HIM AS YET ANOTHER LIVING **CORPSE**...

ALL HAIL **KAGRA,** MASTER OF THE **RED RUBY OF GARLOTH!**

YES, MY SUBJECTS HAVE CHOSEN **WISELY** FROM THE WOMEN "CROP" OF BARGOLL! AND AS EACH OF YOU SHEDS HER BLOOD FOR GARLOTH, ONE OF US WILL WALK THE EARTH AMONG THE LIVING AND THE SUNLIGHT!

UHHHH...

AH! AND HERE I FIND ONE WHOSE BEAUTY **SURPASSES** THAT OF ALL THE OTHERS! FRANKLY, I DID NOT **KNOW** THAT SUCH BEAUTY AS YOURS FLOWERED IN ALL OF BARGOLL!

217

THEN, IN A CHILLING, RASPY WHISPER...

PERHAPS I SHALL HAVE YOU **SPARED** THE SACRIFICE! WE CAN ALWAYS REPLACE YOU WITH ANOTHER WENCH FROM THE SURFACE! THEN WHEN I REGAIN MY **LIFE**, YOU SHALL BECOME MY **BRIDE!**

I'LL **DIE** BEFORE I EVER AGAIN LET YOU TOUCH ME WITH YOUR MOLDER-ING FINGERS!

SA-MASHK!

OOPHF!

FOLLOW ME, MY SISTERS, AND WE'LL YET ESCAPE FROM THIS DEN OF DEATH!

STOP HER!

DEAD FIGURES RESPOND TO KAGRA'S REVERBERATING COM-MANDS... UNBLINKING EYES FOLLOW THE LITHE FIGURE AS SHE SPRINTS ACROSS THE ROOM...

UNTIL SHE CAN RUN NO FURTHER...

THEY ARE COMING FROM **ALL SIDES!** I'M TRAPPED! HOPELESSLY TRAPPED!

SEIZE HER! AND FOR HER **INSOLENCE**, SHE WILL BE THE **FIRST** TO DIE ON THE ALTAR OF GARLOTH!

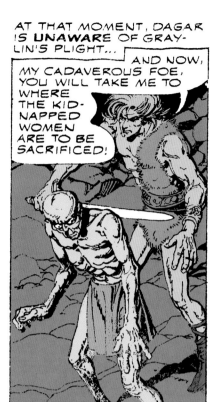

AT THAT MOMENT, DAGAR IS **UNAWARE** OF GRAYLIN'S PLIGHT...

AND NOW, MY CADAVEROUS FOE, YOU WILL TAKE ME TO WHERE THE KIDNAPPED WOMEN ARE TO BE SACRIFICED!

N-NO! IF I REVEAL **THAT** TO YOU, THE MASTER WOULD **DESTROY** ME FOR MY BETRAYAL!

AND **I** SHALL DESTROY YOU ON THE SPOT IF YOU **DON'T!**

VERY WELL, MORTAL! YOUR ARGUMENT HAS **CONVINCED** ME!

AND NONE OF YOUR **TRICKS!** REMEMBER A LIVING DEADMAN WITH **NO HEAD** IS AS GOOD AS A DEAD STEED!

THE DEADMAN SUDDENLY GRABS DAGAR'S SWORD...

DON'T LOOK SO **SURPRISED,** SURFACE MAN! REMEMBER THAT A DEAD MAN...EVEN A **LIVING DEADMAN...** CANNOT BE HURT BY YOUR SHARP BLADE!

BUT **YOU** CAN!

BY SCORPIO'S SOUL!

AND IN ANOTHER MOMENT, BEFORE THE MERCENARY HAS **TIME** TO DRAW HIS **DAGGER...**

IRONIC, WOULDN'T YOU SAY? YOU DYING BY YOUR **OWN** SWORD! HAH! HAH! HAH!

BUT DAGAR'S CHILDHOOD WAS SPENT IN *TRAINING* AND DEVELOPING HIS REFLEXES TO LIGHTNING PEAK!

OOOF!

THAK-GASHK!

YOU WERE FAST, WARRIOR! BUT EVEN **WITH** YOUR SWORD YOU SHALL NOT SUBDUE ME A SECOND TIME! NO, **THIS TIME** YOU **DIE!**

AS THE DEADMAN MAKES HIS THREAT, HE LUNGES FORWARD. AGAIN, DAGAR'S MOVEMENTS ARE AS SWIFT AS A SABRE-TOOTH CAT... AND THE ROCK'S WEIGHT AND **MOMENTUM** CARRY THE LIVING CORPSE INTO SPACE...

NOW THAT HE AND THAT EARTH-LIZARD HAVE BEEN RETURNED TO THE WORLD OF THE DEAD, I CAN LOOK FOR GRAYLIN!

BUT I FEAR I MAY ALREADY BE TOO LATE!

BUT GRAYLIN IS STILL VERY MUCH ALIVE... AND KICKING.

UNGGH!

I AM LUCKY THAT THE LIVING DEAD ARE SLOW MOVING! PERHAPS WHILE THIS ONE IS DAZED I CAN GET PAST HIM!

I NOTICED THIS OPENING BEFORE! NOW IF IT ONLY LEADS SOMEWHERE AWAY FROM HERE!

STOP HER! SHE MUST BE SACRIFICED!

BEFORE ANY OF THE WALKING DEAD CAN ENTER THE PASSAGEWAY, GRAYLIN HAS MADE SEVERAL DETOURS...

IT SEEMS AS IF I'M SAFE FROM THEM! I ONLY WISH THE OTHER WOMEN COULD HAVE FOLLOWED ME!

AND...

NOW WHERE AM I?

THAT SOUND...

GRAYLIN! I'M SORRY IF I STARTLED YOU!

DAGAR!

SILENCE PERVADES THE CHAMBER AS THE WARRIOR DRAWS HIS WOMAN TO HIM... HOLDING HER TENDERLY WITH POWERFUL HANDS THAT HAVE SLAIN MONSTERS...

YOU ARE SAFE, GRAYLIN! BUT I HAVE GIVEN MY WORD THAT I WOULD ALSO FREE THE OTHER WOMEN!

THOSE ARE WORDS I'D HOPED TO HEAR YOU SAY!

BUT THE PROBLEM REMAINS! HOW DO WE FIGHT OFF AN ENTIRE BAND OF LIVING DEADMEN?

IF THE WOMEN WERE FREE THEY WOULD FIGHT!

WAIT, DAGAR! I MAY HAVE THE ANSWER! THE SECRET TO DEFEATING THE DEADMEN COULD BE IN THEIR EYES... WHICH HAVE EVOLVED TO ACCOMMODATE THEIR EXISTENCE IN THIS DARK, SUNLESS WORLD!

"THEY HAVE BEEN IN THESE DEPTHS FOR SO LONG THAT THEY CANNOT ENDURE THE LIGHT! THAT IS WHY THEY COULD ONLY KIDNAP THEIR SACRIFICIAL VICTIMS AT NIGHT..."

LOOK OVER THERE!

YES! THOSE **ANIMAL BONES** MIGHT JUST BE WHAT WE NEED!

THEN WE'LL NEED THE **LIGHT** ON OUR SIDE! **TORCHES** WOULD BE THE ANSWER!

BUT WHERE DO WE GET **WOOD** FOR TORCHES DOWN HERE?

AFTER FASTENING CLOTH FROM GRAYLIN'S GARMENT OVER THE BONES, DAGAR MAKES THE PRECARIOUS DESCENT TO THE VERY CORE OF THE VOLCANO...

AND NOW WE HAVE TORCHES!

THE WARRIOR GIVES THE WOMAN HIS **DAGGER.** THEN GRAYLIN LEADS HIM THROUGH THE TUNNEL THAT HAD PROVIDED HER ESCAPE...

YOU HEAR THAT **CHANTING?** THE RITUAL OF GAR-LOTH MAY HAVE ALREADY **BEGUN!**

EERIE CHANTING, SPOKEN BY A GROUP OF CREATURES THAT SHOULD BE DEAD, FILLS THE GREAT CHAMBER. AND IN THE CENTER OF THE ROOM, OCCUPYING A PLACE OF PROMINENCE, IS A GLOWING SCARLET JEWEL...THE RED RUBY OF GARLOTH...

THIS IS THE NIGHT WHICH WE HAVE LONG AWAITED! FOR ON THIS NIGHT EACH OF US SHALL SACRIFICE A VICTIM WHOSE **DEATH** WILL GRANT US LIFE! BRING ME THE FIRST WOMAN!

AND THE FIRST TO DIE WILL BE **SARY**, THE FRIEND OF THAT BLACK-HAIRED WITCH YOU FOOLS LET ESCAPE!

N-NO!

SARY TRIES TO RESIST...BUT THE DEADMEN ARE **STRONG**. IN ANOTHER MOMENT SHE IS BRUTALLY THROWN ACROSS THE COLD STONE **ALTAR**...

HELPLESS... SQUIRMING UNDER THE TIGHT ROPES THAT HOLD HER TO THE CRUDE ALTAR, SARY WATCHES IN HORROR AS KAGRA RAISES A STONE KNIFE IN HIS BONY HAND...

HEAR YOUR SERVANT, O **GARLOTH**, DEMON OF THE DARK GODS! AND ACCEPT THE DEATH OF THIS INNOCENT VICTIM IN EXCHANGE FOR THE **TRUE LIFE** OF YOUR PRIEST!

BUT BEFORE THE SACRIFICIAL KNIFE CAN TOUCH THE GIRL'S FLESH...

STOP! UNLESS YOU'D PREFER BEING SACRIFICED... TO ME!

WHAT?! IT IS THAT ACCURSED WENCH AND SOME OTHER MORTAL! KILL THEM WHERE THEY STAND!

KAGRA HAS NOT RECKONED WITH THE INGENUITY OF HIS ADVERSARIES... NOR THE BLAZING **WEAPONS** THEY WIELD...

Y//// THE **LIGHT!**

I CANNOT **STAND** IT! THE **P-PAIN**... AS IF THE **SUN** ITSELF HAS COME DOWN FROM THE SKY! **EEEEEAAAHH!**

I WILL FIGHT OFF THESE **DAZED CORPSES,** GRAYLIN!

AND **I** WILL TAKE ADVANTAGE OF ALL THIS CONFUSION...

...FIRST BY FREEING **SARY!**

GRAY-LIN!

WITHIN MOMENTS...

YOU TAKE MY **TORCH!** THEN BOTH OF YOU CAN HOLD OFF THE DEADMEN WHILE YOU FREE THE OTHER WOMEN! BUT I...

...I WILL SHOW THIS **VULTURE** WHO CALLS HIMSELF "**MASTER**" THE CONSEQUENCES OF ABDUCTING MY **WOMAN!**

KAGRA GASPS AT THE SIGHT OF THE GOLDEN-HAIRED **AVENGER**, WHOSE FACE IS TWISTED LIKE THE VISION OF SOME RAGING **BEAST**...

THE LEADER OF THE DEADMEN MOANS AND TRIES TO STAND, BUT AS HE AGAIN SLUMPS TO THE ROCK FLOOR...

BY THE DARK GODS!

AA-UUHH!

KRa-DofR!

IF I AM TO DEFEAT ALL OF THE LIVING DEAD, I MUST FIRST DESTROY THE **SOURCE** OF THEIR POWER!

BUT AS THE WARRIOR'S FINGERS FIRMLY GRIP THE **RED RUBY OF GARLOTH**...

ARGHH! THE JEWEL FEELS LIKE **FIRE**!

DAGAR'S BODY ACHES FROM THE SEARING JEWEL. HIS MIND SWIRLS, HIS LEGS BEGIN TO COLLAPSE...

AND HE BEGINS TO **FALL**...

DAGAR FIGHTS TO CLEAR HIS NUMBED MIND...

NO! CAN'T GIVE IN... MY VOW TO FREE THE WOMEN... MUST BE KEPT...

THOUGH IT MEANS THAT THE RUBY BURNS ME TO A CINDER!

THE SURFACEMAN TAKES THE RED RUBY OF GARLOTH! PREVENT HIM!

STILL CLUTCHING THE BURNING RUBY, DAGAR USES THE FLAT OF HIS BLADE TO AT LEAST **STUN** THESE UNKILLABLE CREATURES...

AND AS DAGAR BATTLES AGAINST SEEMINGLY HOPELESS ODDS, GRAYLIN FREES THE LAST OF THE CAPTIVES...

THERE! BUT NOW I THINK I'LL BE NEEDING THE USE OF MY **TORCH** AGAIN!

FOR IT APPEARS THAT THE ONE WHO HAS SAVED ME SO OFTEN IN THE PAST COULD NOW USE MY HELP!

GRAYLIN! I WELCOME YOUR HELP! MY HEAD IS DAZED... MY BODY'S AFLAME!

AS THE DEADMEN FLEE FROM GRAYLIN'S TORCH...

LEAD THE WOMEN UP THE CRATER WHILE I DESTROY THE JEWEL!

PRESENTLY, TWO TORCHES ILLUMINATE THE TUNNEL WHICH CONNECTS THE SACRIFICIAL CHAMBER TO THE CRATER...

BRIEF MINUTES LATER, THE GROUP SCALES THE BOWL-LIKE WALLS THAT LEAD TO FREEDOM...

WE WILL WAIT WITH THE TORCHES UNTIL THE OTHERS HAVE REACHED THE SURFACE!

YES, THOUGH I DOUBT WE'LL HAVE ANY MORE TROUBLE FROM THE LIVING DEAD!

DAGAR, HOWEVER, CANNOT MAKE THAT SAME ASSURING CLAIM...

THE JEWEL DRAINS ME OF ENERGY! BUT I STILL MAY OUTRUN THE STIFFLY-MOVING DEAD-MEN!

FASTER, YOU FOOLS! FASTER!

THOUGH IT CAUSES HIM SEVERE **PAIN**, DAGAR MANAGES TO REACH THE RIM OF THE FUMING, BUBBLING ABYSS...

SSSSTTTT!

ONLY **SECONDS** REMAIN! YOU **MUST** STOP HIM! FOR THAT RUBY IS **ALL** THAT KEEPS US IN THE SEMBLANCE OF LIFE!

NO! HE HAS THROWN IT INTO THE PIT!

SPPLLLSHHH!

THE **RUBY OF GARLOTH** DISSOLVES IN THE MOLTEN FURY OF THE ACTIVE VOLCANO! AND AS THE MYSTIC JEWEL IS INCINERATED FOR ALL TIME, KAGRA AND HIS MINIONS ARE ROBBED OF THEIR FLEETING "LIFE"... **PEACEFULLY**, WITHOUT **PAIN**...AS THOUGH THEY HAD **NEVER** BEEN OTHER THAN LIFELESS CORPSES...

IT IS **DONE!** NOW I CAN RETURN TO THE SURFACE, WHERE I'LL ENJOY A BREATH OF **FRESH AIR!**

BUT AS DAGAR LEISURELY WALKS AWAY FROM THE RIM OF THE PIT, HE DOES NOT NOTICE THAT **SOMETHING** IS TAKING ON A GHASTLY **SHAPE**... AND RISING TO THE **SURFACE** OF THAT SIZZLING CAULDRON OF ROCK...

GGRRRGLLL.. SSSTT!

THEN DAGAR **HEARS** IT... SOMETHING ENORMOUS LOOMING BEHIND HIM, WITH A HIDEOUS UNEARTHLY **ROAR** SEEMINGLY ORIGINATING IN THE DEPTHS OF HADES...

WITLESS MORTAL **FOOL!** DO YOU NOT REALIZE THAT IN DESTROYING THE RUBY, YOU HAVE FREED **GARLOTH,** A DEMON OF THE DARK GODS, FROM HIS EARTHLY **PRISON?** AND THAT YOUR **REWARD** FOR FREEING ME IS **DEATH?**

THE SWORD IS DAGAR'S **ONLY** WEAPON AGAINST THE DEMON... AND THOUGH HE HACKS AWAY...

MY BLADE DOES NOT EVEN **FAZE** GARLOTH!

THE FUTILE ANTICS OF YOU MORTALS NEVER CEASE TO **AMAZE** ME! YOU ALWAYS ASSUME THAT STEEL FORGED ON EARTH CAN SLAY A DEMON OF THE DARK GODS!

CHOKING FROM THE SULPHUROUS **FUMES** NOW RISING MORE STRONGLY FROM THE PIT, DAGAR SEES THE FLOOR DROP FROM HIM... AND FEELS THE HEAT ISSUE FROM THE **MOUTH** OF GARLOTH!

BUT BEFORE THOSE DEMON JAWS CAN CLAMP DOWN UPON THE HELPLESS WARRIOR...

WHAT IS THAT **SOUND?** AND THIS SUDDEN **PREMONITION** THAT I AM IN **DANGER?**

BBmmmm-rummblle!

BUT YOU **SHALL LEARN SOMETHING** OF GARLOTH THIS NIGHT, MORTAL! YOU SHALL LEARN THAT HIS FAVORITE **FOOD** IS WITLESS FOOLS SUCH AS YOURSELF!

HAH! HAH! HAH! RUMMMBBLLLL!

LOOKING DOWN INTO THE VOLCANIC PIT, GARLOTH BEHOLDS THE **RESULT** OF HIS OWN RELEASE... HE SEES HOW THE MYSTIC POWERS, WHICH FOR SO LONG HAD BEEN CONTAINED WITHIN THE RUBY, HAVE NOW BURST **FREE**... AND HAVE **REACTED** WITH THE MOLTEN MATERIALS... REACTED EXPLOSIVELY...

BA-RUMBBBLLL-SPLIISSHH!

AND **MT. BARGOLL** VOMITS ITS FIERY **FURY** INTO THE NIGHT SKY...

BRRAAA-KROOOOOOOO!!!

AN **ERUPTION!**

AND **DAGAR** HAS NOT YET COME OUT OF THE VOLCANO! OH, **SARY**...HE **MUST** HAVE BEEN KILLED!

BUT AS THE VOLCANO CONTINUES TO LAUNCH A MOLTEN HOLOCAUST FROM ITS CRATER, DAGAR YET **LIVES**... BUT PERHAPS NOT FOR LONG...

I SPOTTED THIS TUNNEL WHEN **GARLOTH** LIFTED ME! BUT THE LAVA HAS **ALSO** FOUND THIS AS A ROUTE OF ESCAPE!

WAIT! THERE IS WHAT APPEARS TO BE AN **OPENING!** HAVE TO RUN **FASTER**, OR I'LL BE **BROILED** LIKE A HOG ON A SKEWER!

MERE MOMENTS LATER, A WEARY MERCENARY BRACES HIMSELF AGAINST THE QUAKING WALL OF THE VOLCANO...

ANOTHER SECOND AND I'D HAVE BEEN A **PART** OF THAT LAVA!

SRLOOOBBLL!

GRAYLIN REJOICES AS SHE SEES THAT HER WARRIOR HAS ESCAPED THE SEETHING CATACLYSM. AND AS DAGAR STANDS AT HER SIDE, THEY WATCH THE GHOSTLY IMAGE OF **GARLOTH** FOREVER DISSIPATE AMID THE COILING SMOKE AND MIST...

SOON, DAGAR AND GRAYLIN LEAD THE WOMEN BACK INTO THE TOWN OF BARGOLL...

BUT YOU ONLY FIGHT FOR GOLD, DAGAR! WERE YOU PAID TO SAVE THE WOMEN?

YES, I WAS PAID!

BUT ENOUGH TALK OF FEES! WE'LL GET YOUR HORSE! I WISH TO LEAVE THIS TOWN...TRAVEL FAST AND FAR...UNTIL THE VOLCANO'S STENCH OF DEATH LEAVES MY NOSTRILS!

the END

233

GOLD KEY®

90279-410

DAGAR

TALES OF SWORD AND SORCERY

DAGAR
THE INVINCIBLE

25¢

TWO WARRIORS COMBINE THEIR MIGHT AGAINST A GIANT FOE...

NIGHT OF THE SERPENT

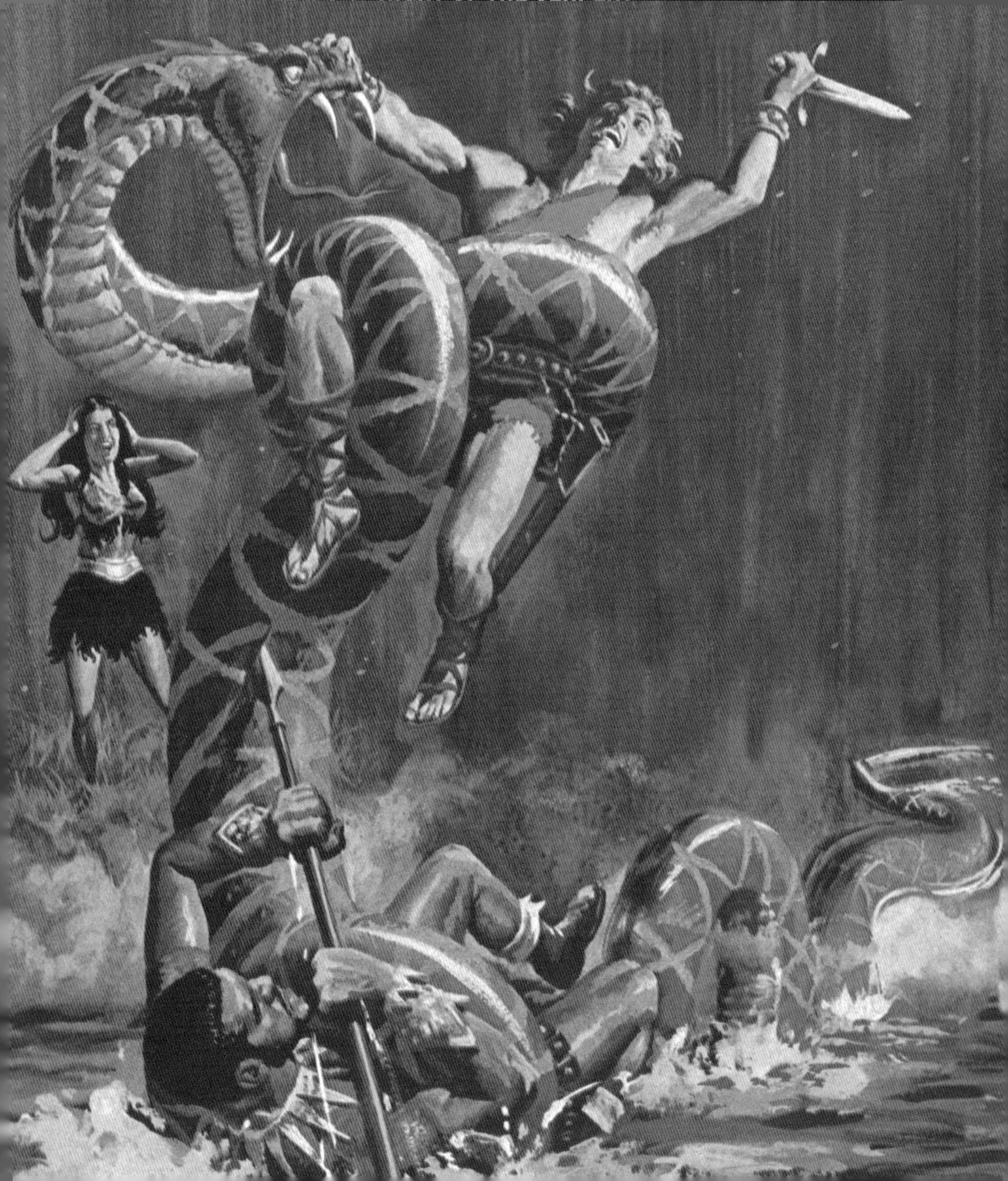

DAGAR
THE INVINCIBLE

NIGHT OF THE SERPENT

THE GUTTERAL ROARS OF PRIMEVAL *CONFLICT* BLARE THROUGH THE MOON-BATHED SWAMPS THAT SURROUND THE CITY OF *YANG-DORR*... AND THE GIANT GROUND SLOTH, BY NATURE A PEACEFUL CREATURE, STRUGGLES FUTILELY AGAINST THE FANGED *HORROR* THAT SLITHERS ABOUT ITS SHAGGY BULK...

TWO FIGURES OBSERVE THE AWESOME SPECTACLE AS THE SLEEK REPTILIAN MONSTROSITY COILS ABOUT THE GREAT MAMMAL... THE FAIR-SKINNED *GRAYLIN*, AND HE WHO IS CALLED *DAGAR THE INVINCIBLE*...

90279-410
DAGAR #9 - 747

GLEAMING SCALES SHIMMER IN THE MOONLIGHT AS THE ENORMOUS SERPENT *SQUEEZES* AND READIES ITS DAGGER-LIKE *FANGS*...

...TO *STRIKE!*

HSSSS! GRRRAAAA! ROAARRRR! SSSS!

FOR LINGERING MOMENTS THE ANGUINE MONSTER *FASTENS* UPON THE MEGATHERIUM... THEN RELEASES ITS SHAGGY VICTIM, WHICH STRUGGLES TO NURSE ITS WOUNDS IN THE NEARBY STREAM...

BUT ONLY *DIES* AS ITS TAINTED BLOOD RUSHES FROM ITS WOUNDS AND MIXES WITH THE COOL RUNNING WATERS...

DAGAR... WHAT HAPPENED TO THE *SERPENT?* IT WENT INTO THE UNDER-BRUSH AND SEEMS TO HAVE JUST *VANISHED!*

BUT THAT SERPENT *INFECTED* OUR INTENDED KILL WITH ITS VENOM! AND I HAD A PARTICULAR *APPETITE* FOR SLOTH! HMM... WELL, I SUPPOSE WE CAN EAT IN YANG-DORR!

I DON'T *CARE* IF THE SNAKE DISAPPEARED, GRAYLIN... AS LONG AS IT DOES NOT *RETURN!*

238

DAGAR, *MUST* YOU GO TO THAT CITY AND PUT YOUR SWORD UP FOR *HIRE?* IF YANG-DORR IS TO OUR LIKING, CAN'T WE MAKE IT OUR *HOME* AND *QUIT* THIS LIFE OF CONSTANT DANGER?

YOU KNOW WE ARE BOTH *OUTCASTS!* I AM THE LAST MAN OF TULGONIA, A NATION *SLAUGHTERED* BY THE SORCERER SCORPIO! AND YOU WILLINGLY LEFT YOUR OWN PEOPLE, WHO TRIED *SACRIFICING* YOU TO A RACE OF VAMPIRES!

NO, WE'VE LEFT OUR HOMES *BEHIND* US! NEITHER OF US CAN EVER SETTLE DOWN ANYWHERE, GRAYLIN! IF YOU ARE TO BE MY COMPANION, YOU'LL HAVE TO *ACCEPT* THAT!

AS DAGAR AND GRAYLIN, MOUNTED ON THEIR HORSES *KASA* AND *TARNU*, PROCEED TOWARD *YANG-DORR*...

CAREFUL WHERE YOU GUIDE TARNU! THERE ARE MORE *DANGERS* IN THIS SWAMP THAN ONE VANISHING SERPENT!

THERE IS *OTHER* ACTIVITY IN A *CLEARING* OF THE STEAMING SWAMP... FOR THIS IS THE TEMPORARY HOME OF THE *ZARGANI*, A TRIBE OF NOMADIC BLACK WARRIORS WHOSE PROWESS WITH THE *SPEAR* AND *BATTLEAXE* HAS OBVIATED THEIR USE OF THE SWORD...

AND WHILE THE ZARGANI ATTEND TO MATTERS OF THE TRIBE, THEIR *WARRIOR CHIEFTAIN* AND HIS WIFE ARE STROLLING BESIDE THE RIVER...

TORGUS! I FIND IT DIFFICULT TO BELIEVE WE'VE BEEN WED FOR *TWO YEARS!* YOU TREAT ME LIKE A *BRIDE!*

THAT IS UNDERSTANDABLE FOR A WIFE SUCH AS YOU, RENYA!

I AM THIRSTY, TORGUS! WOULD YOU PLEASE GET ME SOME WATER, AS YOU DID DURING OUR MARRIAGE CEREMONY?

OF COURSE, MY BELOVED!

THUS, THE STRAPPING CHIEF OF THE ZARGANI CUPS HIS MIGHTY HANDS... REPEATING AN ACT OF THEIR WEDDING ...SYMBOLIC OF THE SHARING OF LOVE WHICH, LIKE THE WATERS OF THE STREAM, WOULD CONTINUE TO FLOW...

BUT BARELY HAS THE TINGLING WATER TOUCHED RENYA'S LIPS, WHEN...

RENYA!

T-TORGUS... I FEEL LIKE... B-BURNING UP... I...

TORGUS HAS SLAIN *MONSTERS* WITH HIS MIGHTY STRENGTH...BUT NOW HE CAN ONLY *WATCH* AS HIS WIFE'S EYES CLOSE AND HER ONCE VIBRANT BODY DROPS LIMPLY IN HIS MUSCULAR ARMS...

...AND TORGUS LEARNS THAT EVEN A WARRIOR CHIEFTAIN CAN SHED TEARS.

THE TALKING AND LAUGHTER IN THE CAMP OF THE ZARGANI ARE SUDDENLY DISPLACED BY A *HUSH*, AS TORGUS SILENTLY WALKS IN THEIR MIDST...

WHAT HAS HAPPENED, MY CHIEFTAIN?

TORGUS DOES NOT REPLY...BUT CONTINUES TO WALK TOWARD ONE PARTICULAR *TENT*...

THE TENT OF THE AGED TRIBAL *SEER*...

ONLY *YOU* CAN HELP RENYA, OLD ONE! SHE SEEMS TO HAVE DRUNK *POISONED WATERS!*

EVEN I CANNOT BRING LIFE TO THE DEAD, MY CHIEFTAIN! BUT WE MUST BE *CAREFUL* IN THESE MORE ENLIGHTENED TIMES, FOR OFTEN THE *APPEARANCE* OF DEATH CAN *DECEIVE* US! HMM...YES...

WHAT DO YOU SEE—?

RENYA IS *NOT* DEAD! THERE IS YET A *FLICKER* OF LIFE WITHIN HER! BUT THAT FLICKER IS SWIFTLY *FADING!* SHE *WILL* DIE BEFORE ANOTHER *SUNSET*, UNLESS...

UNLESS *WHAT*, ANCIENT ONE?

PERHAPS YOUR ANSWER IS *HERE*, TORGUS...IN THE SMOKE FROM THIS ENCHANTED INCENSE! *OBSERVE*, THEN, FOR THE SMOKE CONTAINS PROFOUND *IMAGES* FOR THOSE THAT HAVE A *DESIRE*... AND A *NEED*... TO SEE!

241

"BEHOLD, TORGUS, THIS **SERPENT**... A MONSTER OF THE EVIL GODS OF DARKNESS ... FOR IT IS THIS SCALY HORROR WHOSE VENOM POISONED THE WATER WHICH YOUR RENYA DRANK..."

"AND NOW BEHOLD **YANG-DORR**, A CITY BORDERING THE INNERMOST RIM OF THIS SWAMPLAND. IN YANG-DORR YOU SHALL FIND RENYA'S **ONLY** POSSIBLE SALVATION FROM A FAST-APPROACHING **DEATH**..."

"THERE LIVES THE SORCERER **NAR-KAL**, A FOLLOWER OF THE **DARK GODS**, AND POSSESSOR OF THE MYSTIC **ORB OF ORG-RA**...

"ONLY THE **ORB** CAN SAVE THE FLEETING LIFE OF RENYA, IF YOU CAN SECURE IT IN **TIME!**"

THEN I MUST GO TO YANG-DORR, **SEIZE** THE ORB AND **SAVE** MY BELOVED...OR **PERISH** IN THE ATTEMPT! THIS SWEARS **TORGUS** BY ALL THE GODS OF THE ZARGANI!

THE MORNING SUN RISES STEADILY IN THE CLOUDLESS SKY AS DAGAR THE MERCENARY AND THE WOMAN HE LOVES STRIDE ALONG A BACKSTREET OF YANG-DORR...

IT IS DIFFICULT TO BELIEVE THAT NO ONE HAS YET WANTED TO **HIRE** ME, GRAYLIN! COULD IT BE THAT AT LAST WE'VE FOUND A CITY WHERE **EVERYONE** HAS THE COURAGE TO FIGHT HIS OWN BATTLES?

I AM **NOT** COMPLAINING, DAGAR!

HO THERE, MERCENARY! COULD YOU SPARE SOME *COINS* FOR THREE *CRIPPLED* BEGGARS?

NO! I AM IN NEED OF MONEY *MYSELF* THESE DAYS! BESIDES, YOU HARDLY LOOK *CRIPPLED* TO ME!

BUT I HAVE HEARD THAT MERCENARIES *ALWAYS* CARRY MUCH GOLD... PAID THEM FOR THE USE OF THEIR COURAGE AND SWORD! PERHAPS YOUR *LADY* ALSO HAS A SIZABLE DONATION FOR US!

I SAID *NO!*

THEN IF THE MERCENARY WON'T SURRENDER HIS GOLD OUT OF THE KINDNESS OF HIS *BRAVE HEART*, LET'S *PERSUADE* HIM A BIT!

AYE! IT WILL BE GOOD TO CAST OFF THIS *BEGGAR'S DISGUISE!*

IT IS THREE OF US AGAINST ONE MAN... AND ONE *FRAIL FEMALE!*

THE ATTACK IS *LIGHTNING SWIFT*. THERE IS NO *TIME* FOR DAGAR TO DRAW HIS SWORD:... BUT WITH ADVERSARIES SUCH AS *THESE*, THERE IS REALLY NO *NEED!*

Thunk!

Thump!

AND WHAT OF THAT "ONE *FRAIL FEMALE*"?

I HAVE NEVER *KILLED*...SO YOU'LL HAVE TO BE CONTENT MEETING THE *FLAT* SIDE OF MY BLADE!

MERE MOMENTS LATER...

NOW DO YOU AND YOUR THIEVING ACCOMPLICES STILL FEEL LIKE ATTACKING STRANGERS? *I* HAVE NO QUALMS ABOUT USING THE *SHARP* SIDE OF *MY* SWORD!

THE REPLY OF THE THREE STREET THIEVES IS IMMEDIATE AND WORDLESS...

THEY ANSWER BY RUNNING LIKE THE FRIGHTENED HYENAS THEY ARE! I DOUBT WE'LL BE TROUBLED BY *THEM* AGAIN!

BUT WHY DID *YOU* JOIN IN THE BRAWL? FIGHTING IS *MAN'S* WORK!

IF I AM TO BE COMPANION TO A *WARRIOR,* I *WON'T* BE A HELPLESS DAMSEL WHO DOES NOTHING WHILE THE MAN SHE *LOVES* IS OFF SLAY-ING *DRAGONS!*

YET, EVEN AS DAGAR AND GRAYLIN DEBATE THE ROLES ASSIGNED THEM BY THEIR PRIMITIVE SOCIETY, THEIR ACTIONS DO NOT GO *UNNOTICED*...FOR THEIR IMAGES HAVE COME INTO SHARP *FOCUS* WITHIN A GLOWING OCCULAR SPHERE...

...OFF SLAYING *DRAGONS!*

SO THERE IS A *MERCENARY* IN YANG-DORR! BUT OF WHAT USE ARE *SWORDSMEN* TO THE POSSESSOR OF THE *ORB OF ORG-RA?*

FOR WHILE I, *NAR-KAL*, POSSESS THE MAGICAL *EYE* FROM THE IDOL OF THE GOD *ORG-RA*, I AM THE MOST POWERFUL MAN IN ALL YANG-DORR!

YET EVEN AS THE SORCERER NAR-KAL FEELS THE EERIE ENERGY THROBBING THROUGH HIS BEING, HIS THOUGHTS RETURN TO A TIME WHEN HE WAS BUT A COMMON MAN...

...A MAN DESIRING POWERS BEYOND HIS NATURE...A MAN WHO PERFORMED A CLANDESTINE *RITUAL* IN THE SWAMPS, REQUESTING A BOON OF THE *DARK GODS*...

NAR-KAL'S PRAYERS WERE *ANSWERED!*

AS NAR-KAL GRASPED THE LEGENDARY SPHERE, HE FELT *POWER* COURSE THROUGH HIS VEINS... AND HEARD *WORDS* SPEAKING TO HIS BRAIN...

YOU NOW WIELD THE *ORB OF ORG-RA!* BUT IT SHALL GIVE YOU POWER *ONLY* THROUGH YOUR *FAMILIAR!*

THIS SHALL BE YOUR *FAMILIAR*, MORTAL...THIS SLITHERING REPTILE WHICH ORDINARILY HAUNTS THE SUBTERRANEAN TUNNEL BENEATH THESE SWAMPS!

AS OF THIS FATEFUL NIGHT, A *MYSTIC BOND* EXISTS BETWEEN YOU AND THE SERPENT...

Hüüsssš!Ahhhhhhh!

Ssssssttt!

...A BOND THAT LINKS YOU *TOGETHER* IN THE EYES OF THE *DARK GODS!*

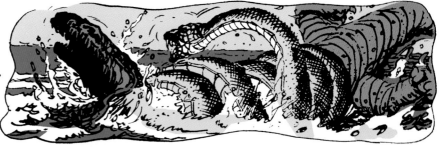

AND AS NAR-KAL'S THOUGHTS AGAIN RETURN TO THE *PRESENT...*

FOR EVERY *KILL* THE SERPENT MAKES, I CAN FEEL MYSELF GETTING *STRONGER!* WHEN MY POWER HAS REACHED ITS *PEAK,* PERHAPS I'LL PUT THE ENTIRE *COUNTRY* UNDER MY RULE!

NIGHT BLACKENS THE SKY ABOVE YANG-DORR. AND AS THE FULL MOON SHINES UPON THE HOUSE OF NAR-KAL, A CAT-LIKE FIGURE CREEPS SILENTLY ACROSS THE ROOFTOP...

THE FIGURE GRACEFULLY DESCENDS THE SIDE OF THE BUILDING... AND FINDING THE DOOR TO THE SORCERER'S DWELLING UNDERSTAND-ABLY *LOCKED,* PROVIDES *ANOTHER* MEANS OF ENTRANCE...

THEN STEALTHILY MOVING THROUGH THE SHADOWY HOUSE OF NAR-KAL, THE DETERMINED *TORGUS* HEARS SOUNDS COMING FROM AN ADJOINING ROOM... THE SOUNDS OF CUMBERSOME *ARMOR.* REASSURINGLY CLUTCHING THE HANDLE OF HIS WEIGHTY *AXE.* TORGUS *TURNS...*

TORGUS'S EYES SHIFT TO EACH OF THE ONRUSHING SENTRIES, SEEING A MACE DESCEND UPON HIM WITH CRUSHING IMPACT. BUT THE CHIEFTAIN IS *SWIFT*...

WUNSSSS...

EVEN AS HE BLOCKS *ONE* BLOW, HIS HEAD DOES NOT TURN IN TIME TO AVOID A HEAVILY ARMORED *GLOVE*...

UNGGH!

SPla-krunk!

NOR DOES IT AVOID A *SECOND* SWING OF THAT METALLIC FIST...

CHOK

ARGHH!

AS TORGUS RAISES HIS HEAVY AXE, THE PAIN WHICH HAD BEEN RIPPING THROUGH HIM SEEMS TO *VANISH*...FOR ALL THAT CONCERNS HIM IS THE WOMAN WHO AWAITS EITHER HIS TRIUMPHANT RETURN...OR THE COMING OF *DEATH*. BUT AS HE SWINGS HIS WEAPON...

HUH—?! WHAT *WITCHCRAFT* IS THIS?!

KRACA-4K!!

247

THOSE GUARDS WERE NOTHING BUT *EMPTY SUITS OF ARMOR,* BROUGHT TO LIFE THROUGH *MAGIC!* I SUSPECT NAR-KAL WAS CONFIDENT THAT THEY WOULD STOP *ANY* INTRUDER!

AND IF SUCH IS THE CASE, HE MIGHT NOT HAVE THOUGHT OF PUTTING *OTHER* GUARDS IN THIS PLACE!

HMM...THERE IS A STRANGE *LIGHT* COMING FROM BEHIND THOSE DRAPES...

YES...AS I SUSPECTED! IT IS THE *ORB OF ORG-RA,* JUST AS IT APPEARED IN THE SEER'S VISION!

THEN I *HAVE* THE MEANS OF SAVING MY BELOVED RENYA! ALL THAT REMAINS NOW IS TO GET THE ORB IN HER PRESENCE BEFORE THE *DAWN!*

YOU PRESUME TOO MUCH, THIEF! FOR THOUGH YOU MANAGED TO DEFEAT MY LIFELESS *SENTRIES,* YOU HAVE YET TO FACE ME *DIRECTLY!*

NAR-KAL!

BUT AS NAR-KAL GESTURES...

YOU SHOULD HAVE BEEN *STRUCK* BY A SPELL! BUT *NOTHING* HAPPENED!

OBVIOUSLY YOU HAVE *NO POWER* AS LONG AS *I* HOLD THE ORB OF ORG-RA! HOWEVER, IF YOU'D CARE TO OPPOSE ME *PHYSICALLY*...

N-NO, I...

EVEN AS THE WARRIOR THUNDERS AWAY FROM THE HOUSE OF NAR-KAL ON HIS MAGNIFICENT CHARGER, THE POWER-STRIPPED SORCERER MAKES A GRIM VOW...

GO THEN, BARBARIAN THIEF! BUT YOU'VE NOT HEARD THE *LAST* FROM NAR-KAL!

BUT WHAT CAN I DO TO *STOP* SUCH A ONE?

WAIT! OF *COURSE!* THERE IS THAT *MERCENARY* WHO CAME TO YANG-DORR...THE MERCENARY WHO COMPLAINED OVER THE LACK OF EMPLOYMENT! IF HE IS YET IN TOWN...

WITH A REPUTATION SUCH AS NAR-KAL'S, IT IS A SIMPLE TASK TO ELICIT *ANSWERS* FROM THE PEOPLE OF THE CITY. THUS, BEFORE LONG, HIS QUERIES BRING HIM TO AN *INN*...

THE INN IS ALIVE WITH THE RAUCOUS SOUNDS OF MUSIC AND LAUGHTER AND MUGS SLAMMING AGAINST WOODEN TABLES. AS NAR-KAL ENTERS THE PLACE OF MERRIMENT, HIS EYES SINGLE OUT TWO FIGURES WHOM HE *RECOGNIZES*...

YOU *SEE*, GRAYLIN! *SOME* WOMEN NEITHER STAY AT HOME *NOR* GO OFF AND FIGHT WITH THEIR *MEN!*

HUH?!

Clink--link! Kink!

YOU MAY *HAVE* ALL THAT GOLD... AND *MORE* LATER ON! THAT IS, *IF* YOU'D CARE TO *WORK* FOR IT!

WHAT WOULD YOU HAVE ME DO?

THIS NIGHT A LOWLY *THIEF* BROKE INTO MY HOME AND STOLE A TREASURED *FAMILY HEIRLOOM*... THE *ORB OF ORG-RA!* I WANT IT *BACK!*

ORB OF ORG-RA? THINGS WITH SUCH *PECULIAR* NAMES USUALLY SMELL OF *SORCERY!* I HAVE *NO* REGARD FOR MAGIC! BUT RIGHT *NOW* I HAVE EVEN *LESS* REGARD FOR *THIEVES!*

THEN YOU'LL TAKE THE JOB?

YES, I'LL RETRIEVE YOUR SO-CALLED *ORB* IN RETURN FOR YOUR *GOLD!* BUT FIRST, I'LL GET GRAYLIN SAFELY TUCKED IN A ROOM AT THE INN WHERE...

DAGAR, NO!

I'M GOING *WITH* YOU! UNLESS YOU'D PREFER MY STAYING IN THIS CITY WHERE *THIEVES* AND *CUTTHROATS* MAKE BOLD ASSAULTS IN BROAD DAYLIGHT! WELL—?

SOON, *THREE* FIGURES RIDE THROUGH THE SWAMPLAND. FOR ONE WITH *DAGAR'S* TRAINING, PERCEIVING THE "THIEF'S" *TRAIL* IS SIMPLE...

AND AS THE TRAIL APPEARS *FRESHER*...

YOUR THIEF IS *NEAR!* AND SINCE *I'M* THE ONE EARNING THIS GOLD, I'M GOING AFTER HIM *ALONE!* FASTER, KASA!

WHILE NOT FAR AWAY...

I LOST PRECIOUS *TIME* WHEN MY HORSE FELL EXHAUSTED! BUT NOW THAT HE'S *RESTED,* WE CAN GO ON!

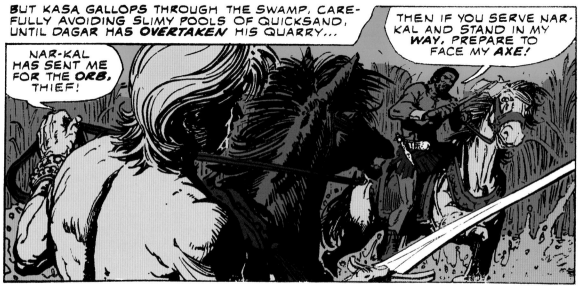

BUT KASA GALLOPS THROUGH THE SWAMP, CAREFULLY AVOIDING SLIMY POOLS OF QUICKSAND, UNTIL DAGAR HAS *OVERTAKEN* HIS QUARRY...

NAR-KAL HAS SENT ME FOR THE *ORB,* THIEF!

THEN IF YOU SERVE NAR-KAL AND STAND IN MY *WAY,* PREPARE TO FACE MY *AXE!*

THEY RIDE HARD TOWARD ONE ANOTHER— *DAGAR*, DEDICATED TO RETURNING THE ORB OF ORG-RA TO ITS PROPER OWNER, THUS WINNING A SACK OR TWO OF *GOLD*...

...*TORGUS*, CONCERNED ONLY WITH *RETAINING* THAT SAME COVETED ORB AND GETTING IT TO HIS DYING WIFE BEFORE THE DAWN.

AND WHEN TWO SUCH DETERMINED FORCES MEET *HEAD-ON*...

Ka-rash!

YOU REALLY THINK TO FIGHT OFF A *WAR AXE* WITH BUT A *BROADSWORD?!*

MY GRANDFATHER'S SWORD HAS NOT FAILED ME *YET!*

AS THE TWO RELENT-LESS FIGHTERS TUMBLE TO THE GROUND... AND THE ORB OF ORG-RA ROLLS FREE... TORGUS CAPITALIZES ON THE CONFUSION...

Whack!

HE RAISES HIS DEADLY BATTLEAXE, READY TO STRIKE...

BUT THE TULGONIAN WARRIOR HAS BEEN TRAINED SINCE CHILDHOOD TO REMAIN *ALERT*...

...AND *FIGHT BACK!*

NOW, MERCENARY, YOU *DIE!*

YET EVEN WHILE THE VALOROUS BLACK CHIEFTAIN PREPARES TO FOLLOW THROUGH ON HIS THREAT, TWO *OTHER* RIDERS HAVE ENTERED THE SCENE OF BATTLE...

THE *ORB!* LET THOSE FOOLS BATTER THEMSELVES INTO OBLIVION! THE ORB IS NOW MINE FOR THE *TAKING!*

MY BELOVED WIFE WILL *DIE* IF I DON'T GET TO HER IN TIME WITH THE *ORB!* AND NEITHER YOU NOR NAR-KAL AND ALL HIS DARK GODS WILL *PREVENT* ME!

WHAT ARE YOU SAYING?! PERHAPS THERE IS *MORE* TO THIS BUSINESS THAN NAR-KAL *TOLD* ME!

YOU *HAVE* ME, MERCENARY! WHY HAVEN'T YOU *SLAIN* ME?

BECAUSE I THINK THERE IS MUCH TO *TALK* ABOUT BEFORE THIS CONTINUES!

AFTER TORGUS HASTILY *EXPLAINS* WHAT HAS HAPPENED...

IT APPEARS AS IF I'VE BEEN FIGHTING THE *WRONG MAN!* YOUR CAUSE IS *JUST*, TORGUS, WHILE NAR-KAL SERVES THE *DARK GODS!*

DAGAR WILL *AID* YOU IN GETTING THE ORB TO YOUR WIFE!

WAIT, BARBARIANS! BEFORE YOU MAKE *ANY* PLANS ON RETURNING *ANYWHERE*, YOU'D BEST *CONSIDER* THE SITUATION!

FOR AGAIN I HOLD THE *ORB*... AND AGAIN I FEEL ITS SURGING *POWER!* NOW I *USE* THE ORB TO SUMMON FORTH A CREATURE THAT WILL RID ME OF YOU *BOTH!*

THERE IS NO TIME TO PONDER THE IMPORT OF NAR-KAL'S WORDS... FOR ALREADY THERE COMES A *RUMBLING* FROM BELOW, AS THOUGH SOMETHING *ENORMOUS* WAS MOVING BENEATH THE EARTH. THEN THE EARTH *CRACKS*...SPLITS APART... AND DAGAR AND TORGUS BEHOLD A FAMILIAR REPTILIAN HORROR...

BY THE WARRIOR GODS!

THE *SERPENT!*

HISSSS! GRASHHHH! RRRRRESSSSSSSSSSY!

ITS SILVERY SCALES GLEAMING IN THE MOONLIGHT, THE GREAT SERPENT COILS ABOUT TORGUS AND DAGAR. A BRIEF IMAGE OF THE POWERFUL GROUND SLOTH HELPLESS IN THE REPTILE'S GRASP FLASHES IN THE TULGONIAN'S MIND, AND HE WONDERS HOW THE SMALLER HUMANS CAN *ESCAPE* A SIMILAR FATE, BUT THEN DAGAR REMEMBERS THAT HE IS A *MAN*... A MAN WITH *DETERMINATION!*

DON'T GIVE UP THE *FIGHT*, TORGUS! WE CAN *YET* DEFEAT THIS MONSTER!

IF IT DOESN'T (*UHHH!*) *CRUSH* US FIRST!

GRRRAARRRGG! HSSSTT! SSSTAARRRGGGG!

AND WHEN *YOU* HAVE BEEN CRUSHED LIKE A BUG, DAGAR, I'LL RETRIEVE MY BAG OF GOLD AND WIN ON *ALL* COUNTS!

PERHAPS DAGAR WILL BE *GLAD* THAT I CAME ALONG AFTER ALL! EH, SORCERER?

WHAT—?!

I...CAN'T SEE!

WHAT IS WRONG? ARE YOU TOO *BUSY* TO WORK ANOTHER SPELL?

BUT THEN, YOU *CAN'T* WORK ANY MAGIC IF YOU NO LONGER HOLD THE *ORB!*

OWW!

SplaK!

MECHANICALLY, NAR-KAL'S EYES FOLLOW THE MOVEMENT OF THE GLOWING SPHERE... AS IT FLIES THROUGH THE AIR, ONLY TO LAND UPON THE MURKY SURFACE OF AN OMINOUS DARK *POOL...*

THE DARK GODS *CURSE* YOU, WOMAN! THAT'S *QUICKSAND...* AND WITHIN MOMENTS THE ORB OF ORG-RA WILL SINK FOREVER BENEATH THE SURFACE!

THEN IF THE ORB MEANS SO *MUCH* TO YOU...

AAAIIIIEEEEEEEEEE!

...YOU MAY GO IN *AFTER* IT!

HELP ME! I'M BEING PULLED *UNDER!*

HELP YOU? WHEN YOU SENT THAT MONSTER TO MURDER THE MAN I LOVE?

THEY SAY THAT IF YOU REMAIN CALM, YOU CAN *SWIM* IN QUICKSAND! AND IF I CAN SWIM TOWARD THE *ORB*, I CAN YET *SAVE* MYSELF!

LEAVING THE STRUGGLING SORCERER, GRAYLIN RETURNS TO THE MAN OF HER HEART... REPULSED AT THE SIGHT OF TWO WARRIORS IN THE THROES OF THE SERPENT'S CRUSHING GRIP...

SHARP FANGS DRIP POISONOUS SALIVA AS THE SERPENT'S BODY CONTINUES TO TIGHTEN AROUND THE TWO STRUGGLING WARRIORS...

DAGAR, I FEAR WE'RE *DOOMED!*

A MAN IS *NEVER* DOOMED, AS LONG AS HE HAS THE STRENGTH TO SWING HIS WEAPON!

RRRGRRRAAAR... SSSSST!

AND WITH A LOOK OF TRIUMPH SEEMINGLY *MIMICKING* THE HIDEOUS FACE OF THE MONSTROUS SNAKE, NAR-KAL *REACHES* THE SHINING EYE...

I *HAVE* IT! AGAIN I SHALL HAVE *POWER!*

257

BUT TWO WARRIORS *CONTINUE* TO BATTLE THE MONSTER...

UTILIZING THEIR WEAPONS WITHOUT RELENT...

UNTIL...

ITS BODY DESTROYED BY THE COMBINED EFFORTS OF BOTH WARRIORS, THE SERPENT *DIES*...THEN *RELAXES*...

WE'VE DONE IT, TORGUS!

BY THE GODS! *LOOK!*

UNTIL NOW I DID NOT REALIZE THE TRUE *IMPORT* OF THE BOND BETWEEN MYSELF AND THE SERPENT! FOR ITS VERY *DEATH* IS CAUSING *ME* TO DIE...AND *NOTHING* CAN...SAVE ME! NOT EVEN...

...THE *ORB* OF... *ORG-RA*...

I *MUST* SALVAGE THE ORB...OR RENYA WILL *DIE!*

IT'S *TOO LATE*, TORGUS! YOU'LL *NEVER* REACH THE ORB!

THE VALIANT BLACK WARRIOR STRUGGLES IN THE SUCKING QUAGMIRE, BUT...

THERE *MAY BE A WAY* TO SAVE HIM! BUT IT WILL REQUIRE THE COMBINED WORK OF YOU, KASA AND MYSELF!

QUICKLY, DAGAR REMOVES A *ROPE* FROM HIS HORSE'S SADDLE...

REMEMBER, GRAYLIN! IT IS *YOUR* TASK TO SEE THAT KASA PULLS! OTHERWISE...

THEN PLUNGING INTO THE GREENISH BROWN POOL, THE MERCENARY BLINDLY GROPES ABOUT... GRASPING ONLY OOZING SLIME, UNTIL...

I'VE REACHED AN *ARM!* LET'S HOPE IT'S THAT OF TORGUS! NOW, *PULL!*

KASA MOVES FORWARD, MUSCLES STRAINING...

I COULD NOT REACH THE ORB! YOU SHOULD HAVE LEFT ME TO PERISH!

THE DARK GODS MUST BE LAUGHING AT THIS IRONY! FOR IN SLAYING THE SERPENT, WE INADVERTENTLY SLEW NAR-KAL... *LOST* THE ORB... AND DOOMED RENYA! I VOWED TO SAVE HER OR *DIE* TRYING...

OH, DAGAR! IT WAS *I* WHO FORCED NAR-KAL INTO THE QUICKSAND! I...NEVER KILLED BEFORE! B-BUT WHEN I SAW WHAT NAR-KAL HAD *DONE* TO YOU...

WE *ALL* DID THE ONLY THINGS POSSIBLE! FOR HAD THE SERPENT KILLED US, OR HAD NAR-KAL SURVIVED ALONG WITH THE ORB, RENYA WOULD JUST AS SURELY HAVE PERISHED! I AM THE VICTIM OF A SADISTIC *FATE*!

AND NOW I SHALL RETURN TO MY PEOPLE, DAGAR... AND TELL THEM THAT I CAN NO LONGER BE THEIR CHIEF! FOR I HAVE FAILED TO SAVE THE WOMAN I LOVE...AND THUS AM NOT *FIT* TO LEAD THEM!

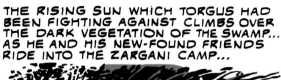

THE RISING SUN WHICH TORGUS HAD BEEN FIGHTING AGAINST CLIMBS OVER THE DARK VEGETATION OF THE SWAMP... AS HE AND HIS NEW-FOUND FRIENDS RIDE INTO THE ZARGANI CAMP...

BEFORE I ADDRESS MY PEOPLE WITH WORDS I DREAD TO SPEAK, I WISH TO LOOK UPON THE BODY OF MY BELOVED... FOR THE FINAL TIME!

BUT AS TORGUS ENTERS THE SEER'S TENT, EXPECTING TO VIEW THE LIFELESS FORM OF HIS WIFE...

IT IS NOT POSSIBLE!

YOU ARE *ALIVE*... AND SEEM HEALTHY! BUT HOW CAN IT BE?!

DON'T QUESTION THE FAVORS OF THE GODS, MY LOVE! JUST *HOLD* ME!

THE MAGIC INCENSE REVEALED *ALL* TO ME, MY CHIEFTAIN! SINCE THE SERPENT WAS A CREATURE OF THE *DARK GODS,* ITS POISON WAS *MAGICAL* BY NATURE! THUS BY DESTROYING THE SNAKE AND NAR-KAL, THE *EFFECTS* OF THE VENOM WERE ALSO DESTROYED!

AND AS *TORGUS* PROUDLY WALKS WITH HIS BEAUTIFUL *RENYA* TO RESUME THE DUTIES OF *WARRIOR CHIEF* OF THE *ZARGANI...*

YOU SEE, WE ACTUALLY *SAVED* RENYA AND DIDN'T KNOW IT! AND I THINK IT BEST THAT THE *ORB OF ORG-RA* IS AT THE BOTTOM OF THAT QUAGMIRE, WHERE IT WILL DO NO MORE HARM!

WE ALSO HAVE THIS BAG OF *GOLD!* SOME SORCERERS *ARE* GOOD FOR *SOMETHING!*

the END

MAC RABOY'S FLASH ⚡ GORDON

Thrill to the celestial dangers of space travel and the science
fiction action of yesteryear's Flash Gordon weekly series! Continuing
Dark Horse Comics' tradition of fine reprint books, this tome is the first
ever collection of Flash Gordon strips written and illustrated by acclaimed
Green Lama and Captain Marvel, Jr. artist Mac Raboy. Ming the Merciless,
the traitorous Klag, a mysterious creature known as "The Mind," and a
host of villains and dangers oppose the hardy, heroic Flash and it's
up to him to save the day!

VOLUME 1
ISBN 978-1-56971-882-7

VOLUME 2
ISBN 978-1-56971-911-4

VOLUME 3
ISBN 978-1-56971-978-7

VOLUME 4
ISBN 978-1-56971-979-4

$19.95 each!

AVAILABLE AT YOUR LOCAL COMICS SHOP OR BOOKSTORE!
To find a comics shop in your area, call 1-888-266-4226.
For more information or to order direct visit darkhorse.com or call 1-800-862-0052 Mon.–Fri. 9 AM to 5 PM Pacific Time
*Prices and availability subject to change without notice

EDGAR RICE BURROUGHS'
Tarzan

Swing into adventure with these thrilling tales of Edgar Rice Burroughs' iconic jungle hero, Tarzan, King of the Apes!

CONAN®

THE CHRONICLES OF CONAN

Roy Thomas, Barry Windsor-Smith, Gil Kane, John Buscema, Neal Adams, Howard Chaykin, and others

Volume 1: Tower of the Elephant and Other Stories
ISBN 978-1-59307-016-8 | $15.99

Volume 2: Rogues in the House and Other Stories
ISBN 978-1-59307-023-6 | $15.99

Volume 3: The Monster of the Monoliths and Other Stories
ISBN 978-1-59307-024-3 | $15.99

Volume 4: The Song of Red Sonja and Other Stories
ISBN 978-1-59307-025-0 | $15.99

Volume 5: The Shadow in the Tomb and Other Stories
ISBN 978-1-59307-175-2 | $15.99

Volume 6: The Curse of the Golden Skull and Other Stories
ISBN 978-1-59307-274-2 | $15.99

Volume 7: The Dweller in the Pool and Other Stories
ISBN 978-1-59307-300-8 | $15.99

Volume 8: Brothers of the Blade and Other Stories
ISBN 978-1-59307-349-7 | $16.99

Volume 9: Riders of the River-Dragons and Other Stories
ISBN 978-1-59307-394-7 | $16.99

Volume 10: When Giants Walk the Earth and Other Stories
ISBN 978-1-59307-490-6 | $16.99

Volume 11: The Dance of the Skull and Other Stories
ISBN 978-1-59307-636-8 | $16.99

Volume 12: The Beast King of Abombi and Other Stories
ISBN 978-1-59307-778-5 | $16.99

Volume 13: Whispering Shadows and Other Stories
ISBN 978-1-59307-837-9 | $16.99

Volume 14: Shadow of the Beast and Other Stories
ISBN 978-1-59307-899-7 | $16.99

Volume 15: The Corridor of Mullah-Kajar and Other Stories
ISBN 978-1-59307-971-0 | $16.99

Volume 16: The Eternity War and Other Stories
ISBN 978-1-59582-176-8 | $16.99

Volume 17: The Creation Quest and Other Stories
ISBN 978-1-59582-177-5 | $17.99

Volume 18: Isle of the Dead
ISBN 978-1-59582-382-3 | $17.99

Volume 19: Deathmark and Other Stories
ISBN 978-1-59582-515-5 | $17.99

Volume 20: Night of the Wolf and Other Stories
ISBN 978-1-59582-584-1 | $18.99

Volume 21: Blood of the Titan and Other Stories
ISBN 978-1-59582-704-3 | $18.99

CONAN MINISERIES

Conan and the Jewels of Gwahlur HARDCOVER
P. Craig Russell
ISBN 978-1-59307-491-3 | $13.99

Conan and the Demons of Khitai
Akira Yoshida and Paul Lee
ISBN 978-1-59307-543-9 | $12.99

Conan: Book of Thoth
Kurt Busiek, Len Wein, and Kelley Jones
ISBN 978-1-59307-648-1 | $17.99

Conan and the Songs of the Dead
Joe R. Lansdale and Timothy Truman
ISBN 978-1-59307-718-1 | $14.99

Conan and the Midnight God
Josh Dysart, Will Conrad, and Jason Shawn Alexander
ISBN 978-1-59307-852-2 | $14.99

Conan: The Blood-Stained Crown and Other Stories
Kurt Busiek, Fabian Nicieza, Cary Nord, Eric Powell, Bruce Timm, and others
ISBN 978-1-59307-886-7 | $14.99

Conan: The Spear and Other Stories
ISBN 978-1-59582-523-0 | $14.99

CONAN THE PHENOMENON

Paul M. Sammon
ISBN 978-1-59307-653-5 | $29.99

THE CHRONICLES OF KING CONAN

Volume 1: The Witch of the Mists and Other Stories
ISBN 978-1-59307-477-7 | $18.99

Volume 2: Vengeance from the Desert and Other Stories
ISBN 978-1-59582-670-1 | $18.99

CONAN ONGOING SERIES

Volume 0: Born on the Battlefield
TPB: ISBN 978-1-59307-981-9 | $17.99
HC: ISBN 978-1-59307-980-2 | $24.99

Volume 1: The Frost Giant's Daughter and Other Stories
Kurt Busiek and Cary Nord
ISBN 978-1-59307-301-5 | $15.99

Volume 2: The God in the Bowl and Other Stories
Kurt Busiek and Cary Nord
ISBN 978-1-59307-403-6 | $15.99

Volume 3: The Tower of the Elephant and Other Stories
Kurt Busiek, Cary Nord, and Michael Wm. Kaluta
ISBN 978-1-59307-547-7 | $15.99

Volume 4: The Hall of the Dead and Other Stories
Kurt Busiek, Mike Mignola, Tim Truman, and Cary Nord
ISBN 978-1-59307-775-4 | $17.99

Volume 5: Rogues in the House and Other Stories
Timothy Truman, Cary Nord and Tomás Giorello
ISBN 978-1-59307-903-1 | $17.99

Volume 6: The Hand of Nergal
Timothy Truman and Tomás Giorello
TPB: ISBN 978-1-59582-178-2 | $17.99
HC: ISBN 978-1-59582-179-9 | $24.99

Volume 7: Cimmeria
TPB: ISBN 978-1-59582-283-3 | $17.99
HC: ISBN 978-1-59582-341-0 | $24.99

Volume 8: Black Colossus
TPB: ISBN 978-1-59582-533-9 | $17.99
HC: ISBN 978-1-59582-507-0 | $24.99

Volume 9: Free Companions
ISBN 978-1-59582-592-6 | $17.99

Volume 10: Iron Shadows in the Moon
ISBN 978-1-59582-713-5 | $17.99

SAVAGE SWORD OF CONAN

Roy Thomas, Barry Windsor-Smith, John Buscema, Alfredo Alcala, Pablo Marcos, and others

Volume 1
ISBN 978-1-59307-838-6 | $17.99

Volume 2
ISBN 978-1-59307-894-2 | $17.99

Volume 3
ISBN 978-1-59307-960-4 | $19.99

Volume 4
ISBN 978-1-59582-149-2 | $19.99

Volume 5
ISBN 978-1-59582-175-1 | $19.99

Volume 6
ISBN 978-1-59582-375-5 | $19.99

Volume 7
ISBN 978-1-59582-510-0 | $19.99

Volume 8
ISBN 978-1-59582-582-7 | $19.99

Volume 9
ISBN 978-1-59582-648-0 | $19.99

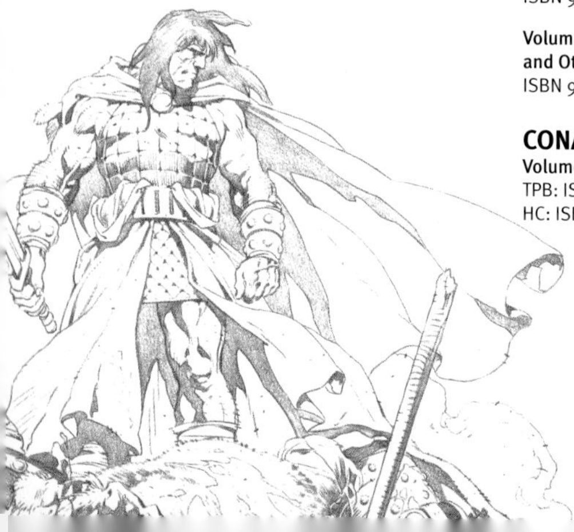

AVAILABLE AT YOUR LOCAL COMICS SHOP OR BOOKSTORE
To find a comics shop in your area, call 1-888-266-4226. For more information or to order direct visit darkhorse.com or call 1-800-862-0052. Mon.–Fri. 9 AM to 5 PM Pacific Time. *Prices and availability subject to change without notice.

SIR... MAY I SPEAK WITH YOU?

...OLDIERS ...ESCEND ...PON THE ...O ...URES, ...T NO ...RCENARY ...LLS THAT ...Y TO A ...INGING ...ORD! NO ...RBARIAN ...ES ...NEATH A ...OPPING ...E...

THEY ARE ONLY *IMAGES*, CONJURED UP BY MAGIC! THAT MEANS THAT MOGRA IS ALSO A TRAITOR! SLAY ALL *THREE* OF THEM!

...S DAGAR STRUGGLES TO BREAK FREE ...F LUPOF'S UNBREAKABLE GRIP, HE ...ELS THE GROWTH OF SHARP POINTS ...GGING INTO HIS FLESH...

...HAS THE STRENGTH ...F AN ANIMAL... BY ...HE GODS! HE'S NOT **HUMAN!**

DON'T LOOK SO **SURPRISED**, SURFACE MAN! REMEMBER THAT